THE *Mind* OF

MODERN
RUSSIA

Historical and Political Thought
of Russia's Great Age

Edited by HANS KOHN

HARPER TORCHBOOKS ❦ *THE ACADEMY LIBRARY*

HARPER & ROW, PUBLISHERS

NEW YORK, EVANSTON, AND LONDON

THE MIND OF MODERN RUSSIA

To
my colleagues and students
at the City College of New York
in appreciation of
their friendly fellowship and open-minded scholarship

Quand ils ont longtemps et glorieusement vécu les peuples, quoi qu'ils fassent, ne sauraient rompre avec leur passé; ils subissent son influence au moment même où ils travaillent à le détruire; au sein de leurs plus éclatantes transformations, ils restent, pour l'essentiel de leur caractère et de leur destinée, tels que les a fait leur histoire. Il n'y a point de révolution, si hardie et si puissante qu'elle soit, qui abolisse les longues traditions nationales. Il importe donc grandement, non seulement pour la satisfaction des esprits, mais pour la bonne conduite des nations dans leurs affaires, que ces traditions soient bien connues et bien comprises.

—FRANÇOIS GUIZOT, *Essai sur l'histoire de France,* Préface.

Preface

François Guizot, who lived through the French revolutions of the last decade of the eighteenth and the first half of the nineteenth century, was more fortunate as historian and moralist than as statesman and politician. With a profound insight into national history, he wrote that "when nations have existed for a long and glorious time, they cannot break with their past, whatever they do; they are influenced by it at the very moment when they work to destroy it; in the midst of the most glaring transformations they remain fundamentally in character and destiny such as their history has formed them. Even the most daring and powerful revolution cannot abolish national traditions of long duration. Therefore, it is most important, not only for the sake of intellectual curiosity but also for the good management of international affairs, to know and to understand these traditions."

In its historical setting, the Union of Socialist Soviet Republics, ruled from the Kremlin in the heart of Moscow, cannot be understood without a knowledge of the political and social thought of its predecessors: the Tsardom of Muscovy, which had its origin and center in the very same Kremlin; and the Russian Empire, which Peter the Great founded with St. Petersburg as its capital. In many ways the Russia of today combines characteristic features of its two ancestors. It tries to answer the pressing new problems which post-Petrinian Russia had to face—Russia's relationship to Europe and her progressive Westernization—by a return not only to the ancient capital but also to some of the principles of old Muscovy.

The century from the end of the Napoleonic wars to the
First World War forms the brightest page in Russia's millenary history: it was Russia's great age. During the Napoleonic wars Russian armies decisively influenced the course
of European history. From the moment that they crossed
the Elbe and the Rhine and entered Paris, the Russians
debated the relationship between Russia and the West and
their common or opposite destiny. The intercourse with
Europe stimulated Russian intellectual life to an unprecedented degree. With astonishing rapidity European culture
was assimilated by the Russian educated circles and transformed and enriched by Russia's peculiar gifts. Thus the
new Russian literature could make a great and lasting con-
tribution to European letters and sensibility. The Russian
novel of the nineteenth century equaled as a human document and as an artistic achievement the West's highest accomplishments.

Then as today, the backward conditions of Russia made
a free political life impossible. Under these circumstances,
literature became the outlet for the debate about Russia's
character and mission. In Russia's great age the creative
individuality of the thinker and writer, though limited in
the ways of expression until 1905, remained essentially free.
This freedom even under an autocratic government, this
possibility of spiritual and intellectual opposition to the
government—which vanished in the unfortunate years
after Lenin's seizure of power—was the foundation of Russia's great age.

The debate about Russia and the West, which went on
throughout the nineteenth century, forms the background
against which Russia in the middle of the twentieth century
and her relationship to the West can be understood. The
following pages offer to the students of modern history, of
political theory, and of international relations some source
material (most of it difficult of access otherwise) for the

knowledge and understanding of the national traditions which have formed the Russian character and Russian history. It was thought preferable to present as full selections as possible of a few writers, instead of offering many short passages which could hardly do justice to their authors. The titles given to the excerpts are of my own choosing, to bring out the salient thought in each, and do not necessarily correspond to the titles of the original writings. A list of sources may be found at the end of the book. Because of the vastness of the source material, the selection naturally remains open to many justifiable objections. I can only hope that other works will supplement this first venture. But in many years of teaching I have found such a selection of readings lacking, and fellow teachers, fellow students, and the growing number of those seriously interested in an understanding of Russia may find the book useful. Russian intellectual history and political thought make fascinating reading and will reveal some less known aspects of the Russian problem and of the wealth and diversity of cultural attitudes and human personalities.

By numbers and by historical importance, the Russians are the foremost Slav nation. European history until the eighteenth century was the history of the Latin and Teutonic peoples; the Slav peoples entered it only two hundred years ago. Since then their political and cultural participation has steadily grown. Slav and non-Slav writers during that time have often predicted, some with hopeful pride, others with dark forebodings, the advent of a Slav century or a Slav era. In the nineteenth-century Russian mind, Russia's relation to the other Slavs played a dominant role. As Slav thought in general is less known in the West than is Russian literature, one representative Czech and one representative Polish voice about Russia and the Western Slavs were included. On the other hand, for reasons of space, the great Russian novelists, available in many English editions, were not included—though Dostoevsky presents the Slavophil point of view and Turgenev the Western point of view, inventively and cogently.

In the preparation of this book and of some of the translations I had the good fortune of the assistance of my friends Hugo Knoepfmacher, Wallace Sokolsky, and Ruben Weltsch, and of Mr. Mark Field of Harvard University. I am pleased to thank also Miss Gertrude Richman, Miss Ruth Sender, and Miss Barbara Benjamin for their ever friendly and conscientious help with the manuscript.

HANS KOHN

Autumn 1954
New York City

Table of Contents

The *Mind* of Modern Russia

I

Russia's Great Age:
Encounter with Europe

Since the end of antiquity, Europe has been divided into East and West: Constantinople and Rome, the Eastern and the Western Empires, Greek Orthodox and Roman Catholic Christianity. After the fall of Constantinople to the Turks, at the close of the Middle Ages, Russia emerged as the most powerful representative of the East. In the West, with the development of the parliamentary system and the beginnings of the industrial revolution, England became, more than geographically, the typically Western country.

In some spheres, similarities between the two countries are not lacking. After the seventeenth century Britain's face was only half turned toward Europe; the other half looked westward, across the Atlantic Ocean to New England and the growing empire. At about the same time Russia began to divide her attention between Europe and the wide vista eastward over the Asian land masses. The British and the Russians were both hardy pioneer races: the former peopled and developed northern America from the Atlantic to the Pacific; the latter explored and settled the endless plains of northern Asia and advanced to the Pacific, into China and northwestern America. Yet, the two nations followed contrary directions in their political ideas and social structure.

The "tight little island" has been in modern times the classical home of individual liberty and middle-class enterprise; neither was greatly known in the immense Eastern empire.

This opposition in the intellectual climate and political thought of the two peoples is essentially a modern development. Medieval England was not a seafaring nation, nor were her people endowed with greater liberties than other Europeans. Medieval Russia, which was centered around Kiev and Novgorod, the Dnieper River, and the approaches to the Black and Baltic Seas, communicated with the West and shared in some of its political and social institutions. The change came with the fall of Kiev to the Tartars in 1240. As its result the center of gravity in Russia moved east to newly colonized lands around Moscow. The centuries of Tartar domination cut Russia off from Europe. Renaissance and Reformation initiated a movement in Europe in which Russia no longer shared. The growth of constitutional liberty and religious tolerance in seventeenth-century England, the ascendancy of the middle classes, and the spirit of commercial enterprise made Britain more and more the leader of the West and laid the foundations of her power. In Moscow strong Renaissance rulers molded Russia in an opposite tradition and turned her East. They attempted to base Russian power on autocracy and uniformity to a degree unknown anywhere in Europe.

Thus, Russia and the West grew farther apart from the thirteenth to the seventeenth centuries: two worlds, closed and incomprehensible to each other. The Eastern and Western minds did not meet. The result was an astonishing discrepancy in the development of the two parts of Europe. While the West forged ahead in science and the arts, in production of wealth and improvement of government, Russia stagnated intellectually and economically. Only in the eighteenth century did she make a determined effort to meet Europe again. Out of this encounter grew Russia's great age: a fertilization of her intellectual life and the beginnings of social change.

The eastward trend in Russian history from Kiev to Moscow, to the gates of the East, shows certain similarities to later German developments, which shifted another center of gravity from old cultural centers in the West to newly colonized marches in the East. The Russian lands and, centuries later, the German lands were unified by their eastern outposts, Moscow and Prussia, and both drew their strength not from the Western spirit of liberty but from military discipline and devotion to the absolute head of the state. But the Rhine was an integral part of the West to a degree never known on the Dnieper, and the lands east of the Elbe were infinitely nearer to the cultural heart of Europe than the Volga. In modern times Germany became the great intermediary between Russia and the West.

As the empire of Moscow grew away from Europe in its political ideals and social structure, the Russian Church loosened its ties with its mother church in Byzantium and became more and more a national church. It did not use Greek as its language, as the West used Latin; its Slavonic liturgy cut it off from the universal Greek Church and from the invigorating contact with ancient civilization. Deeply devoted to the Orthodox faith, the Russians became convinced that they alone lived in undefiled purity, that they were the only truly Christian people. The fall of Constantinople, the capital of the Eastern Roman Empire and of the Greek Orthodox Church, to the Mohammedan Turks in 1453 was interpreted by the Russians as God's punishment upon Byzantium for not having been strict enough in maintaining the purity of the faith and for having accepted, at the Council of Florence in 1439, union with Rome and the Latin infidels. Moscow remained uncompromisingly hostile to the West. God had rejected the pagan Rome of Augustus on the Tiber and the Christian Rome which Constantine built in Byzantium as unworthy of bringing peace and justice to the world and of guiding it to the true faith. By the purity of its Orthodoxy, Moscow was chosen to be the Third Rome, and Russia to be Holy Russia.

While Moscow assumed the Roman heritage of world government, its princes established an autocracy. The ruler was regarded as the sole owner of the land. All the people without distinction were entirely subject to him, liable to compulsory and universal service to the state, which was identical with the prince and was everything. Neither nobles nor burghers had any rights against the prince as did their counterparts in the West. No rank or law protected against the lawless arbitrary whim of the ruler.

Peter the Great, who ruled from 1689 to 1725, attempted to Westernize and to secularize Russia and to provide her with the resources she needed to occupy a dominant position in the international world of modern times. He wished to increase the productiveness of Russian labor, to stimulate the spirit of enterprise, and to release the people from the deadening shackles of lawless despotism. But, deeply suspicious of Europe and always involved in war, he was in a hurry to achieve reforms for which Russia was in no way ready. His ruthless Russian despotism and the Russian inertia that he encountered drove him to use force and regimentation to a degree that not only kept Russia outside Europe but defeated the purpose which he dimly sensed as fundamental, of arousing the Russians to a spirit of individual liberty, dignity, and responsibility.

In the words of a great Russian historian, Peter was faced with an insoluble problem: "Even when his doings were beneficent in intention they were accompanied by a repellent display of force, since his reforms were a threefold struggle between a despotism, a people, and a people's instincts, a struggle in which, using his authority as a menace,

he constantly strove to spur a community of serfs into spontaneous action."

Peter initiated a new period of Russian history. He transferred the capital from half-Asiatic Moscow, from which
the river-ways led to the Caspian Sea, to a site on the Baltic
Sea, nearer to the West. Here he built a new city, named
after him, which he intended as a symbol of the new Westernized Russia. But half a century more had to pass before
Catherine II (1762–1796), a princess of German descent,
freed the nobility and transformed Russia from a purely
Oriental patriarchal state into a nation which at its top
resembled contemporary Europe. From that time on, the
discrepancy between the proclaimed Western ideals and
the continuing semi-Asiatic reality grew, and with it the
gulf between government, society, and the people. The
government distrusted the educated classes and the people.
The educated classes became in their outlook and way of
life alienated from the peasants and the merchants. All the
problems which Westernization a century later brought to
India and China were adumbrated in Russia, the first non-
Western society to come under the impact of modern Western civilization.

At the beginning of the nineteenth century, Russia was
not of Europe, nor was she outside Europe. Military expe-
ditions, above all the victory over Napoleon, established her
as a factor of great importance and even general fear for
Europe. She seemed more powerful than any other state,
vaster than any other empire, but at the same time culturally and politically archaic and backward. She became a
problem to Europe but above all to herself. Could the new
freedom learned from the West be reconciled with the
maintenance of order and unity in the vast unprepared empire? Would not European liberty transplanted to the so

different soil of Russia lead to chaos? Had Peter's reforms fathered a better Russia, or had they destroyed Russia's foundations, exposing her to the destructive influences of infidel Europe? The Russian historian Nikolai Karamzin asked in 1812: "Has the name Russian still the inscrutable force for us which it formerly had? Our ancestors, even if they enjoyed many advantages of foreign customs, remained always of the opinion that the Orthodox Russian is the most perfect citizen on earth and Holy Russia the first state. May one call that an error, yet how it promoted the love of the fatherland and its moral strength! Now, however, after more than a century of foreign education, we call all the Europeans, whom we formerly called infidels, our brothers. I ask, for whom will it be easier to subdue Russia, for infidels or brothers? Peter is responsible for it."

All through the nineteenth century the question of the relations of Russia and Europe was ever present in the Russian mind. Russia was clearly predestined to a great future, but her course toward it and her goal remained an awe-inspiring mystery. None expressed this feeling more beautifully than Nikolai Gogol in his *Dead Souls* (1842), comparing Russia to a troika, a small sleigh drawn by three fast horses abreast over the hardened crystalline snow covering the endless plains.

Ah, Russia, from my beautiful home in a strange land I still can see you! In you everything is poor and disordered and homely. . . . Yet what secret, what invisible force draws me to you? . . . What is it that your boundless expanses presage?

Do they not presage that one day there will arise in you ideas as boundless as yourself? Do they not presage that one day you, too, will know no limits? Do they not presage that one day, when again you shall have room for daring exploits, there will spring to life the heroes of old? . . . Yes, each time that there arises in Russia a movement of thought, it becomes clear that such a movement sinks deep into the Slavonic nature while it would have but skimmed the surface of other nations. . . .

Russia of mine, are you not also speeding like a troika which nothing can overtake? Is not the road smoking beneath your wheels, and are not the bridges thundering as you cross them, everything left behind, while the spectators, struck with the portent, stop to wonder whether you be not a thunderbolt launched from heaven? What does that awe-inspiring progress of yours foretell? What is the unknown force which lies within your mysterious steeds?

Surely the winds themselves must abide in their manes, and every vein in their bodies must be an ear stretched to catch the celestial message which bids them, with iron-girded breasts, and hoofs which barely touch the earth as they gallop, fly forward on a mission of God?

Whither are you speeding, Russia of mine? Whither? Answer me! But no answer comes—only the weird sound of your collar-bells. Rent into a thousand shreds, the air roars past you, for you are overtaking the whole world, and shall one day force all nations, all empires to stand aside, to give way to you!

Could such a nation become simply part of Europe, following its lead and accepting its values and standards, or was she to remain conscious of and to cultivate her unique character? Russia asked all these questions at a time when Europe herself was in a state of transition. Did not even some Western intellectuals look longingly to an idealized past; did they not condemn modern civilization which apparently alienated man from the true sources of existence and deprived him of the strength of faith? Was the Slav peasant not close, in all essential concerns, to the ideal man envisaged by Jean Jacques Rousseau and Johann Gottfried Herder, and infinitely superior to the Western bourgeois? Did not Russia provide a better soil for the fruition of the hopes of Western romantic reactionaries and socialist revolutionaries, both equally opposed to middle-class society? Did not Russia possess a living tradition of an organic community of fraternity and harmony, whereas Western society was held together, in competition and exploitation, by the coldness of law and the brutality of force?

The German romantic rejection of the West was adopted, with similar arguments, by many Russians, who however included Germany in the rejected West. From France and Germany in the first half of the nineteenth century, the conflicting and turbulent intellectual trends of modern Europe suddenly poured into Russia with its entirely different social structure and political tradition. Unfamiliar with the social and intellectual realities of the West but taken with the freedom and utopian perfectionism of the realm of ideas, many Russians viewed Europe with a critical eye which perceived weaknesses more easily than the intrinsic strength. With their inclination to go to extremes and to hold middle-class common sense in very low esteem, the Russians in their discussion of Western ideas felt themselves easily superior to the West.

The more the discussion of these ideas moved in a vacuum, the more heated it became. Everything seemed possible. The magic world of romanticism and social utopianism received its sanction in an extravagant misinterpretation of the character of the Russian people or of Russian history, or of both. Romantic reaction with its idealization of the past, and socialist revolutionism with its concentration upon the future, both had originated in the West. There, however, they remained intellectual stimuli within the framework of a developing society. In Russia they became absolutized. In Europe they were generally found in opposite camps until the twentieth century; in nineteenth-century Russia they frequently inspired the same men and movements. The two ideologies expressed an identical contempt for Western parliamentary constitutions, for middle-class, middle-of-the-road mentality, and for the strength of creative compromise.

Thomas G. Masaryk, the Czech scholar who knew Russia and the West equally well, deplored in his *Russia and Europe* (1913) the lack of criticism and moderation in Russian thought, its addiction to dogma and myth. He found therein no difference between Orthodox theologians and

Westernized rationalists; the latter, in turning away from traditional Orthodoxy, only changed the object of their faith. Similarly, a century earlier, Alexander Herzen recognized the deep affinity between the Russian autocratic government and the Russian revolutionary socialism. "One has remarked that an opposition which leads a frontal attack upon a government has always something of its character in an inverted sense. I believe that there is some justification for the fear which the Russian government begins to feel of communism: communism is the Russian autocracy turned upside down."

The hopes of reforms aroused among the educated classes in Russia by the contact with Europe in the Napoleonic wars and by the liberalism of the earlier part of the reign of Alexander I (1801–1825) were dashed by the failure of the uprising of December 14, 1825. The uprising itself was the last link in the chain of post-Napoleonic military uprisings which started in Spain in 1820. The young men who participated and who are known in history as Decembrists were mostly officers and scions of high Russian nobility. The savage repression which followed under Alexander's brother and successor, Nikolai I (1825–1855), postponed the necessary reforms, inevitable though they were, and failed to prepare the people for them. The task was difficult. Russia then, and even half a century later, had no strong, independent middle class and little capital and industry to alleviate the agrarian problem and the low standard of productivity.

When the Crimean War broke out in 1854, it was regarded by many Russians as the beginning of the final struggle between Russia and Europe. It was to settle the Eastern Question—the possession of Constantinople—and inaugurate the era of Russian world leadership. In reality, the war revealed the backwardness of the proud empire. Alexander II (1855–1881) introduced some of the reforms necessary to bring Russia into line with nineteenth-century Europe, but they lost much of their beneficial effect because of the incompetence of the bureaucracy and the impatience of the intelligentsia.

The word "nihilism," which Nietzsche introduced twenty years later to Europe, was first popularized in the early 1860's in the novel *Fathers and Children* by Ivan Turgenev. The spokesman of the young generation does not find "a single convention of our present-day existence, in family or social life, that does not call for complete and ruthless rejection." The nihilists, who called themselves "new men" or "thinking realists," were as unrealistic and absolutist in their negativism and materialism as the most extreme representative of the old order. A boundless optimism inspired them: "We are still ignorant, but we shall learn—and learning will liberate us. We shall become happy, we shall become brothers and sisters." But through the dialectics of extremism, they arrived at the very opposite of liberty. "After having started from unlimited liberty," Shigalev says in *The Possessed,* by Fedor Dostoevsky, "I finally arrived at unlimited despotism."

The Russian nihilists of the sixties turned materialism into a peculiar sort of dogmatic theology, anticipating the communists of the twentieth century. Of this theological tinge of Russian materialism, Nikolai Berdyayev, a leading modern Russian religious philosopher, wrote:

It became a dogma of moral obligation, and behind it was concealed a distinctive nihilist asceticism. A materialist catechism was framed and was adopted by the fanatical circles of the left Russian intelligentsia. Not to be a materialist was to be taken as a moral suspect. If you were not a materialist, then you were in favor of the enslavement of man both intellectually and politically. Science, by which was to be understood principally the natural sciences, which at that time were presented in materialist colors, became an object of faith; it was turned into an idol. . . . The nihilists were not men of science. They were men of dogmatic belief. The methodical doubt of Descartes suits the nihilists, and indeed the Russian mind in general, but little. The typical Russian cannot go on doubting for very long; his inclination is to make a dogma for himself quickly, and to surrender himself to it wholeheartedly and entirely. A Russian sceptic is a Western type in Russia. There was nothing sceptical in Russian materialism; it was a faith.

In nihilism still another Russian Orthodox trait was reflected; the lack of an understanding for the autonomy of cultural activities. Ascetic Orthodoxy doubted the justifiability of culture; it was inclined to see sinfulness in cultural creativeness. This found expression in the painful doubt felt by the great Russian writers about the justifiability of their own literary work. Religious, moral, and social doubt of the justification of culture is the most characteristically Russian theme. The problem of the cost at which culture is purchased is dominant in the social thought of the seventies. [From *The Origin of Russian Communism*, 1937]

The nihilists and materialists represented only one group among the Russian intellectuals of the nineteenth century. Bitter controversies raged among the conflicting groups. In their intellectual earnestness, they present an attractive and even exciting picture. But in the pre-capitalistic Russian society and under a despotic government, all these men— many of them dedicated souls, many endowed with wide cultural and personal charm—were confined to thought and talk. Detached from social reality and responsibility, they were generally unable to find fulfillment in a comprehensive work or in constructive action. Thus they inclined to revolutionary extremism or succumbed to the feeling of frustration.

The hero of a succession of great literary creations mirrored this aspect of the life of the Russian intelligentsia. He was the "superfluous man" in various garbs, from Byronic romanticism at the beginning of the nineteenth century to *fin de siècle* melancholy at its end. There was a long procession from Eugene Onegin in the verse novel of the same name (1832) by Alexander Pushkin; Petchorin in the novel *A Hero of our Times* (1839) by Mikhail Lermontov; Oblomov in the novel of that name (1857) by Ivan Goncharov; and Turgenev's Rudin (1855); down to the hero of the drama *Uncle Vanya* by Anton Chekhov. These characters all suffered from a feeling of frustration; self-centered and self-pitying, they lacked will-power and energy.

Interestingly enough, the weak and vacillating hero was generally contrasted with a young woman of unusual strength and integrity of character, who showed more purity and dedication and also more practical common sense than the man. Chivalry and the idealization of women had been practiced in the West since the Middle Ages. In Russia they were unknown. Only in the nineteenth century did they become great themes of the Russian cultured classes.

The Russian masses did not share in this belatedly eager adoption and transfiguration of Western forms. Even after the emancipation of 1861, the centuries-old habits of serfdom and traditionalism, of coarseness and of the *knout,* continued to shape their mind. The wide gulf between the educated classes and the primitive masses began to weigh heavily upon the conscience of many members of the former. They felt their portion of guilt for the almost subhuman condition of the people. The repentant nobleman or intellectual was convinced of his duty of "going to the people," the *narod,* to become a *narodnik,* sharing the life of the people and carrying enlightenment and civilization to them. Others went further. Their repentance led them to abnegation and humiliation. They sought forgiveness by bowing down before the peasants, by seeking refuge and wholeness in striking roots again in the soil. All these attitudes in varied interpenetrations underlay the great debate between Russian Westernizers and Russian Slavophils, which began in Moscow in the 1830's. In a different form, it expresses even today the principal tension of the modern Russian mind.

The great debate was started by Peter Chaadayev. He was the first who dared, in the midst of the prevailing intellectual confusion, to scrutinize the very foundations of the Russian condition and to develop a philosophy of Russian history in revolt against both the Russian past and the Russian present. An aristocrat by birth and mind, he was as genuinely a European as he was a Russian. He wrote very little and published even less. Yet his few essays and letters, by the fearlessness of their approach and the penetrating brilliancy of their style, stirred and shook contemporary Russia. As a Russian patriot, he had great hopes for Russia's future. He based these hopes, however, not upon her past but upon her close cooperation with Europe, upon her learning from, and continuing, Europe's heritage. A younger generation, men like Alexander Herzen, Mikhail Bakunin, and Vissarion Belinsky, followed him in looking not to the Russian past but to the West and to the Russian future. But whereas Chaadayev adhered to the old conservative Europe, the younger generation looked to the Europe stirred by the feverish hopes of 1848 and became disillusioned by the want of revolutionary absolutism in the West.

The Slavophils, on the other hand, turned away from old Europe as well as from the new European radicalism. They took a stand completely opposite to that of Chaadayev. One of their forerunners, the romantic philosopher Prince Vladimir Odoyevsky wrote to Stepan Shevyrev: "What Chaadayev says of Russia, I say of Europe, and vice-versa." The Slavophils believed the Russian past with its Orthodox Christianity greatly superior to the European Middle Ages with their Roman Christianity and to modern Europe with its rationalism and individualism. Characteristically, the

Slavophils had a deep faith in the Russian traditions and in
the distinguishing and unique character of Russian history
and development (its *samobytnost,* or to use the correspond-
ing term of German romanticism, *Eigenart*), which they did
not regard as a manifestation of backwardness as compared
with the West; rather they regarded the primitive Russian
peasant masses as the true bearers of Russia's destiny. In the
nineteenth century they idealized rural nature and the
peasant, as the physiocrats and Rousseau had done in eighteenth-century Europe. Similarly, twentieth-century Marxist Russia was to idealize industrial technology and natural
science as nineteenth-century Europe had done. And the
Bolsheviks in the 1930's might have agreed, with a slight
change, with Prince Odoyevsky's words of a century before,
when he wrote, "A Russified Europe, as a new force, will
bring life to senile and decrepit Europe. . . . There are
true signs of the unconscious gravitation of the West
towards the northeast; this tendency is involuntary and is
being developed by the West from within itself."

A small but growing number of Russian liberals understood Europe and wished to integrate Russia fully with the
West and its traditions of liberty under law. One of these
liberals was Ivan Turgenev. In his novel *Smoke* (1867) he
spoke out through the character of Potugin against the Russian superiority complex which deprecated other nations
and admired some home-grown genius whose works were
only an imitation. To a young Russian friend, Potugin con-
fessed: "Yes, I am a Westerner, I am devoted to Europe. I
mean, to put it more exactly, I am devoted to its cultural
standards, to those same cultural standards at which our
people poke such delightful fun these days—its civilization
—yes, yes, that word is still better. And I love it with all my
heart, and I believe in it. . . . Every time you have to turn
to a task, ask yourself: are you serving civilization—in the
exact and strict meaning of the word—are you carrying

through one of its ideas, has your labor that educative, European character which alone is beneficial and fruitful in our day, in our country?"

In a letter to Alexander Herzen, Turgenev wrote in 1862: "You who are an enemy of all mysticism and absolutism are kneeling mystically before the Russian sheepskin [the garment of the muzhik or Russian peasant], and you recognize in it a great blessing, new and original future forms of society—in one word you recognize it as the absolute, that absolute of which you make so much fun in philosophy. All your idols lie in ruins, but how can men live without an idol —and thus let us build an altar to the sheepskin, this unknown God. Fortunately one does not know anything about it, and thus one can again pray, believe, and hope." The unknown and idealized peasant masses, were they not the source of salvation not only for Russia but for the decaying and disintegrating West?

The two greatest writers of the Russian earth, Dostoevsky and Count Leo Tolstoy, rejected Western civilization and turned to the "sheepskin." Yet as if to illustrate the breadth and freedom of the Russian mind in its great age, they did it in a different and almost opposite spirit. Tolstoy shared the rational optimism and the universalist ethics of the European eighteenth century; his open mind embraced Russia and the world. His home in Yasnaya Polyana became a center of pilgrimage for men of all lands. His message was one of humanity and for humanity. He was a pacifist, for Russia and non-Russia alike, and rejected all excuses and subterfuges for Russia's wars and conquests.

Dostoevsky, on the other hand, was a Slavophil, a Russian Orthodox nationalist. To him man's life, in which reason was of little strength, was dark and tragic, an existence of sinfulness, suffering, and repentance. In this Christian pessimism and insistence on salvation through suffering, he sharply differed from Stalinist communism with its exces-

sive secular optimism. But Dostoevsky and Stalinism both
extolled the importance of the Russian people for the salvation of mankind. Dostoevsky regarded the Russian people
as the God-bearing nation (*narod bogonosets*). To heighten
the faith in Russia, he also compared the realities of the
West, with a heavy stress on their imperfections and their
sordid side, to an ideal Russia of truly brotherly love, as it
existed in lofty programs and daring anticipations. He saw
force and violence in the West and seemed not to be aware
that there were few states as warlike and oppressive as the
Russian autocracy. Wars by other nations seemed to him
acts of imperialism, which he bitterly condemned, but he
glorified Russia's wars as wars of liberation and proclaimed
an "imperialism of love" opposed to the Western imperialism of conquest and greed. He despised the poverty and
exploitation in capitalistic Europe without noticing the
incomparably greater oppression and misery of the masses
in Russia. The two worlds of Russia and Europe appeared
incompatible to him, and therefore they could not be
judged by the same standards. He was convinced of an inevitably approaching, decisive struggle between the two
camps. Russia's victory in this apocalyptic war would assure
peace and brotherhood everywhere. "So much that is new
and progressive will begin in human relations that it would
be useless to mourn and to hesitate on the eve of the last
great struggle which will bring about the great regeneration
of all Europe."

Dostoevsky shared the Slavophil conviction that Europe
—the creation of Roman and Teuton conquests, the spiritual product of Catholic rationalism and Protestant individualism—was doomed by the inevitable conflict of races and
classes and the inescapable growth of doubt and loss of faith,
all inherent in Europe's history and mentality. For these
reasons Western society needed legal and constitutional
guarantees for self-protection against its own lust for power

and lack of brotherly feeling. Through her history and true faith, Russia was different. Whereas Western nations needed bloody revolutions and civil wars to abolish serfdom or slavery, Russia had accomplished it in a peaceful way; her very nature prevented the growth of racial conflicts or the occurrence of social upheavals. Therefore, Russia could never build a society disfigured by shortcomings after the Western pattern. She must become either a perfect society, or she cannot exist at all. She must realize absolute justice, and must do it soon. Ivan Karamazov, one of Dostoevsky's most memorable heroes, voiced a general sentiment of the Russian youth when he exclaimed, "I must have justice or I will destroy myself. Not justice in some remote time or space, but here on earth, and so that I can see it myself." In the eyes of the Slavophils and in the eyes of the "progressive" Russian youth alike, Russia was destined to become the model "socialist" country, in which the social problem would be solved.

Many Russian intellectuals regarded the modern West with its middle-class mentality as incapable of social revolution and moral regeneration. Even Westernizers and socialists like Herzen and Bakunin shared the illusion of the Slavophils in transforming the most serious and actual Russian weaknesses into potential glorious national assets. "In the natural simplicity of our peasant life," Herzen wrote, "in our uncertain and unsettled economic and judicial conceptions, in our vague sense of property, in our lack of a strong middle class, and in our extraordinary capacity for assimilating foreign ideas, we have an advantage over nations that are fully organized and exhausted."

The coexistence of revolutionary justice and political autocracy, of a perfect solution of the social problem and the lack of parliamentary institutions and constitutional guarantees, presented no contradiction to the Russian mind. As early as 1851 the French historian Jules Michelet, who through study and inclination was equally familiar with the problems of liberty and of revolution and was deeply interested in the Slavs, pointed to this strange harmonization of apparently opposed attitudes. He was convinced that the West was threatened not so much by Russia's military aggression as by her assumption of the role of a revolutionary power and of a true friend of progress under an absolutist form. Russian propaganda, he wrote, disseminated doubt and confusion in Europe by using and perverting Western concepts of liberty and of help to the oppressed. Autocratic Russia, oppressing her own peasant masses, invaded Poland under the pretense of protecting the peasants there against the nobility. She attacked Turkey in order to establish political and religious freedoms there, although they did not exist in Russia herself. She did it always, Michelet charged, under a magniloquent slogan of disinterestedness, though the slogan varied. Michelet wrote with keen vision, "Yesterday Russian propaganda told us: I am Christianity—tomorrow it will tell us: I am Socialism." According to him, the Russian government, which he characterized as "the petrification of the Terror," maintained a strict separation of Russia from the West in order to prevent among its people the rise of Western individualism and searching criticism, which alone could awaken the Russians to a sense of liberty and avert the danger which they otherwise presented to Western freedom. A century later Michelet's description of 1851 seemed perfectly to fit the East-West relations in Europe.

The two decades following Michelet's warnings were filled with important developments. In 1861 Alexander II emancipated the Russian peasants; ten years later Germany defeated France. The victorious Germans regarded themselves as a "young" race, despising the "decadent" West. Michelet warned them against this assumption. The Russians might imitate the Germans, Michelet wrote in 1871, by regarding them too as an old and finished race. The Germans apparently expected the salvation of the West to come through Berlin's leadership. Might not Moscow, strengthened by the recent administrative reforms, assume this leadership herself? The emancipation of the serfs, which had aroused so many hopes, did not, in Michelet's opinion, prepare a liberal development in Russia, but rather it made possible the emergence of a "socialist" tyrant there, of an autocrat who would become "a messiah of the serfs, a barbarous messiah, terrible to Europe." Michelet called upon the West to unite against this danger. "I solemnly call upon young America," he wrote, anticipating the Atlantic union of a century later. "Let America justify our hope, let her be deaf to all petty interests, free of all petty rancors, devoted to the great general interest of human progress, closely associated with the civilized West, with the cause of liberty which she has supported so recently and which she has made so gloriously victorious."

Michelet pointed out what few people in the West realized even by the 1940's, that the words "liberty" and "democracy" had a different meaning for the West than for many Russians. For even in Russia's great age a Russian writer who lived in England for years and worked to promote the friendship between the two countries, Mrs. Olga Novikov, could write that in spite of all contrary appearances, the Russia of the 1880's represented a truer democracy than the West. "Russia has a nobility, but without any political privileges," she wrote; "General Skobelev, like all Russians, was a democrat and believed, like the overwhelming majority of all Russians, that our democracy required the supreme will of an autocratic concentrated power."

The aristocratic individualist Konstantin Leontyev, who might be regarded as representing the extreme Right, and the anarchist communist Bakunin, who stood for what may be called the extreme Left, were agreed on the one point that Western liberalism had no future in Russia. Leontyev in 1890 had the vision of a Russian autocrat who would organize and lead world revolutionary socialism through a system of enlightened despotism supported by a mystic faith. "It is no minor affair," he said, "to teach our people the spirit of law; such instruction might well take a century. Unfortunately, the great events will not wait so long. Our people love and understand authority better than law. They consider a military chief more accessible and even more sympathetic than a constitutional article or a legal code. A constitution which would weaken authority in Russia would not have the time to inculcate in the Russian the devotion which the English have for legality. Anyway, our people are right. Only a strong monarchical authority, limited solely by its conscience and sanctified by faith, can solve the contemporary problem which seems insoluble—the conciliation of capital and labor. We must draw ahead of Europe on the question of labor, and we must set the example. What the West regards as a genius of destruction, must become with us a creative work. Our people need affirmative faith and material security more than they need constitutional rights and true science."

The deep antagonism which, according to some Russian intellectuals, separated Russia from the West, together with the often overestimated strength and aggressiveness of the Russian state, aroused a wide-spread fear of Russia in nineteenth-century Europe. For a few decades after the defeat of Napoleon Russia appeared all-powerful and thought herself the arbiter of Europe's fate. Friedrich Gentz, Prince Metternich's secretary, described the European situation in 1815 in a way calling to mind that of 1945:

Napoleon's downfall was a pure and unqualified advantage for Russia; for the rest of Europe, and especially for the states bordering on Russia, it was largely balanced by the increased strength that she secured for herself at the expense of the general equilibrium. For this great power there is virtually no further real danger; if she attacks her neighbors her greatest risk is merely that she may fail in her purpose and have to postpone her venture for a more favorable time. The difficulty of penetrating Russia's interior is now so generally recognized that only lunacy and despair could prompt an attempt to conquer this great empire. While the other states of Europe exhausted themselves in the struggle against Napoleon, Russia who first allied herself with him understood well how to extract the most solid benefits from the ephemeral union. It would be easy for her to fall upon her neighbors, for she has so many greedy and ambitious reasons for trying it, and, if the expression be allowed, such substantially centrifugal habits, that war, which others regard as a necessary evil, will always be to the Russians a matter of choice, of emotion, and of speculation.

Yet in spite of the wide-spread fear of Russia, many European governments were on the best of terms with the Russian government during the nineteenth century; fear of Russia was not propagated by foreign offices and often ran counter to official policy. Though some Russian intellectuals continually suspected some plot of a united West against Russia, the government of St. Petersburg was free of such obsessive suspicions of a hostile surrounding world as have more recently characterized the government of Moscow. Fear of Russia was nevertheless kept alive in Europe by Russia's own policy which kept the country separated and inaccessible at a time when frontiers elsewhere lost their forbidding character and passports became unnecessary for travel. Such a policy by its repression of domestic opposition outraged large parts of Western public opinion. Russian persecution, moreover, created waves of emigrants who fed the European antipathy towards the Russian governmental system.

Thanks to this policy of seclusion, Russia was so little known in nineteenth-century Europe that the reports of travelers read like voyages of discovery in distant and fabulous lands. Such a traveler was the French writer Astolphe,

Marquis de Custine, a grandson of the famous General Adam Philippe, Comte de Custine, who fought with distinction under Lafayette in the American War of Independence and later in the French revolutionary wars. The younger Custine visited Russia in 1839; the four volumes which he published in 1843 and which went through many editions and translations were an indictment of the backwardness and servility of Russian society. Custine, whose grandfather and father had died as victims of the French revolutionary terror, went to Russia as a declared enemy of parliamentary government; he returned from there, as so many twentieth-century travelers have, a convinced *partisan des constitutions*. "The more I see of Russia," he wrote, "the more I approve of the Emperor forbidding the Russians to travel and rendering access of his country difficult to foreigners. The political régime of Russia could not withstand twenty years of free intercourse with Western Europe. . . . One has to have lived in this prison without leisure that is called Russia in order to feel all the freedom one enjoys in the other countries of Europe, whatever form of government they may have adopted. . . . When your son is discontented in France, use my formula, tell him to go to Russia. It is a journey useful to every foreigner: whoever has really seen that country will find himself satisfied to live anywhere else."

Half a century later an American journalist, George Kennan, visited Siberia. His book *Siberia and the Exile System*, which appeared in 1891, created a sensation in the Western world. The number of exiles involved was then infinitely smaller than it is today, and the Tsarist government showed itself more sensitive to foreign criticism; fundamentally, however, the situation as revealed by Mr. Kennan has little changed; it is clear how strongly the present Soviet police state is rooted in traditional Russian practices. Under the Tsars, people were exiled to Siberia by administrative process for being "suspected of the intention to put themselves into an illegal situation." "The grotesque injustice, the heedless cruelty, and the preposterous 'mistakes' and 'misunderstandings' that make the history of administrative exile in Russia seem to an American like the recital of a wild nightmare are due to the complete absence, in the Russian form of government, of checks upon the executive power, and the almost equally complete absence of official responsibility for unjust or illegal action. . . . The Russian government has its own press and its own representatives abroad; it can explain, if it chooses, its methods and measures. The Russian revolutionists, buried alive in remote Siberian solitudes, can tell their story only to an occasional traveller from a freer country, and ask him to lay it before the world for judgment." The Soviet government, more efficient than the Tsarist administration, has taken good care that no occasional travelers from a freer country talk to the Siberian exiles. The Russian government itself, from the times of the Grand Dukes of Moscovy on, has set the example of lawlessness. The suspected individual was, and is, "literally and absolutely without any means whatever of self-defense."

This governmental attitude under the Tsars was nevertheless not ruthless enough to cow some of the strong minds and wills among the people into total submission. The spirit of violence and lawlessness prevailing in the empire aroused a counterviolence among the revolutionaries, an almost mystical fervor of devotion to the idea of the revolution. Everything seemed permissible against the enemy. All rules of individual morality were suspended in the struggle. The revolutionaries could admit neither liberty nor law as their guiding principles, nor could they accept democratic decisions: by despotic leadership the inert masses were to be forced into revolution. But terrorism remained confined to a very small circle within the opposition to the existing governmental system. Even the Revolutionary

Executive Committee submitted on March 10, 1881, ten
days after the assassination of Alexander II, a letter to Alexander III in which it déplored the necessity for the bloody
revolutionary struggle and implored the Tsar to create the
conditions of a peaceful evolution in Russia. To that purpose it demanded the convocation of a freely chosen National Assembly, elected under conditions which would
guarantee the fullest liberty of election programs and cam-
paigns. "We declare solemnly before the fatherland and before the whole world that our party will submit without any
reservation to a National Assembly which is elected under
such conditions, and that it will in future never allow itself
to employ force or violence of any kind against a government legitimized by the National Assembly." When such a
National Assembly came into being, in January 1918, the
Soviet government unfortunately did not follow the line
proposed by the Revolutionary Executive Committee in
1881.

After the death of Alexander II, the Russian government
prepared the ground for the catastrophe by adhering stubbornly to a policy of absolutist autocracy. All reforms after
the model of Western parliamentary democracy were scorn-
fully rejected. The leading thinker of the régime, Konstantin Pobedonostsev, was convinced that Western civilization
led necessarily to moral corruption. When the English
translation of his *Moscow Collection* (1896) appeared in
1898, Mrs, Olga Novikov wrote in the preface that to the
author, "as to all of us Russians, the parliamentary theater
of the Western world performs a long tragicomedy, which
occasionally ascends to tragedy and sometimes sinks into
farce. However much you may deplore the fact, we are outside of it, and have never shown less disposition than today
to enroll ourselves in the democratic troupe. We have no
parliamentary party in Russia. No one, even in the abstract,
as a matter of theory, would wish to inoculate the Muscovite

politician with the passion of parliamentary faction." Mrs. Novikov was wrong in both thoughts: Western parliamentary democracy, and not the Muscovite absolutist system, proved its strength and stability; many Russians did long for the introduction of parliamentary democracy into Russia and wished to integrate their country into the Western system.

By the end of the nineteenth century, modern capitalism and the spirit of enterprise began slowly to penetrate into Russia. In widening circles an understanding of reality and responsibility was awakening; the struggle for liberty under law and the education for legal concepts and rights were undertaken in earnest. In the first years of the twentieth century, Russia made surprisingly great progress in all fields. The standards of living were fast rising. New industries were founded, and the cooperative movement among the peasants and popular education among all classes made rapid strides forward. Individual rights and property were more and more protected against the arbitrariness of a still semi-autocratic government; the freedom of inquiry and expression became accepted. In literature and art the best Western standards were reached or surpassed. The seclusion and exclusiveness characteristic of the Russian mind for so many centuries seemed definitely on the way out.

Vladimir Solovev, the greatest philosopher Russia has produced, as a young man came under the influence of Dostoevsky and the Slavophils, but later broke with them. He protested against "the worshipping of one's people as the chosen vessel of. universal truth. . . . For a true and far-sighted patriotism, the most essential, even the only essential question is not the question of Russia's might or mission but that of the sins of Russia."

The large majority of the educated classes thus worked for the full integration of Russia into Europe. But their efforts were crushed between the stupidity of a corrupt government and the backwardness and inertia of the masses. Had the First World War not broken out (Russian nationalist expansion was one of the elements precipitating it), or even so had Russia been among the democratic victors, her progressive Europeanization would have become certain. From the point of view of Western civilization, this would have been one of the decisive and hopeful factors in twentieth-century history. The revolution of March 1917, which overthrew the Russian autocracy in order to introduce constitutional liberty, pointed in that direction. But it was cut short by Nikolai Lenin's military coup of November 1917. Lenin restored autocracy, supported by a burning absolutist faith.

The Anglo-American revolutions in the seventeenth and eighteenth centuries developed against a unique background of English traditions of self-government and individual liberty. Thus they could lead to a continuous flowering of freedom under law. The French Revolution took place in a nation strongly absolutist in the political sense but at the same time culturally the most advanced of the period. Karl Marx expected his revolution to happen in the socially and economically most progressive country of the time. The Russian revolution turned into a disaster because its stage was set among the politically, culturally, and socially most backward masses of Europe, where the traditions of liberty were just beginning to take root. Thus Lenin's total rejection and contemptuous hatred of "bourgeois" Western civilization could strike a responsive cord in many Russian hearts. The masses were not prepared for constitutional liberty; many of the intellectuals harbored an eschatological faith in revolutionary utopianism. The greatest Russian poet of the period, Alexander Blok, suc-

cumbed for a brief moment to the nationalist missionary
appeal of the revolution. On January 30, 1918, before the
misery of the revolution cut off his voice, as it was to cut off
so many other voices of creative Russia, Blok wrote his last
poem, presenting the Russians as "Scythians" prepared to
embrace Europe in fraternal love or to destroy her in an
apocalyptic struggle.

The Westernizing revolution of March 1917 wished to
continue Russia's great age on a more popular and enlightened level, but the sudden relaxation of the restraints of
traditional authority mobilized the un-Europeanized
masses and released forces which Lenin with masterly and
ruthless strategy harnessed towards a revival of the old Muscovite unity of state and church: the state founded by Lenin
soon became more totalitarian than Ivan's had been, and
the Communist party line showed itself more comprehensive and exclusive than the Orthodox dogma. Masaryk, who
was then in Russia, saw from the beginning that Lenin's
revolution destroyed the hope of Russia's integration into
Europe. He found in Lenin more of Bakunin than of Marx.
"Unpolitical, wholly unscientific infallibility is the basis
for the Bolshevik dictatorship," he wrote in 1920, "and a
régime that quails before criticism and fears to recognize
thinking men stands self-condemned."

True, the Marxist dogma came from outside Russia, and
many of its elements originated in the German idealist philosophy and in the English political economy of the early
nineteenth century. But like Byzantine Orthodoxy, Marxism was soon nationalized and became a Russian church.
The new régime took over from Marxism not so much its
economic theories, which the development in the West had
proved wrong and which were inapplicable to a backward
agrarian community, as its eschatological expectation of the
coming perfect social order, the faith in revolution through

which the absolute ideal would be realized and this corrupt
world saved. Marx's secularized eschatology promised salvation according to the tenets of science and through the
means of technology. It offered to the descendants of the
Russian nihilists an apparently utilitarian and rational religion, to the service of which all thought and art, all life and
labor, could be directed.

When Lenin left Switzerland during the First World
War to return to Russia, he wote a farewell letter to the
Swiss workers on April 8, 1917, in which he said, "To the
Russian proletariat fell the great honor to inaugurate the
series of revolutions which are being produced, with objective necessity, by the imperialist war. But we do in no way
harbor the thought of regarding the Russian proletariat as
a chosen revolutionary proletariat among the workers of
other countries." From the beginning Lenin proclaimed
his "one world" goal, and his movement promised to realize
some of the desires and programs of the working class of
nineteenth-century Europe. Under Lenin, Russia seemed
to reach that position of world leadership which some of the
extreme Russian nationalists of the nineteenth century had
claimed for her. The forecast was impressive to many, but
close observers, familiar with Russia and with socialism,
saw from the beginning how alien Leninism was to the
main trend of the European tradition, especially to its
democratic tradition. How could Lenin harmonize his insistence upon the complete dependence of the people on
the party as "the vanguard" of the proletariat and upon the
total discipline within the party, with democracy? Leon
Trotsky, Lenin's principal assistant in the Bolshevik seizure
of power, wrote in 1904 that Lenin's method means that
first the party substitutes itself for the people or the proletariat; then the party organization substitutes itself for
the party as a whole; then the central committee of the organization substitutes itself for the organization; and finally

a single dictator substitutes himself for the central committee.

In 1870, the year of Lenin's birth, Bakunin described the organization of the revolutionary party which "will put itself at the head of the popular masses during the so visibly near destruction of the Russian empire." It will have nothing in common with political or socialist parties as known in the West. It will be a party "strong by its discipline, by the devotion and passionate self-denial of its members and by its passive obedience to all the orders of a central committee . . . in which it is not the individual who thinks, desires, and acts, but the collectivity. A serious member will understand that only such a discipline can create a collective revolutionary force which, supported by the elemental force of the people, will be able to overthrow the formidable strength of the state. . . . Whoever is for this program, will come with us. Whoever is against us, is a friend of the enemies of the people, he is a henchman of the Tsar, he is our enemy. Whoever is not for us, is against us."

Lenin followed Bakunin's lead. His party was not, as parties in Western society are, part of a society, but a dominant all-embracing totality. In reality, it was nothing but the militant instrument of an omnipotent and omniscient autocracy. Masaryk asserted in 1921: "The Bolsheviks have accepted Marxism and pride themselves on being its only orthodox adherents. They do not realize how much they owe to Bakunin, the adversary of Marx. From him they took over their mystic faith in the revolution, in the Russian people, in its unique socialist and communist ability. . . . All the shortcomings which characterized the Russian state, the Russian school, the Russian church, and so on, characterize also the Bolshevik state and régime because they have come from the same people and have undergone the same formation."

Even some of the most orthodox or radical non-Russian

Marxists opposed Lenin's method. Rosa Luxemburg, a leader of German extremist socialists, wrote in September 1918:

Each democratic institution has its limits and shortcomings, a situation shared by all human institutions. But the remedy which Trotsky and Lenin found, namely the annihilation of democracy itself, is still worse than the evil which it wishes to cure: to bury the life source itself, from which alone all the innate insufficiencies of the social institutions can be corrected, the active, unrestrained, energetic political life of the masses. It is a manifest and incontestable fact that without a free press and without the free right of association and meeting the rule of the masses is entirely unthinkable. Liberty only for the adherents of the government, only for the members of one party—be they ever so numerous—is no liberty. . . . Public life gradually dies off. Several dozens of party leaders, men of inexhaustible energy and boundless idealism, direct and rule, but in reality not more than a dozen brilliant men are in real control, and the working class is called from time to time to attend meetings to applaud the speeches of the leaders and to adopt unanimously resolutions proposed by the leaders —this is truly a dictatorship, but not the dictatorship of the proletariat, but one of a handful of politicians.

Once only in their history the Russian people were allowed free elections. These were instituted by the provisional government which originated in the revolution of March 1917. The elections were held in November of that year. The Constituent Assembly thus elected was the realization of the hopes and efforts of many decades, the result of Russia's contact with Europe in her great age. But hardly had the assembly met in Petrograd in January 1918 when Lenin dispersed it by armed force. Two months later, Russia's capital was transferred from the maritime periphery where Peter had placed it at the beginning of Russia's great age, to Russia's ancient capital behind the hallowed walls of the Kremlin. At the very moment when to all outward appearances, Russia professed to appeal to the whole world as never before, she withdrew into herself and again became a closed society, anxiously guarded from contact with the infidel world; once again she became the Third Rome, Holy Russia, which was to lead mankind to salvation. Haughtily she turned against Europe. The encounter between Russia and the West, which had been a period of high intellectual fertility and ferment for both, was closed. With it, Russia's great age was over, at least for the time being.

II

Russia's Place in Universal History
CHAADAYEV

In the second quarter of the nineteenth century, St. Petersburg was the capital of the Russian Empire and the seat of the imperial court, but Moscow was its intellectual center. The oldest Russian university was founded in Moscow in 1755. It was there that the very small circle of highly educated men, almost all of them members of the landowning aristocracy, began to discuss Russia's enigmatic position in the political and intellectual history of Europe. This generation had witnessed Napoleon's defeat in Russia, the victorious march of Russian armies across Europe into Paris, and the dominant role of the Russian Emperor at the Peace Congress of Vienna, which settled the fate of Europe. Russia cast a gigantic shadow over Europe, yet politically and culturally she appeared backward and her people immature.

This discrepancy between appearance and reality struck Peter Yakovlevich Chaadayev, a member of the aristocratic and intellectual circles in Moscow. As a young man he had fought in the Russian army against Napoleon and had served in Europe. He resigned his commission out of a desire for complete personal freedom. From that time on until his death in 1856 he led a solitary life. Neither a radical nor a revolutionary, he was deeply attached to the cultural life of Old Europe and to the conservative Christian pacifism of the Holy Alliance. He was influenced by the French political thinker Joseph Comte de Maistre, who was Sardinian ambassador in St. Petersburg, and by the German philosopher Schelling. Although Chaadayev was a Russian patriot and a monarchist, he did not countenance the facile self-glorification of so many of his Russian contemporaries. He rejected their comforting illusion that the Russian past and the Orthodox Church were infinitely superior to the European past and Western Christianity. He found the face of the Russian masses strangely expressionless, mirroring an inner emptiness.

According to Chaadayev, Russia was retarded as a result of her separation from the universal trend of European history. Russia had vegetated throughout the centuries, unaffected by the civilizing influences of Greek and Roman antiquity, of the Catholic Middle Ages, and of modern times. The ideas of civil rights and duties, individual dignity and freedom, ideas inherent in the air which Occidental peoples breathe, were alien to Russia. "The history of other nations is a story of their emancipation. Russian history is the development of serfdom and of autocracy." How could Russia, a nation which had contributed nothing to the stream of universal civilization, claim the mission of guiding Europe and mankind? Russia must first break her isolation, learn from Europe, and vitalize her faith by contact with the Western Church.

Chaadayev left no written work outside of a few fragmentary essays and a number of personal letters. Only one of his essays, which he called "Philosophical Letter Written to a Lady," was published during his lifetime. But so daring was its content, so deep its sense of moral and human responsibility, so incisive its language, that it created a sensation in a country in which the number of periodicals was extremely small. It appeared in 1836 in a Moscow periodical in a Russian translation, and it was dated from Necropolis, the City of the Dead, a term designating Moscow. It was originally written in 1829 in French, the language of all Chaadayev's writings. The impression that this essay made on the Russian public, living in the enforced silence of the régime of Nikolai I, was described by Alexander Herzen as "a shot that rang out in the dark night; it forced all to awaken." Russian society was outraged. The authorities intervened. The periodical was suppressed, the censor who had passed the article was dismissed, the editor exiled, and the author declared insane by order of the Tsar.

Chaadayev wrote in the following year an essay "Apology of a Madman," which was not published until after his death. It bore as motto Coleridge's lines: "Oh my brethren! I have told most bitter truths, but without bitterness." In it he expressed his hopes for Russia's future. The very fact of her isolation and backwardness might make her the heir of the whole experience of the West, if she learned from Europe and avoided Europe's mistakes. Because Russia was virgin soil, without a past and without spiritual traditions, she enjoyed the freedom of judging and choosing without prejudice. But Chaadayev did not retract his judgment of Russia's past and present; courageously he rejected all narrow or boastful nationalism. Love of truth was superior to, and more beneficial than, love of country.

To these sentiments Chaadayev remained faithful throughout his life. At the beginning of the Crimean War, two years before his death, he circulated a memorandum among his friends, at the very time when patriotic enthusiasm about the war against Europe and confidence in Russian power and victory were at their height. Therein he spoke of the patriotism of his youth and of the great changes which had come over the Russian mind in the period between the end of the Napoleonic War and the Crimean War. "We wished the welfare of our country, we desired good institutions for her, we even sometimes went so far as to wish more liberty for her, if that were possible. We knew that Russia was great and powerful, with much promise for the future. But . . . we were far from imagining that Russia represented some kind of abstract principle comprising the definite solution of the social problem, that she by herself constituted a world apart . . . that she had a special mission of absorbing all the Slav peoples in her bosom, and of bringing about the regeneration of mankind. Above all, we did not think that we were called on to save European civilization which had formerly saved us from our ancient torpor. We treated Europe with civility, nay, even with respect, for we knew that she had taught us many things, and among others, our own history. . . .

"You have changed all that; so be it! Who does not know that the so-called national sentiment has grown to a state of real monomania among our new class of learned men? It was no longer a question of the prosperity of the country or of civilization or progress; it was sufficient to be Russian: this quality included all imaginable blessings, even salvation. . . . The nationalists began to repudiate all the serious and fertile ideas which Europe had taught us, and claimed to have started a new ethics on the soil of Russia. . . . These new patriots mistake their unfinished thoughts, their inarticulate wishes and their vague hopes for a true national policy. They greeted the Crimean War, without any hesitation, as the beginning of the realization of the utopia. Nor did the government lack the docile following of the masses who fall for every patriotic dream which is sold to them in the banal idiom used on such occasions." Whereas the Russian nationalists dreamt of Russia's victory over the decadent West and saw in the Crimean War the beginning of the final victorious struggle between Russia

and the Occident, Chaadayev advised the Russians to sue
for peace as soon as possible.

Chaadayev had an immense influence on the Russian
thought in the first part of the nineteenth century by the
opposition which his views aroused. He had no followers.
From the Slavophils he was separated by his whole evalua-
tion of the Russian past. The Westernizers shared his love
and respect for European civilization, but they revered
"progressive" Europe, the revolutions of 1830 and 1848,
whereas Chaadayev was dedicated to the traditional liberties of Old Europe, much nearer to Burke than to Bentham
in his thought and heart. But like the Westernizers he was
convinced that what Russia needed was ordered liberty and
respect for individual rights and that she could find these
only in cooperation with the West.

More than one hundred years later, another Russian
thinker, Georgii Fedotov, infinitely more familiar with the
Russian past and the Orthodox Church than Chaadayev
was, and with a perspective on the experience with Russian
nationalism and utopian radicalism, expressed the same
thought: that the idea of liberty was an Occidental concept
and experience and had to be learned by Russia from Europe. Only on such basis, Chaadayev and Fedotov knew,
could Russia grow into her great age, to that moral and
intellectual life which was potentially hers.

RUSSIA AND THE WORLD

[From "Letters on the Philosophy of History," 1829–1831]

ONE of the most deplorable things in our strange civilization is that we still have to discover the truths,
often very trivial ones, which other, even less advanced
peoples discovered long ago. We have never moved in con-

cert with other peoples; we do not belong to any of the great families of mankind. We are not part of the Occident, nor are we part of the Orient; and we don't have the traditions of the one or of the other. Since we are placed somewhat outside of the times, the universal education of mankind has not reached us. . . .

All peoples undergo a time of violent agitation, of passionate restlessness, of action without thought. At that time men wander around in the world like bodies without a soul. It is the age of the great emotions, of the large undertakings, of the grand passions of the people. People then move vehemently, without any apparent aim, but not without profit for posterity. All societies pass through these periods, and from them receive their most vivid reminiscences, their miracles, their poetry, and all their most powerful and most fruitful ideas: these reminiscences are the necessary bases of societies. Otherwise the societies would not have any fond memories to cling to; the dust of their earth would be their only tie. The most interesting epoch in the history of mankind is that of the adolescence of the nations, for that is the moment when their faculties develop rapidly, a moment which lingers in their memories and serves as a lesson once they are mature. Over here we have nothing like it. The sad history of our youth consists of a brutal barbarism, then a coarse superstition, and after that a foreign, savage, and degrading domination of the spirit which was later inherited by the national power. We have not known an age of exuberant activity and of the exalted play of moral forces among the people as others have. The period in our social life which corresponds to this moment was characterized by a dull and dreary existence, without vigor or energy, which was enlivened only by abuse and softened only by servitude. There are no charming recollections and no gracious images in our memory, no lasting lessons in our national tradition. If you look over all the centuries in which we have lived and over all the territory which we cover, you will not find a single fond memory, or one venerable monument which forcefully speaks of bygone times or retraces them in a vivid or picturesque manner. We live in the most narrow present, without a past or a future, in the midst of a flat calm. And if at times we strive for something, it is not with the hope and desire for the common good, but with the childish frivolity of the baby who stands up and stretches out his hand to grasp the rattle which his nurse is holding. . . .

The peoples of Europe have a common physiognomy, a family resemblance. Despite their general division into Latins and Teutons, into southerners and northerners, it is plain to anyone who has studied their history that there is a common bond which unites them into one group. You know that not too long ago all of Europe considered itself to be Christian, and this term had its place in public law. Besides this general character, each of these peoples has its own character, but all that is only history and tradition. It is the ideological patrimony inherited by these peoples. There each individual is in full possession of his rights, and without hardship or work he gathers these notions which have been scattered throughout society, and profits from them. Draw the parallel yourself and see how we can profit from this interchange of elementary ideas, and use them, for better or for worse, as a guide for life. Note that this is not a question of studying, of lectures, or of anything literary or scientific, but simply of a relation between minds; of the ideas which take hold of a child in his crib, which are surrounding him when he plays, which his mother whispers to him in her caresses; of that which in the form of various sentiments penetrates the marrow of his bones, the very air he breathes, and which already permeates his soul before he enters the world and society. Do you want to know what these ideas are? They are the concepts of duty, justice, law, and order. They are derived from the same events which have shaped society; they are the integral elements of the social world in these countries.

This is the atmosphere prevailing in the Occident. It is more than history, it is more than psychology; it is the physiology of the European man. What do you have to put in its place over here? I don't know whether one can deduce anything absolute from what we have just said, or whether one can derive strict principles from it. But it is easy to see how this strange situation of a people which cannot link its thought to any progressive system of ideas that slowly evolve one from the other within a society, of a people which has participated in the general intellectual movement of other nations only by blind, superficial, and often clumsy imitation, must be a strong influence on each individual within that people. . . .

God forbid! I certainly do not claim that we have all the vices and that Europe has all the virtues. But I do say that one has to judge a people by studying the general spiritual attitude which is at the base of its existence, and only this spirit can help it to attain a more perfect moral state or an infinite development, and not this or that trait in its character.

The masses are subject to certain forces at the summit of society. They do not think for themselves; but among them there is a certain number of thinkers who do think for themselves, and thus provide an impetus to the collective intelligence of the nation and make it move onward. While the small number meditates, the rest feel, and the general movement takes place. This is true for all the peoples of the earth with the exception of a few brutal races whose only human attribute is their face. The primitive peoples of Europe, the Celts, the Scandinavians, and the Germans, had their druids, their scalds, and their bards; all were powerful thinkers in their own way. Look at the people of North America who are being destroyed by the materialistic civi-

lization of the United States: among them are men of great
depth.

Now, I ask you, where are our sages, where are our thinkers? Which one of us ever thought, which one of us is
thinking today? And yet we are situated between the great
divisions of the world, between the Orient and the Occident, one elbow leaning on China and the other one on
Germany. Therefore, we should be able to combine the
two principles of an intelligent being, imagination and
reason, and incorporate the histories of the whole globe into
our own. However, that is not the role assigned to us by
Providence. Far from it, she doesn't seem to have concerned
herself with us at all. Having deprived the hearts of our
people of her beneficent influence, she has left us completely
to ourselves; she did not want to bother with us, and she
did not want to teach us anything. The experience of the
ages means nothing to us; we have not profited from the
generations and centuries which came before us. From
looking at us it seems as though the moral law of mankind
has been revoked especially for us. Alone of all the peoples
in the world, we have not given anything to the world, and
we have not learned anything from the world. We have not
added a single idea to the pool of human ideas. We have
contributed nothing to the progress of the human spirit, we
have disfigured it. From the first moment of our social existence we have not created anything for the common good
of man. Not a single useful thought has grown in the sterile
soil of our fatherland; no great truth has been brought
forth in our midst. We did not take the trouble to devise
anything for ourselves, and we have only borrowed deceptive appearances and useless luxuries from the devices of
others.

A strange fact! Even in the all-inclusive scientific world,
our history is not connected with anything, doesn't explain
anything, doesn't prove anything. If the hordes of barbar-

ians who convulsed the world had not crossed the country in which we live before swooping down on the Occident, we could hardly have filled one chapter of world history. In order to be noticed we had to expand from the Behring Straits to the Oder. Once, a great man wanted to civilize us, and, in order to give us a taste of the lights, he threw us the mantle of civilization; we picked up the mantle, but we did not touch civilization. Another time, a great prince, in associating us with his glorious mission, led us to victory from one end of Europe to the other; when we returned from this triumphal march across the most civilized countries of the world, we brought back only ideas and aspirations which resulted in an immense calamity, one that set us back half a century. There is something in our blood which repels all true progress. Finally, we have only lived, and we still only live, in order to give a great lesson to a remote posterity which will understand it; today, despite all the talk, our intellectual achievements are nihil. I cannot help but admire this astonishing blank and this solitude in our social existence. It contains the seeds of an inconceivable destiny, and doubtlessly also man's share of that destiny, as does everything which happens in the moral sphere. Let us ask history: she is the one who explains the peoples.

What did we do during the struggle between the energetic barbarism of the northern peoples and religion's high ideals, a struggle out of which rose the edifice of modern civilization? Driven by a fatal destiny, we searched unhappy Byzantium for the moral code which was to educate us, and thus we incurred that people's utter contempt. Shortly before that, an ambitious spirit [Photius] had led this family away from universal brotherhood; thus we adopted an idea which had been disfigured by human passion. At that time everything in Europe was animated by the vital principle of unity. Everything was derived from it, and everything converged on it. The whole intellectual movement of the time tended to bring about the unity of human thought, and all activity originated in this driving need to arrive at a universal idea, which is the essence of modern times. Strangers to this marvelous principle, we became a prey to conquest. Once we were freed from the yoke of the foreigner, we could have profited from the ideas which had blossomed forth during that time among our Occidental brothers, if we had not been separated from the common family. Instead we fell under a harsher servitude, one which was sanctified by the fact of our deliverance.

How many bright lights had already burst forth in the Europe of that day to dispel the darkness which had seemed to cover it! Most of the knowledge on which humanity prides itself today had already been foreshadowed in men's minds; the character of society had already been fixed; and, by turning back to pagan antiquity, the Christian world had rediscovered the forms of beauty that it still lacked. Relegated in our schism, we heard nothing of what was happening in Europe. We had no dealings with the great event taking place in the world. The distinguished qualities which religion has bestowed on modern peoples have made them, in the eyes of sound reason, as superior to the ancient peoples as the latter were to the Hottentots or the Laplanders. These new forces have enriched the human mind; these principles have made submission to an unarmed authority as gentle as it was brutal before. Nothing of all that took place over here. Despite the fact that we were called Christians, we did not budge when Christianity, leaving the generations behind it, advanced along the path which its divine Founder had indicated in the most majestic manner. While the world entirely rebuilt itself, we built nothing; we stayed in our thatched hovels. In one word, the new fortunes of mankind did not touch us. Christians, the fruit of Christianity did not ripen for us. . . .

In the end you will ask me: aren't we Christians, and can

one become civilized only in the way Europe was? Unquestionably we are Christians; aren't the Abyssinians Christians as well? Certainly one can be civilized in a different manner than Europe was: haven't the Japanese been civilized, even more so than the Russians, if we are to believe one of our compatriots? Do you believe that the Christianity of the Abyssinians or the civilization of the Japanese will bring about that order of things of which I just spoke, or that they constitute the ultimate goal of the human race? Do you believe that these absurd aberrations from the divine and human truths will make heaven come down to earth? . . .

All the nations of Europe held hands while advancing through the centuries. Today, no matter how many divergent paths they try to take, they always find themselves together. One does not have to study history in order to understand the family development of these peoples. Just read Tasso, and you will see them all bowing down before the walls of Jerusalem. Remember that for fifteen centuries they spoke to God in the same language, lived under a single moral authority, and had the same belief. Remember that for fifteen centuries, each year, on the same day, at the same hour, with the same words, they all together raised their voices towards the Supreme Being, to extol his glory. A wonderful concert, a thousand times more sublime than all the harmonies of the physical world! Moreover, since that sphere where the Europeans live, the only one where the human race can fulfill its final destiny, is the result of the influence that religion had on them, it is clear that up to now our lack of faith or the insufficiency of our dogmas has kept us out of this universal movement, in which the social ideal of Christianity has been formulated and developed. We have thus been thrown into that category of peoples who will profit only indirectly from Christianity's influence, and at a much later date. Therefore, we must try to revive our faith in every possible way and give ourselves a truly Christian enthusiasm, since it is Christianity which is responsible for everything over there. That is what I meant when I said that this education of the human race has to begin once more for our benefit. . . .

Fundamentally, we Russians have nothing in common with Homer, the Greeks, the Romans, and the Germans; all that is completely foreign to us. But what do you want! We have to speak Europe's language. Our exotic civilization rests so much on Europe's that even though we do not have its ideas, we have no other language but hers; hence we are forced to speak it. If the small number of mental habits, traditions, and memories we have do not link us to any people of this earth, if, in effect, we do not belong to any of these systems of the moral universe, we still, because of our social superficialities, belong to the Occidental world. This link, which in truth is very feeble, which does not unite us so closely to Europe as is commonly thought, and which fails to let every part of our being feel the great movement taking place over there, still makes our future destiny dependent on this European society. Therefore, the more we try to amalgamate with it, the better off we shall be. . . .

Certainly we cannot remain in our desert much longer. Let us do all we can to prepare the way for our descendants. We are unable to bequeath them that which we do not have—beliefs, reason molded by time, a strong personality, opinions well-developed in the course of a long intellectual life that has been animated, active, and fruitful in its results—but let us at least bequeath them a few ideas which, even though we did not find them ourselves, will at least have a traditional element in them, if transmitted from one generation to the next. By this very fact they will have a certain power and a certain profundity which our own ideas did not have. We shall thus be worthy of posterity, and we shall not have inhabited this earth uselessly.

RUSSIA'S INTERCOURSE WITH EUROPE

[From letters to A. I. Turgenev, 1833 and 1835]

Here, my friend, is a letter for the illustrious Schelling which I ask you to forward to him. The idea of writing to him came to me from something you once said about him in one of your letters to her ladyship, your cousin. The letter is open, read it, and you will see what it is about. Since I talked about you in it, I wanted it to reach him through you. It would give me great pleasure if, when you send it to him, you could let him know that I understand German; because I am anxious for him to write to me (if he does me that honor) in the language in which he so often revived my friend Plato, and in which he transformed science into a combination of poetry and geometry, and by now perhaps into religion. And heavens! It is time that all this became one thing. . . .

Please don't be offended, but I prefer your French letters to your Russian ones. There is more free rein in your French letters, you are more yourself. Moreover, you are good when you are completely yourself. . . . Besides, you are essentially a European. You know that I know something about it. You should really wear the garb of a Frenchman. . . .

Like all peoples, we too are galloping today, in our own way if you like, but we are speeding, that is certain. I am sure that in a little while the great ideas, once they have reached us, will find it easier to realize themselves in our midst and to incarnate themselves in our individuals than anywhere else, because here they will find no deep rooted prejudices, no old habits, no obstinate routines to fight. It seems to me that the European thinker should not be totally indifferent to the present fate of his meditations among us. . . .

What? You live in Rome and don't understand it after all

that we have told and retold each other about it! For once, understand that it is not a city like all the others, a heap of stones and of people; it is an idea, it is an immense fact. One should not look at it from the top of the Capitol or from the gallery of St. Peter, but from that intellectual summit which brings so much delight when one treads on its sacred soil. Rome will then be completely transfigured right before your eyes. You will see the large shadows by which these monuments project their prodigious teachings over the whole surface of the earth, and you will hear a powerful voice resound from this silent body and tell you ineffable mysteries. You will know that Rome is the link between ancient times and new times, because it is absolutely necessary that there be one spot on earth to which, at times, every man can turn in order to rediscover materially and physiologically all the memories of the human race, something sensible, tangible, in which the thought of the ages is summed up in a visible manner—and that spot is Rome. Then these prophetic ruins will tell you all the fates of the world; their tale will be a whole philosophy of history for you, a whole doctrine, and more than that, a living revelation. . . . But the Pope, the Pope! Well, isn't the Pope another idea, a completely abstract thing? Look at the figure of that old man, carried on his litter, under his canopy, always in the same manner for thousands of years, as though it were nothing. Seriously, where is the man in all that? Isn't he an all powerful symbol of time, not of that time which passes but of the time which does not move, through which everything else passes but which itself remains motionless, and in which and by which everything happens? Tell me, don't you absolutely want a single intellectual monument on the earth, one which lasts? Don't you need something more in the way of human achievement than the pyramid of granite which knows how to fight the law of death, but nothing else?

That great play which is put on by the peoples of Europe, and which we attend as cold and impassive spectators, makes me think of that little play by Mr. Zagoskin whose title is *The Dissatisfied,* which is to be given here and will be attended by a cold and impassive audience. The dissatisfied! Do you understand the malice of that title? What I don't understand is where the author found the characters for his drama. Thank God, here one sees only perfectly happy and satisfied people. A foolish well-being and a stupid satisfaction with ourselves, those are our outstanding traits at the present time; it is remarkable that at the moment when all that the Christian peoples inherited from paganism, the blind and excited nationalism which makes them each other's enemies, is fading away, and when all the civilized nations are beginning to give up their self-complacency, we take it upon ourselves idiotically to contemplate our imaginary perfections. . . .

Take any epoch you like in the history of the Occidental peoples, compare it to the year we are in now [1835], and you will see that we do not embrace the same principle of civilization that those peoples do. You will find that those nations have always lived an animated, intelligent, and fruitful life; that they were handed an idea at the very beginning, and that it is the pursuit of that idea and its development which make up their history; and finally that they have always created, invented, and discovered. Tell me, what idea are we developing? What did we discover, invent, or create? It is not a question of running after them; it is a question of an honest appraisal of ourselves, of looking at ourselves as we are, to cast away the lies and to take up the truth. After that we shall advance, and we shall advance more rapidly than the others because we have come after them, because we have all their experience and all the work of the centuries which precede us. The people in Europe are strangely mistaken about us. There is Mr. Jouffroy, who

tells us that we are destined to civilize Asia. That is all very
well; but, I beg you, ask him what Asian peoples have we
civilized? Apparently the mastodons and the other fossilized
populations of Siberia. As far as I know, they are the only
races we have pulled out of obscurity, and that thanks only
to Pallas and Fischer. Some Europeans persist in handing
us the Orient; with the instinct of a kind of European nationalism they drive us back to the Orient so as not to meet
us any longer in the Occident. Let us not be taken in by
their involuntary artifice; let us discover our future by ourselves, and let us not ask the others what we should do. It is
evident that the Orient belongs to the masters of the sea;
we are much farther away from it than the English, and we
no longer live in an age when all Oriental revolutions come
from the middle of Asia. The new charter of the India Company will henceforth be the true civilizing element of Asia.
On the contrary, it is Europe to whom we shall teach an
infinity of things which she could not conceive without us.
Don't laugh: you know that this is my profound conviction.
The day will come when we shall take our place in the
middle of intellectual Europe, as we have already done in
the middle of political Europe; and we shall be more powerful, then, by our intelligence than we are today by our material forces. That is the logical result of our long solitude:
great things have always come from the desert.

THE LEGACY OF PETER THE GREAT

[From "Apology of a Madman," 1837]

For three hundred years Russia has aspired to consort
with Occidental Europe; for three hundred years she has
taken her most serious ideas, her most fruitful teachings,
and her most vivid delights from there. For over a century
Russia has done better than that. One hundred and fifty
years ago the greatest of our kings—the one who supposedly

began a new era, and to whom, it is said, we owe our greatness, our glory, and all the goods which we own today—dis-
avowed the old Russia in the face of the whole world. He
swept away all our institutions with his powerful breath; he
dug an abyss between our past and our present, and into it
he threw pell-mell all our traditions. He himself went to the
Occidental countries and made himself the smallest of men,
and he came back to us so much the greater; he prostrated
himself before the Occident, and he arose as our master and
our ruler. He introduced Occidental idioms into our language; he called his new capital by an Occidental name; he
rejected his hereditary title and took an Occidental title;
finally, he almost gave up his own name, and more than
once he signed his sovereign decrees with an Occidental
name.

Since that time our eyes have been constantly turned
towards the countries of the Occident; we did nothing more,
so to speak, than to breathe in the emanations which
reached us from there, and to nourish ourselves on them.
We must admit that our princes almost always took us by
the hand, almost always took the country in tow, and the
country never had a hand in it; they themselves prescribed
to us the customs, the language, and the clothing of the
Occident. We learned to spell the names of the things in
Occidental books. Our own history was taught to us by one
of the Occidental countries. We translated the whole literature of the Occident, we learned it by heart, and we adorned
ourselves with its tattered garment. And finally, we were
happy to resemble the Occident, and proud when it con-
sented to count us as one of its own.

We have to agree, it was beautiful, this creation of Peter
the Great, this powerful thought that set us on the road we
were to travel with so much fanfare. It was a profound wisdom which told us: That civilization over there is the fruit
of so much labor; the sciences and the arts have cost so much

sweat to so many generations! All that can be yours if you cast away your superstitions, if you repudiate your prejudices, if you are not jealous of your barbaric past, if you do not boast of your centuries of ignorance, if you direct your ambition to appropriating the works of all the peoples and the riches acquired by the human spirit in all latitudes of the globe. And it is not merely for his own nation that this great man worked. These men of Providence are always sent for the good of mankind as a whole. At first one people claims them, and later they are absorbed by the human race, like those great rivers which first fertilize the countryside and then pay their tribute to the waters of the ocean. Was the spectacle which he presented to the universe upon leaving his throne and his country to go into hiding among the last ranks of civilized society anything else but the renewed effort of the genius of this man to free himself from the narrow confines of his fatherland and to establish himself in the great sphere of humanity?

That was the lesson we were supposed to learn. In effect we have profited from it, and to this very day we have walked along the path which the great emperor traced for us. Our immense development is nothing more than the realization of that superb program. Never was a people less infatuated with itself than the Russian people, such as it has been shaped by Peter the Great, and never has a people been more successful and more glorious in its progress. The high intelligence of this extraordinary man guessed exactly the point of our departure on the highway of civilization and the intellectual movement of the world. He saw that lacking a fundamental historical idea, we should be unable to build our future on that impotent foundation. He understood very well that all we could do was to train ourselves, like the peoples of the Occident, to cut across the chaos of national prejudices, across the narrow paths of local ideas, and out of the rusty rut of native customs; that we had to raise ourselves, by one spontaneous outburst of our internal powers, by an energetic effort of the national conscience, to the destiny which has been reserved for us. Thus he freed us from previous history which encumbers ancient societies and impedes their progress; he opened our minds to all the great and beautiful ideas which are prevalent among men; he handed us the whole Occident, such as the centuries have fashioned it, and gave us all its history for our history, and all its future for our future.

Do you not believe that if he had found in his country a rich and fertile history, living traditions, and deep-rooted institutions, he would have hesitated to pour them into a new mold? Do you not believe that faced with a strongly outlined and pronounced nationality, his founding spirit would have demanded that that nationality itself become the necessary instrument for the regeneration of his country? On the other hand, would the country have suffered being robbed of its past and a new one, a European one, being put in its place? But that was not the case. Peter the Great found only a blank page when he came to power, and with a strong hand he wrote on it the words *Europe* and *Occident:* from that time on we were part of Europe and of the Occident.

Don't be mistaken about it: no matter how enormous the genius of this man and the energy of his will, his work was possible only in the heart of a nation whose past history did not imperiously lay down the road it had to follow, whose traditions did not have the power to create its future, whose memories could be erased with impunity by an audacious legislator. We were so obedient to the voice of a prince who led us to a new life because our previous existence apparently did not give us any legitimate grounds for resistance. The most marked trait of our historical physiognomy is the absence of spontaneity in our social development. Look carefully, and you will see that each important fact in our history is a fact that was forced on us; almost every new idea is an imported idea. But there is nothing in this point of view which should give offense to the national sentiment; it is a truth and has to be accepted. Just as there are great men in history, so there are great nations which cannot be explained by the normal laws of reason, for they are mysteriously decreed by the supreme logic of Providence. That is our case; but once more, the national honor has nothing to do with all this.

The history of a people is more than a succession of facts, it is a series of connected ideas. That precisely is the history we do not have. We have to learn to get along without it, and not to vilify the persons who first noticed our lack. From time to time, in their various searches, our fanatic Slavophils exhume objects of general interest for our museums and our libraries; but I believe it is permissible to doubt that these Slavophils will ever be able to extract something from our historic soil which can fill the void in our souls or condense the vagueness of our spirit. Look at Europe in the Middle Ages: there were no events which were not absolutely necessary in one way or another and which have not left some deep traces in the heart of mankind. And why? Because there, behind each event, you will find an idea, because medieval history is the history of modern thought which tries to incarnate itself in art, in science, in the life of man, and in society. Moreover, how many furrows of the mind have been plowed by this history! . . .

The world has always been divided into two parts, the Orient and the Occident. This is not merely a geographical division, it is another order of things derived from the very nature of the intelligent being—Orient and Occident are two principles which correspond to two dynamic forces of nature; they are two ideas which embrace the whole human organism. . . .

The Orient was first, and it spread waves of light all over the earth from the heart of its solitary meditations; then came the Occident, which, by its immense activity, its quick word, its sharp analysis, took possession of its tasks, finished what the Orient had begun, and finally enveloped it in its vast embrace. But in the Orient, the docile minds, who were prostrated before the authority of time, exhausted themselves in their absolute submission to a venerated principle, and one day, imprisoned in their immovable syntheses, they fell asleep, without any inkling of the new fates in store for them; whereas in the Occident the minds proudly and freely advanced, bowing only to the authority of reason and of God, stopping only before the unknown, with their eyes always fixed on the unlimited future. And you know that they are still advancing, and you also know that since the time of Peter the Great we believe that we are advancing with them.

But here comes another new school. It no longer wants the Occident; it wants to destroy the work of Peter the Great and again follow the desert road. Forgetting what the Occident has done for us, ungrateful towards the great man who civilized us, towards the Europe which taught us, this school repudiates both Europe and the great man; and in its hasty ardor, this newborn patriotism already proclaims that we are the cherished children of the Orient. Why, it asks, do we have to look for lights among the peoples of the Occident? Don't we have in our midst the germs of an infinitely better social order than Europe has? Why don't we leave it to time? Left to ourselves, to our lucid reason, to the fertile principle which is hidden in the depth of our powerful nature, and above all to our saintly religion, we shall soon go beyond those peoples who are a prey to errors and to lies. For what should we envy the Occident? Its religious wars, its Pope, its chivalry, its Inquisition? Truly beautiful things! Is the Occident the native land of science and of all deep things? It is the Orient, as is well known. Let us then withdraw to the Orient, which we touch everywhere and from which erstwhile we derived our beliefs, our laws, and our virtues, all that made us the most powerful people in the world. The old Orient is fading away: well, aren't we its natural heirs? Henceforth it is among us that these wonderful traditions will perpetuate themselves, that all these great and mysterious truths, with whose safekeeping we were entrusted from the very beginning, will realize themselves. Now you understand whence came the storm which beat down upon me the other day, and you see how a real revolution is taking place in our midst and in our national thought. It is a passionate reaction against the Enlightenment and the ideas of the Occident, against that enlightenment and those ideas which made us what we are, and of which even this reaction, this movement which today drives us to act against them, is the result. But this time the impetus does not come from above. On the contrary, it is said that in the upper regions of society the memory of our royal reformer has never been more venerated than it is today. The initiative, then, has been entirely in the hands of the country. Whither will this first result of the emancipated reason of the nation lead us? God only knows! If one truly loves one's country, it is impossible not to be painfully affected by this apostasy on the part of our most highly developed minds towards the things which brought us our glory and our greatness; and I believe that it is the duty of a good citizen to do his best to analyze this strange phenomenon.

We are situated to the east of Europe; that is a positive fact, but it does not mean that we have ever been a part of the East. The history of the Orient has nothing in common with the history of our country. As we have just seen, the history of the Orient contains a fertile idea which, in its time, brought about an immense development of the mind, which accomplished its mission with a stupendous force, but which is no longer fated to produce anything new on the face of the earth. . . .

Believe me, I cherish my country more than any of you. I

strive for its glory. I know how to appreciate the eminent qualities of my nation. But it is also true that the patriotic feeling which animates me is not exactly the same as the one whose shouts have upset my quiet existence, shouts which have again launched my boat—which had run aground at the foot of the Cross—on the ocean of human miseries. I have not learned to love my country with my eyes closed, my head bowed, and my mouth shut. I think that one can be useful to one's country only if one sees it clearly; I believe that the age of blind loves has passed, and that nowadays one owes one's country the truth. I love my country in the way that Peter the Great taught me to love it. I confess that I do not feel that smug patriotism, that lazy patriotism, which manages to make everything beautiful, which falls asleep on its illusions, and with which unfortunately many of our good souls are afflicted today. I believe that if we have come after the others, it is so that we can do better than the others; it is so that we may not fall into their faults, their errors, and their superstitions. . . . I believe that we are in a fortunate position, provided that we know how to appreciate it. It is a wonderful privilege to be able to contemplate and judge the world from the height of independent thought, free from unrestrained passions and petty interests which elsewhere disturb man's view and pervert his judgment. More is to come: I am firmly convinced that we are called on to resolve most of the social problems, to perfect most of the ideas which have come up in the old societies, and to decide most of the weighty questions concerning the human race. I have often said it, and I like to repeat it: in a way we are appointed, by the very nature of things, to serve as a real jury for the many suits which are being argued before the great tribunals of the human spirit and of human society.

III

The Slav and World Mission of Russia

POGODIN

Mikhail Petrovich Pogodin, though only six years younger than Chaadayev, belonged to another generation. He was the son of a serf, a self-made man, who through zealous industry became an outstanding journalist and editor. In 1830 he was named professor of history at Moscow University. He represented that Russian-centered nationalism and that utopian expectation of Russia's future which Chaadayev combated and scorned. Pogodin was inspired as a youth by the romantic nationalism and anti-Westernism which then swept Central and Eastern Europe. He was overawed by the greatness of the Russian Empire after its victory over Napoleon. The grandeur and might of Russia were to Pogodin incontrovertible proof that Russia possessed herself a glorious past independent from Europe. This past appeared to guarantee an even greater future planned for Russia by Providence.

For many years Pogodin, together with his friend Stepan Petrovich Shevyrev, formed the center of Moscow's literary life. Shevyrev, who was professor of literature at the University of Moscow, cooperated with him in editing and publishing several periodicals; the most important was *Moskvit-yanin,* which appeared from 1841 to 1856. More than anyone else, Pogodin drew the attention of the Russians to the other Slav peoples, especially to those who lived in the Habsburg and Ottoman Empires. He was one of the fathers of Russian Pan-Slavism. Like most of his friends, he never doubted that the other Slavs looked upon Russia with love and devotion, as upon an older brother, and that it was Russia's mission to "liberate" the other Slavs from Western influence and to guide them to their true fulfillment. Between 1835 and 1853 Pogodin visited Europe five times in order to establish a closer contact with the Western Slavs and to promote Pan-Slavism.

When in 1837 the heir to the throne, the future Tsar Alexander II, visited Moscow, Pogodin addressed to him an essay "Letter on Russian History," which expressed his characteristic nationalist and Pan-Slav sentiments. They will sound familiar to readers of some similar Russian statements which emanated from Moscow in the middle of the twentieth century. Russia's world mission and her Slav leadership by the 1950's had become official policy. One century before, they represented only the dreams and aspirations of some Russian intellectuals. The "Letter on Russian History" never reached the Prince because the director of education for the Moscow district to whom it was submitted did not forward it. Pogodin did not publish it until 1867. But his hopes for Russia's mission had in no way been dimmed. Though the country had undergone the painful experience of the Crimean War, Pogodin was convinced that the liberation of the Russian serfs, the distribution of the land, and the liberal reforms of Alexander II served as an auspicious pledge for Russia's future greatness.

THE WEALTH AND STRENGTH
OF RUSSIA

[From "Letter on Russian History," 1837]

RUSSIA, what country can compare with her in magnitude? Which one merely by half? . . . A population of sixty million people, that increases by a million every year! Where is there a people as numerous as that? . . . Let us add to it thirty million more of our brothers and cousins, the Slavs . . . in whose veins flows the same blood as ours, who speak the same language as we do, and who feel, therefore, according to the law of nature, as we do. In spite of geographical and political separation, the Slavs form by origin and language a spiritual entity with us. Hence, we may subtract their number from the population of the neighboring countries of Austria and Turkey and of the rest of Europe, and add it to our figure. What will be left to Europe, and what will fall to us? My thinking stops, the spirit seizing me. . . .

The ninth part of the inhabited earth, almost the ninth part of all mankind! . . . Yet the size of the land, the numbers of people, are not the only conditions of strength. Russia is a country that contains all kinds of soil, all climates, from the hottest to the coldest, from the scorched land around Erivan to icy Lapland—a country that even in her present state of development abounds in all products which are indispensable for maintenance, welfare, and enjoyment, a world in itself, self-contained, independent, with no need of supplementation. Many of her products are of a kind that each by itself could in the course of time have been the source of wealth for whole empires. . . .

We possess mountains of gold and silver, metals almost

exhausted elsewhere in Europe, and vast untapped deposits in reserve. One might request any amount of iron and copper and it would be delivered to the Fair of Nijnii Novgorod the following year. Grain—we feed all Europe in years of famine. Timber—we could rebuild all the cities of Europe, if they were burnt—which God forbid! Flax, hemp, and hides—we give them clothes and shoes. Only yesterday we started to produce sugar, and soon, it is said, we shall not need any more of it from abroad. And wine— the long-stretched shores of the Black and Caspian seas, the Crimea, Bessarabia, are waiting for wine growers, and already the vintners of Burgundy and Champagne are purchasing land in these regions. Moreover, we export wool— and yet the Novorossiisk Region, the old domain of nomads, possesses so many fat pastures that countless flocks will thrive there in the future, and we shall not have to envy the Merinos of Spain and England. Wide regions are fit for silk culture. Shall I speak of cattle, fish, salt, and furs? What do we lack? What is it that we cannot obtain at home? What is it that we could not furnish to others? And all this is, as it were, on the outside, on the surface, near, before our eyes, under our hands, but if we look further, if we dig deeper, . . . Are there not persistent rumors that beds of bituminous coal of several versts thickness have been discovered, that marble, diamonds, and other precious stones have been found?

Those are raw products, but where is there a country more fit for the establishment of factories, since labor is so cheap and the needs and demands of workers so moderate? What a short time ago it was that we started thinking of factories—and yet how well they have developed! Did we not have proof of it at the latest exhibition of our national industry? What about the progress of our spinning, cloth, and cotton mills, our chemical industry? And where could commerce flourish more briskly than here in this country with its immense turnover, and its proximity to the sea-shores, to foreign countries needing our goods, and to the rich Asian lands of Persia, India, and China? In what should Russia fear the rivalry of the English, in spite of all their steamboats on the Euphrates and the Nile and their rail-roads at Suez and Panama?

True, much of what I mention here is not yet in exist-ence, but everything is within possible reach and, what is more, within easy reach. And indeed, which of these things could not be realized tomorrow, if necessary, and if ordered by supreme command? There are physical resources at our disposition, in quantity and quality as nowhere else in Eu-rope, either in the past or in the present, and there is unlim-ited possibility of their future development. . . .

As to the spiritual resources, I wish to point out a peculiar trait of the Russian people, their *tolk* [insight, good sense, fairness] and their *udal* [boldness, courage], for which there are no words in any other European language—their sen-sibleness, vitality, patience, devotion, their stamina in time of emergency, this happy union of qualities of northern and southern men. Education in Europe is a matter of caste, al-though allegedly open to everybody; the lower classes there —with a few exceptions—are remarkable for a certain dull-ness of wit, as the traveler finds out at first glance.

But what is the capacity of the Russian man? In order to give some examples, I wish to draw attention to such things as we see before our eyes every day. We see a muzhik with his heavy hands called in for military service: he has just been taken from behind the plow, he cannot look straight at anything. This "bumpkin," this real Russian bear, can-not take a step without knocking against something. He may be thirty, sometimes nearly forty years old. But his hair will be cut, and a year later he cannot be recognized. He marches in the first platoon of the guard, he carries his rifle no worse than any drum major, in an agile, easy, skillful, even elegant manner. And more, a bugle is put in his hand, or a fagot or a flute, and he becomes a regimental musician and plays so well that foreign artists come to listen to him. This soldier when placed in gunfire, will stand and not falter, when sent to death, will go without thinking. He suffers everything possible: he would don a sheepskin in hot summertime and go barefooted in icy cold, he would live off biscuit for weeks, and he is not inferior to a horse in case of forced marches. Charles XII, Frederick the Great, and Napoleon, unbiased judges indeed, preferred him to all soldiers of the world, extended to him the palm of victory.

The Russian peasant himself manufactures everything he needs, with his own hands; his ax and chisel take the place of the machine, and many industrial goods are being made in peasant huts. Look what patterns come from the hands of pupils in drawing or architectural schools! How proficient in physics and chemistry are peasant children in the technical and agricultural schools! How gifted are the youngsters in the Moscow School of Art!

How many remarkable inventions have never been exploited, just because of the lack of communication and publicity? Deep understanding for the Holy Scriptures and original thinking about problems of theology and philosophy are often found among simple people. The young Russian scholars who at the beginning of the reign of the present Tsar went abroad have won the recognition of outstanding European professors; these in admiration of the fast and brilliant success of their Russian students have granted them a place of honor among their rank. All that is proof of the national talents of the Russians. What a spiritual strength in addition to the physical!

All these physical and spiritual forces form a gigantic machine, constructed in a simple, purposeful way, directed by the hand of one single man, the Russian Tsar, who with one motion can start it at any moment, who can give it any direction, any speed he wishes. But let us keep in mind that that machine is moved by more than mechanical function. No, it is all animated by one feeling, an ancient legacy from our ancestors: allegiance, limitless confidence, and devotion to the Tsar, their God on earth.

I ask: who can compare with us? Whom will we not force into submission? Is not the political fate of the world in our hands whenever we want to decide it one way or the other?

The truth of my words will be even more manifest if one considers the conditions in other European countries. . . . In contrast to Russian strength, unity, and harmony, there is nothing but quarrel, division, and weakness, against which our greatness stands out still more—as light against shadow. . . .

I do not know if it is not too hazardous and paradoxical a statement, that those countries [i.e., France and England] were stronger in the past than they are at present, stronger in words than in deeds, that the right of the individual and the constitution, which indisputably may have its good sides too, have developed from their historic roots at the expense of political strength, that the state machinery has become complex and extremely cumbersome, so that every decision, in passing a multitude of stages, persons, and public bodies, loses its natural force and freshness and misses the right time. I do not know what great actions could yet be undertaken even in these two great countries. Must they not admit that Napoleon and Waterloo represented the culminating point of their strength—*ne plus ultra*. . . .

What is impossible to the Russian Emperor? One word, and a whole empire has ceased to exist—one word, and another empire has been wiped out from the earth—one word, and in their place a third empire is rising, stretching from the Eastern Ocean to the Adriatic Sea. One hundred thousand soldiers more, and the Caucasus will be pacified; its savage sons will serve with the Russian cavalry together with

Kalmuks and Bashkirs, and yet its new generation will be educated in the Russian Cadet Corps in other customs and in another way of thinking. One thousand soldiers more, and a highway is opened towards the border towns of India, Bokhara, and Persia. The Tsar can reverse even the history of the past according to his will: although we did not participate in the Crusades, did he not liberate Jerusalem by a note to the High Porte, by a mere article of a treaty? [Allusion to the Treaty of Unkiar Skelessi of July 5, 1833.] We did not discover America, although we did discover one-third of Asia; but does not our gold, the output of which increases from year to year, supplement the discovery of Columbus, does it not promise to become a counterpoison against poison?

It is well known that our present Emperor, Your Most August Father, does not think of any conquest of that kind, but I cannot help, I dare not fail to, remark as a historian that the Russian Ruler now, even without such a plan, without such a wish, without any preparation, without any intention, quietly seated in his office at Tsarskoe Selo, is nearer to the universal monarchy than Charles the Fifth and Napoleon ever were in their dreams. Europe itself is well aware of that, although ashamed to admit it. That untiring attention that follows every step of ours in Europe, that incessant suspicion at our slightest moves, that muffled grumbling of jealousy, envy, and malice which issues from newspapers and magazines, are they not the most convincing proof of Russia's strength? Yes, the future of the world depends on Russia—spoken, so God wills. What a glorious prospect!

But, my Lord, there is another glory, a pure, beautiful, sublime, sacred glory, the glory of the good, of love, of knowledge, of right, of happiness. What does power matter? Russia does not admire feats of power, any more than a millionaire is impressed by thousands. She stands calmly and silently—and the world is trembling before her, intriguing and busy about her. Russia can do everything. What more does she want? The other glory is more flattering and more desirable. We can shine forth in that glory, too.

Whoever impassionately contemplates the European countries must admit with all regard for their remarkable constitutions, with all gratitude for the service they have rendered to mankind, and with all respect for their history that they have outlived their time and spent their best strength, which means that they cannot produce, cannot achieve anything greater than they did before, be it in the field of religion, law, science, or art. But have they really accomplished everything? Does not history show, on the contrary, that the development in every single country—as compared with the totality of human life—was merely partial, one-sided, incomplete; that in Germany, for instance, the idea prevailed, in religion as well as in other fields; in Italy, feeling; in France, sociability; in England, personality? Yet where is there a full universal development? If we further compare the nations of the entire world, of the old and of the new, we see that each nation has one outstanding quality but is inferior to the rest in other concerns. There must be, however, a synthesis.

Let me consider it still from another higher, ethical point of view. Who dares pretend that the goal of humanity has been achieved or kept in sight by any of the states of Europe? In one country we see more knowledge, in another more production, more comfort, in a third more welfare, but where is the "sacred good"? Corruption of morals in France, laziness in Italy, cruelty in Spain, egoism in England, are characteristic of these countries. Are these by any chance compatible with the idea of civic, not merely individual, happiness, with the ideal society, the City of God? It is the Golden Calf, the mammon, to which without exception all Europe pays homage. Should there not be a higher level of a new European civilization, of Christian civilization? America, on which our contemporaries had pinned their hopes for a time, has meanwhile clearly revealed the vices of her illegitimate birth. She is no state, but rather a trading company, like the East India Company which independently owned territory. America cares solely for profit; to be sure, she has grown rich, but she will hardly ever bring forth anything great of national, let alone of universal, significance. There are no fruits ripening in the countries of the world.

I repeat: where is the "sacred good"? Kollár, the famous Slavic poet of our time, predicts in one of his poetic reflections the coming glory of the Slavs, in particular in the arts. "It is impossible," he exclaims, "that so great a people, so great in numbers, spread over so wide a space, of such talents and qualities, with such language, should accomplish nothing for the good of humanity. Providence does not contradict itself. Everything great is destined for great purposes."

It seems to me one can extend the meaning of Kollár's prophecy and say that the future belongs altogether to the Slavs.

There is in history a succession of nations: one after another steps forth, standing guard, as it were, and does its service to mankind. So far the Slavs have been missing in that illustrious sequence. Their time, therefore, is come to start their course, to begin their noble work for mankind, and to display their highest capacities.

But which of the Slav tribes occupies the first rank today? Which tribe can by its number, its language, and the totality of its qualities be considered the representative of the entire Slav world? Which offers the best pledge for the future goal? Which shows most clearly that it has the conditions for reaching that goal? Which indeed? . . .

My heart trembles with joy, oh Russia, oh my Fatherland! Is it not you? Oh, if it were only you! You, you are chosen to consummate, to crown the development of humanity, to embody all the various human achievements (which hitherto have been accomplished only separately) in one great synthesis, to bring to harmony the ancient and modern civilizations, to reconcile heart with reason, to establish true justice and peace. You alone can prove not only that science, liberty, art, knowledge, industry, and wealth are the goal of mankind, but that there is something higher than scholarship, trade and education, freedom and riches —the true enlightenment in the spirit of Christianity, the Divine Word, which alone can impart to Man earthly and heavenly happiness. . . .

IV

Slav Protests Against Russia's Mission

MICKIEWICZ and HAVLÍČEK

From the time of Pogodin to the last years of Stalin, for well over a century, Pan-Slavism has played a dominant role in the Russian mind. The Russians not only claimed the role of protector and leader of all Slavs, but also they stressed an alleged common Slav mind or mentality, so much so that for many Russians, "Russian" and "Slav" became synonymous.

It is important to point out that the other Slavs never recognized these Russian claims. Leading non-Russian Slavs warned the Russian Pan-Slavs that their hopes for a close political and intellectual union of all the Slavs were ill-founded. They rejected Russian Pan-Slavism as Pan-Russian, which would subject all Slav peoples to undisputed Russian leadership and finally to Russification. The non-Russian Slav peoples who lived within the Russian Empire, the Ukrainians, the Belo-Russians, and the Poles, were subject to a process of ruthless Russification in the second half of the nineteenth century. The Russian concern for the other Slav peoples seemed to spring from the recognition that only by absorbing them into the Russian sphere, only by pushing Russian control westward to a line running from Stettin on the Baltic Sea to the eastern shores of the Adriatic Sea, could Russia be safe from Western influence and strong enough to fulfill her mission.

The Russians felt closest to the Balkan Slavs, with whom they shared the Byzantine heritage of the Orthodox faith. On the other hand they felt most doubtful about the militantly Catholic Poles, whom they regarded as a Western outpost directed against Russia. They were more hopeful about the Czechs and Slovaks as possible allies in the struggle against the West. The Russian Pan-Slavs interpreted the Hussite movement, a fifteenth-century religious reform movement among the Czechs, as an uprising against the West and its Roman Church and as a reassertion of true Slav consciousness. It was, in fact, among the Czechs and Slovaks that the modern Pan-Slav movement started. It was set off by Jan Kollár, who published in 1824 the famous cycle of poems *Slávy Dcera* (*The Daughter of Slava*) and called for the cultural and literary solidarity of all the Slavs.

Most Polish national leaders and writers in the nineteenth century regarded Russian Pan-Slavism, and Russian thought in general, with hostility. They believed that Poland was Europe's bulwark against semi-Asian Russia. Whereas the Russian Slavophils had no doubt that Russia was the true Slav people and at the same time the true Christian people, the predestined savior of Europe and civilization, some of the greatest Polish poets extolled Poland in a similar way. After Poland's autonomy under the Russian Tsar had been lost in the uprising of 1830–31, the national fervor of Polish exiles proclaimed that Poland must rise again and that renascent Poland must propagate the democratic idea among the Slavs and must give the signal for the general emancipation of the European peoples.

By none was this faith expressed more strongly than by the greatest Polish poet, Adam Mickiewicz, whose poetic and prophetic visions deeply influenced Polish patriotism. He was born and brought up in Lithuania, a country which at the beginning of modern times had united with culturally more advanced Poland under the Lithuanian dynasty of Jagiello. In the eighteenth century Lithuania and the greater part of Poland were absorbed by the Russian Empire. Mickiewicz, Lithuanian by descent, Polish by culture, and Russian by political nationality, was accused of an anti-Russian conspiracy and was exiled, by order of the Russian government, to the interior of Russia. He was never to see his native land again. The five years he spent in Russia were decisive for the development of his poetry. He lived there in comparative liberty, received with great friendliness by Pushkin and by Russian literary society. He left Russia for Italy, where his Catholic faith became fervent. The Polish uprising of 1830–31 began while he was in Italy, and although he did not participate in it, it turned him into a fiery patriot who gave "the most powerful literary expression that exists of the loathing felt by the Poles for their Russian oppressors."

Mickiewicz moved in 1832 to Paris. His creative poetical work ceased in 1834. The last two decades of his life he spent as an active and indefatigable propagandist of the Polish national cause. A romantic in his poetry and in his politics, he had now the ambition to become the messianic seer and national teacher of the Poles. In a pseudo-biblical prose work *The Books of the Polish Nation from the Beginning of the World to the Martyrdom of the Polish Nation,* which appeared in 1832, he presented an idealized picture of Polish history in the setting of a treacherous and idolatrous world. Mickiewicz believed that Poland had been partitioned and crucified for its whole-hearted devotion to the liberty and brotherhood of all peoples. The neighboring monarchies, especially the Russians, could not tolerate such a nation. But Mickiewicz was confident that Poland's mar-

tyrdom would end and the nation rise again from its grave.
Its resurrection would bring liberty and peace not only to
Poland but to mankind.

While Mickiewicz and other great Polish poets succumbed to the exalted romantic mysticism of the 1830's,
Czech national leaders showed a more realistic attitude in
the late 1840's. But Poles and Czechs were united in the
opposition to Russia's claim of the leadership of all Slav
peoples or of mankind. This feeling of independence was
shared by the Yugoslavs, who in the first part of the nineteenth century were generally called Illyrians. The Czechs
in 1848 felt nearer to the West than to Russia. They wished
to strengthen the Austrian Empire, to which they belonged,
as a federation of equal nationalities, and they feared subjection to Russian rule and influence as much as to that of
Germany.

František Palacký, the leading Czech patriot of the period
and the country's first great historian, in his *History of the
Czech Nation* interpreted the Hussite movement as a pioneer struggle for the liberty of conscience and for the equality of men against spiritual and social authoritarianism.
Though the Hussites were defeated by German Catholic
armies, they sowed, according to Palacký, the seeds for the
future growth of liberty and enlightenment in Western
Europe. Western emancipation from authoritarianism
owed much to the Hussite Czechs. Thus the Czechs belonged intellectually to the West. In his political program
Palacký stood not only for the liberal demands of 1848 but
also for federalism as the basis for the coexistence of several
nationalities within larger political and economic units. He
did not believe that the small nations of Central and Central Eastern Europe could find security and prosperity in
national independence. But he never envisaged a federation
of the Czechs, or the other Austrian Slavs, with Russia.

In a famous letter to the Committee for calling a German

National Assembly to Frankfurt in 1848, Palacký rejected
the invitation to participate in the assembly, not only because as a Czech he could not take part in a movement dedicated to the creation of a strong and centralized German
nation, but also because he was afraid that the Frankfurt
assembly would weaken Austria. As a Czech he wished to
strengthen Austria, "an empire whose preservation, integrity, and consolidation is, and must be, a great and important matter not only for my own nation but for the whole of
Europe, indeed, for mankind and civilization itself." He
saw a danger to Czech and Slovak survival not only in German expansion or Magyar aggression but also in Russian aspirations.

Russia, Palacký wrote in words strangely anticipating the
mood of 1948, carried on her conquests under the cover of
promoting world peace and social justice. "You know," he
wrote in 1848, "which power it is that occupies the whole
great eastern part of our continent. You know that this
power which already has grown to vast dimensions increases
by its own strength, every decade, to a far greater extent
than is possible for Western countries. Being inaccessible
at its own center to almost any attack, this power has become, and has for a long time been, a threat to its neighbors.
Although it has an open access to the north, it is always
seeking, as if by natural instinct, to expand southwards, and
will continue to do it. Every further step taken on this path
threatens at an ever accelerating pace to found a universal
monarchy, that is to say, an infinite and inexpressible evil,
a misfortune without measure or bound, which I, though
heart and soul a Slav, would deeply regret for the good of
mankind, even though that universal empire called itself a
Slav one." This "universal empire," which Palacký regarded as the core of the Russian aspirations, was envisaged
by Pogodin, Danilevsky, and Dostoevsky. They wished to
found it upon the all-inclusive community of the only true

faith, which would enable its faithful to spread everywhere the principles of justice and peace.

None recognized more clearly the dangerous illusion of Pan-Slavism and of an alleged affinity of Czechs and Russians than the greatest democratic Czech journalist, Karel Havlíček. In his youth he visited Poland and Russia, then as today a closed and little known country, and lived in Moscow in the house of Shevyrev, Pogodin's friend. There he gained a better understanding of the Eastern Slavs and their attitudes and problems than other Czechs of the 1840's had. After his return from Russia, when he became editor of the *Prague News*, a Czech newspaper, he published there in 1846 an article, "Czech and Slav," in which he realistically faced the backwardness of Russia and Poland. Russia did not appear to him to be a country which could or should spread its light to other Slavs and to Europe. He was convinced that Russia urgently needed enlightenment from the West and that the Czechs, a Western people themselves, should turn for guidance to the West. He was one of the first to understand the Ukrainian aspirations for liberty, which most Russians disregarded or rejected. Much of what Havlíček wrote in his article in 1846 has retained its validity even to the present day.

THE BOOKS OF THE POLISH NATION

[From Mickiewicz' prose work, 1832]

IN THE beginning there was belief in one God, and there was freedom in the world. And there were no laws, only the will of God, and there were no lords and slaves, only patriarchs and their children.

But later men renounced the one God, and made for

themselves idols, and bowed down to them, and slew in their honor bloody offerings, and waged war for the honor of their idols.

Therefore God sent upon the idolaters the greatest punishment, which is slavery.

And one half of the people became the slaves of the other half, although all had sprung from one Father. For they had renounced that origin and had devised for themselves various Fathers; one said that he sprang from the earth, and another from the sea, and others from other things.

And when, thus warring, some were taking others into slavery, they all fell together into the slavery of the Roman Emperor.

The Roman Emperor called himself God, and proclaimed that there was no other law in the world except his will; what he approved, that was to be called virtue, and what he condemned, that was to be called sin.

And philosophers were found who strove to prove that the Emperor in so doing did well. . . .

And all the people of the earth became slaves, and there was never such slavery in the world, either before or after, save in Russia in our own days.

For even among the Turks the Sultan must respect the law of Mahomet, nor can he interpret it himself, but for that there are Turkish priests.

But in Russia, the Emperor is the head of the faith, and in what he commandeth men to believe, in that they must believe.

And it came to pass that when slavery had grown strong in the world, there came on a turning point for it; even as the solstice, the turning point of night, in the longest and darkest night, such was the turning point of slavery in the time of the Roman bondage.

At that time there came to earth Jesus Christ, the Son of

God, teaching men that all are born brethren, children of one God.

And that he is the greatest among men, who serveth them and who sacrificeth himself for their good. And whosoever is better in any way, so much the more ought he to sacrifice. But Christ, being best of all, was to sacrifice his blood for them through the bitterest sufferings. . . .

And whosoever sacrificeth himself for others shall find wisdom and riches and a crown on earth, in heaven, and everywhere.

But whosoever sacrificeth others for himself, that he may have wisdom, and office, and riches, shall find folly and wretchedness and damnation on earth, in hell and everywhere.

And finally Christ said: "Whosoever will follow after me shall be saved, For I AM TRUTH AND JUSTICE." And when Christ taught in this manner, the judges who judged in the name of the Roman Emperor were terrified; and they said: "We drove out justice from the earth, and behold it returneth: let us slay it and bury it in the earth."

Then they martyred the holiest and most innocent of men, and laid him in the tomb, and they cried out: "Justice and truth are in the world no longer; who now will rise against the Roman Emperor?"

But they cried out foolishly, for they knew not that having committed the greatest sin, they had already filled up the measure of their iniquities; and their power came to an end at the time when they exulted most.

For Christ arose from the dead, and, having driven out the emperors, he set up his cross in their capital city; and at that time the lords freed their slaves and acknowledged them as brothers, and the kings, anointed in the name of God, acknowledged that the law of God was over them, and justice returned to the earth.

And all the nations that believed, whether they were Germans, or Italians, or French, or Poles, looked upon themselves as one nation, and this nation was called Christendom.

And the Kings of the different nations looked upon themselves as brothers, and marched under the one sign of the cross.

And he who was a man of knightly rank rode out to war against the heathen in Asia, that he might protect the Christians in Asia and win back the sepulcher of the Savior.

And they called this war in Asia the War of the Cross. . . .

Then the kings, renouncing Christ, made ready new gods that were idols, and set them up in the sight of the people, and bade them bow down to them and fight for them. . . .

And the nations forgot that they had sprung from one Father. And the Englishman said: "My father is *ship* and my mother is *steam*." And the Frenchman said: "My father is *continent* and my mother is *bourse*." And the German said: "My father is *workshop* and my mother is *pothouse*."

And those same people who said that it was folly to fight for the faith against the pagans, those same people fought for a scrap of paper called a treaty, fought over a seaport, over a city; like serfs who fight with clubs over the boundary of an estate which they do not possess but which their lords possess.

And those same people who said that it was folly to go to distant lands in the defense of their fellow men, those same people sailed over the sea at the bidding of their kings, and fought over a factory, over a bale of cotton, and over a sack of pepper. And the kings sold them for money into lands across the sea.

And the people became corrupt, so that from among the Germans, and the Italians, and the French, and the Spaniards, only one Christian man was to be found, a wise man and a knight. He was by birth a Genoese.

He exhorted them that they should cease fighting at home, but should rather win back the sepulcher of the Lord and Asia, which had become a desert plain, but which might be a populous and fair country in Christian hands. But all laughed at that man of Genoa and said: "He dreams, and is foolish."

Therefore that godly man departed himself for the war; but in that he was alone, and poor, he therefore wished first to discover lands where gold is produced; and after having gathered riches from there, to hire an army and reconquer the Holy Land. But all when they heard him cried out: "He is mad."

Yet God saw his good intent, and blessed him; and that man discovered America, which became the land of freedom, a holy land. That man was called Christopher Columbus, and he was the last knight of the cross in Europe, and the last who undertook an enterprise in the name of God, and not for himself.

But in Europe meanwhile idolatry had increased. And just as the pagans worshiped at first different virtues in the form of idols, and then different vices, and then men and beasts, and then trees, stones, and different figures that they drew, so also it happened in Europe.

For the Italians devised for themselves an idol goddess, whom they called *Political Balance of Power*. And this idol the pagans of old had not known, but the Italians were the first to establish its worship among themselves, and fighting over it they became weak and foolish and fell into the hands of tyrants.

Then the kings of Europe, seeing that the worship of this goddess *Balance of Power* had exhausted the Italian nation, introduced her quickly into their kingdoms and spread abroad her worship and bade men fight for her.

And the Prussian king drew a *circle* and said: "Lo, here

is a new God." And they bowed down to this *circle* and called this worship *political rounding*. . . .

Finally in idolatrous Europe there rose three rulers; the name of the first was *Frederick the Second* of Prussia, the name of the second was *Catherine the Second* of Russia, the name of the third was *Maria Theresa* of Austria.

And this was a satanic trinity, contrary to the Divine Trinity, and was in the manner of a mock and a derision of all that is holy.

Frederick, whose name signifieth *friend of peace*, contrived wars and pillage throughout his whole life, and . . . in mockery of wisdom wrote a book which he called *Anti-Machiavelli*, or the adversary of Machiavelli, but he himself acted according to the teaching of Machiavelli.

Now *Catherine* signifieth in Greek pure, but she was the lewdest of women, and it was as though the shameless Venus had called herself a pure virgin.

And this Catherine assembled a council for the establishing of laws, that she might turn lawmaking into a mockery, for the rights of her neighbors she overthrew and destroyed.

And this Catherine proclaimed that she protected freedom of conscience or tolerance, that she might make a mock of freedom of conscience, for she forced millions of her neighbors to change their faith. And *Maria Theresa* bore the name of the most meek and immaculate Mother of the Savior, that she might make a mock of humility and holiness. . . .

The names of these three rulers, *Frederick, Catherine,* and *Maria Theresa*, were thus three blasphemies, and their lives three crimes, and their memory three maledictions.

Then this trinity, seeing that not yet were the people sufficiently foolish and corrupt, fashioned a new idol, the most abominable of all, and they called this idol *Interest*, and this idol was not known among the pagans of old.

And the nations became corrupt, so that among them was found only one man who was a patriot and a soldier.

He exhorted them that they should cease warring for *Interest*, but rather that they should protect the freedom of their neighbors; and he himself went away to war, to the land of freedom, to America. The name of this man is Lafayette. And he is the last man of the men of old in Europe in whom there still dwelleth the spirit of self-sacrifice, the remnant of the Christian spirit.

Meanwhile all nations were bowing down to *Interest*. And the kings said: "If we spread abroad the worship of this idol, then as nation fighteth with nation, so afterwards city will fight with city, and then man with man.

"And people will again become savage, and we shall again have such power as savage kings had of old, idolaters, and such as Negro kings and cannibal kings now have, that they may eat their subjects."

But the Polish Nation alone did not bow down to the new idol, and did not have in its language the expression for christening it in Polish, neither for christening its worshippers, whom it calls by the French word *egoists*.

The Polish Nation worshiped God, knowing that he who honoreth God giveth honor to everything that is good. . . .

Its kings and men of knightly rank never assaulted any believing nation, but defended Christendom from the pagans and barbarians who brought slavery.

And the Polish kings went to the defense of Christians in distant lands, King Wladislaw to Varna, and King Jan to Vienna, to the defense of the east and the west.

And never did their kings and men of knightly rank seize neighboring lands by force, but they received the nations into brotherhood, uniting them with themselves by the gracious gift of faith and freedom.

And God rewarded them, for a great nation, Lithuania, united itself with Poland, as husband with wife, two souls in one body. And there was never before this such a union of nations. But hereafter there shall be.

For that marriage and union of Lithuania and Poland is the symbol of the future union of all Christian peoples in the name of faith and freedom.

And God gave unto the Polish kings and knights freedom, that all might be called brothers, both the richest and the poorest. And such freedom there never was before. But hereafter there shall be.

The king and the men of knightly rank received into their brotherhood still more people; they received whole armies and whole tribes. And the numbers of brothers became as great as a nation, and in no nation were there so many men free and calling one another brothers as in Poland.

And finally, on the Third of May [1791, the day of the proclamation of the Polish Constitution], the king and the knightly body determined to make all Poles brothers, at first the burghers, and later the peasants. . . .

And finally Poland said: "Whosoever will come to me shall be free and equal, for I am FREEDOM."

But the kings when they heard of this were terrified in their hearts and said: "We drove out freedom from the earth, and behold it returneth in the person of a just nation that doth not bow down to our idols! Come, let us slay this nation." And they plotted treachery among themselves.

And the King of Prussia came and kissed the Polish nation and greeted it, saying: "My Ally," but already he had sold it for thirty cities of Great Poland, even as Judas for thirty pieces of silver.

And the two other rulers fell upon and bound the Polish Nation. And Gaul was judge and said: "Verily I find no fault in this nation, and France my wife, a timid woman, is tormented with evil dreams; nevertheless, take for yourselves and martyr this nation." And he washed his hands.

And the ruler of France said: "We cannot ransom this innocent nation by our blood or by our money, for my blood and my money belong to me, the blood and the money of my nation belong to my nation."

And this ruler uttered the last blasphemy against Christ, for Christ taught that the blood of the Son of Man belongeth to all our brother men.

And when the ruler had uttered these words, then the crosses fell from the towers of the godless capital, for the sign of Christ could no longer shine upon a people worshiping the idol *Interest*.

And this ruler was called Casimir-Périer [French Prime Minister in 1831 opposed French intervention for the Poles], a Slavic first name and a Roman last name. His first name signifieth corrupter or annihilator of peace, and his last name signifieth, from the word *périre* or *périr*, destroyer or son of destruction. And these two names are anti-Christian. And they shall be alike accursèd among the Slavic race and among the Roman race. . . .

And they martyred the Polish Nation and laid it in the grave, and the kings cried out: "We have slain and we have buried Freedom."

But they cried out foolishly, for in committing the last sin they filled up the measure of their iniquities, and their power was coming to an end at the time when they exulted most.

For the Polish Nation did not die, its body lieth in the grave, but its soul hath descended from the earth, that is from public life, to the abyss, that is to the private life of people who suffer slavery in their country and outside of their country, that it may see their sufferings.

But on the third day the soul shall return to the body, and the Nation shall arise and free all the peoples of Europe from slavery.

And already two days have gone by. One day ended with

the first capture of Warsaw [by the Russians in 1795], and
the second day ended with the second capture of Warsaw
[by the Russians in 1831], and the third day shall begin, but
not end.

And as after the resurrection of Christ blood sacrifices
ceased in all the world, so after the resurrection of the
Polish Nation wars shall cease in all Christendom.

CZECH AND SLAV

[From Havlíček's article, 1846]

Simultaneously with the awakening of the national spirit
and some higher activities in our [Austrian-Czech] fatherland, there came also the Slav idea, or rather this idea made
itself felt again, but this time with greater strength and
greater hope than before. As often happens, this Slav idea,
like all other great and new ideas, became fashionable with
us, so that some years ago almost everybody called himself a
Slav, ashamed, as it were, of something as small as our Czech,
Moravian, Silesian, or Slovak. Everybody called the Russians, Poles, Illyrians, and other Slavs his brothers and was
concerned for their well-being, at least as much as for the
growth of his own nation; and those who were the most
practical ones felt in their heart the firm conviction that as
time went on all eighty million Slavs (and all the other millions who meanwhile would accrue) would have in common
one literary language, the same sympathies and all the other
matters, which it is presently not advisable to discuss; in
short that they all would become a single nation in the same
sense in which the French and others were single nations. . . .

The purpose of this article is to correct these errors as far
as possible in the minds of my countrymen, to remove the
harmful, and thereby to strengthen the useful, aspects of the
Slav idea. I consider that my words will become more ac-

ceptable if I prove them from my own life experience: if we wish to combat prejudices we can do it best if we acknowledge that we shared them formerly. One always believes an experienced man more.

In my student days at the university in Prague, when a young man is most inclined to wax enthusiastic for a new idea, when most youth fall in love with girls and a few with ideas, I too was struck by the Slav idea. . . . We recited with low and high voices sonnets from *Slávy Dcera*, we even wrote (but didn't print) sonnets, we got hold of the grammars of various Slav tongues, and regarded it as a great honor to be able to sing two Polish songs, one Russian, and two Illyrian ones. In this blessed time, having as far as possible learned from books the languages, history, and customs of the Slav peoples, I firmly decided to travel in their lands and to get acquainted with all our Slav brothers personally in their countries.

I learned to know Poland and I did not like it. With a feeling of hostility and pride I left the Sarmatian country, and in the worst cold season I arrived in a sleigh in Moscow, being warmed mostly by the Slav feeling in my heart. The freezing temperature in Russia and other aspects of Russian life extinguished the last spark of Pan-Slav love in me. Cosmopolitanism was always completely alien to me, and so I returned to Prague as a Czech, a simple determined Czech, even with some secret sour feeling against the name Slav, which a better knowledge of Russia and Poland had made suspect to me. After some time, when I had somewhat forgotten the unpleasant impression, I again quieted down, and I was able . . . to balance my unpleasant personal experiences and my former poetic enthusiasm. In short, I formed for myself principles about Slavdom and Czechdom, and these I now wish to put before my readers for their consideration.

Above all, I express my firm and unchangeable conviction that the Slavs, that is the Russians, the Poles, the Czechs, the Illyrians, and so on, are not one nation. These words are like a declaration of war and so strong that they need further explanation. . . . Just as Spaniards, Portuguese, Frenchmen, and Italians are together Romance nations, and Germans, Danes, Swedes, Norwegians, and Dutch are Teutonic nations, so we, the Poles, the Illyrians, the Russians, and so on, are Slav nations; and the name Slav is and should forever remain a purely geographical and scientific name, in no way however a name implying the heart and the sympathy with which every nation pronounces its name.

No decent man should be a cosmopolitan (who says that he loves everybody, loves nobody), and it would be ridiculous to feel Indo-European patriotism and to write enthusiastic poetry about it; equally invalid, though to a lesser degree, is a Pan-Slav patriotism. Should somebody object that the differences among the Slav nations are not so great as among the Romance or the Teutonic nations, then we must simply disagree. Even if there be slighter differences among the various Slav languages than among the various Teutonic and Romance languages (though the Dutch tongue is nearer to German than Russian is to Czech, and between French and Italian there is no greater difference than between Russian and Czech), we must not forget that nationality is determined not only by language but also by customs, religion, form of government, state of education, sympathies, and so on, and that the differences among the different nations are based upon these characters. If we take all that in due consideration, then we cannot say that Russians and Czechs, Poles and Russians, Illyrians and Poles, show a greater affinity than any two Teutonic or Romance nations. . . .

We cannot expect unity even among closely related Slav nations. On the contrary, the closer they live together the more disunity we may expect. Let us take the world as it is, and expect friendship and unity among people and nations only when this is advantageous for both sides. . . .

We hold it to be our sacred duty to declare clearly that a Czech who accepts another Slav nationality sins as much against his fatherland as he would if he were to become a Frenchman or a German. . . .

If the whole Slav world were our fatherland, if all Slavs were one nation, then we should long have accepted the Russian language as literary language, which so far certainly no wise man among us has suggested. It must be the first principle of our nationality that we shall never wish to abandon our language and shall never exchange it voluntarily for another, even the most closely related language. Whoever thinks differently is not with us but against us. . . .

I turn now to the most important part of my discussion, to the condition which really decides the whole future of Pan-Slavism. That is the relationship among Russians, Ukrainians, and Poles. . . . If we survey briefly the history of the Eastern Slavs and the fate of these three great Slav nations, then we shall see how each in turn tried to establish its primacy over the two others, which can perhaps be explained geographically by the fact that no natural frontiers exist between them. First Kiev and the Ukrainians ruled; there the first great power rose, so that it seemed that Poland and present-day Russia would be incorporated in it. Soon, however, the great empire of Vladimir [Monomakh] fell and with it the prospects of independence for the Ukrainians. Now Poland and Russia simultaneously began to rise. At first, because their centers, Cracow and Moscow, were very remote from each other, they paid no attention to each other's activities. Later, however, they expanded towards each other until finally two very similar and yet very dissimilar giants met: similar in the anarchy and injustice of their domestic constitutions, different in their faith, the one an autocracy, the other an aristocracy. Soon . . . such national enmity grew between them that each one began to try to destroy the other, and thus even today the two nations stand one against the other. . . .

At the beginning, I sided with the Poles against the Russians. As soon as I recognized the true state of affairs in Poland, as soon as the veil which poetically hid from me the prosaic misery and corruption of the nation (that is, the Polish nobility) dropped from my eyes, my affection changed to dislike, and for a psychologically understandable reason the Russians appeared to me to be better than the Poles. This, however, did not last long. I soon recognized that Peter is like Paul, Russia like Poland. My Slav sympathy disappeared, and I learned to regard the Russians and the Poles, in spite of the affinity of language, origin, and customs, as nations alien to us Czechs. . . . We must not look on the Russian-Polish relations with such a blind eye as the greater part of Europe does; we should not think of an innocent lamb and a wolf, but know that there wolf meets wolf, and we shall say later that the lamb among them is the Ukrainian. The Poles themselves formerly tried to destroy Russia, and the Russians now try the opposite. . . . The Ukraine is the apple of discord which fate threw between these two nations. . . . Thus the suppression of Ukrainian liberty revenges itself on Poland and Russia. . . . The Poles and the Russians buried the national spirit of the Ukraine and began to divide the great body, and, as generally happens in such cases, they began to fight and have not yet ceased. Both the Russians and the Poles regard the Ukrainian language as a dialect of their own language. . . . Thus we have seen three great Eastern Slav nations, each one of which hates the other two, and also has a just reason for it. Nobody can speak reasonably of brotherhood there. Nevertheless, the Pan-Slav idea has been accepted even by

these nations. That might seem to contradict me: in reality
the way in which Poles and Russians understood and accepted Pan-Slavism will prove that they don't deserve our
sympathy.

The Russians (and I do not speak here of the government,
because I cannot know its trend of thought) have taken up
the idea of Pan-Slavism. In the whole world, but above all in
Europe, the Russians are either disliked or rejected (and
that almost always for good reasons): it was therefore sur-
prising but most agreeable to them to find at least some
friends in the West. Thus they declared immediately their
friendship and brotherhood with us and the Illyrians but
regarded themselves as the older brother, as our com-
mander. The Russian Pan-Slavs believe that we and the
Illyrians would like to be under their domination!! They
are firmly convinced that they will one day control all Slav
lands!!! They now look forward with joy to their future
vineyards in Dalmatia. These gentlemen have started everywhere to say and write Slav instead of Russian, so that later
they will again be able to say Russian instead of Slav. . . .

I cannot describe here in detail everything that I heard in
Russia about the Slav world: I can, however, testify that the
Russians think of the other Slavs in no brotherly fashion,
but dishonestly and egoistically. . . . I admit that I prefer
the Magyars, who are open enemies of the Czechs and Illyrians, to the Russians, who approach us with a Judas embrace—to put us into their pockets. We are Czechs, and we
wish to remain Czechs forever, and we do not wish to become either Germans, or Magyars, or Russians, and therefore we shall be cool to the Russians, if we do not wish to
be hostile to them.

But let us be equally cool towards the Poles. They are like
the Russians, but with tied hands. It is well known that
formerly the Poles did not wish to know anything of the
Slavs. Only when the Polish democrats and emigrants in

France came upon the happy thought that perhaps the other Slavs could jointly with the Poles make light-hearted revolutions and thus serve them in their poorly calculated plans, did they begin to fraternize with us, and in their easy and sanguine temper they began to imagine how they would be the leaders among the Western liberal Slavs and how we should fight for them against everyone they hate! . . .

Finally, it is also significant that the Russians and the Poles exclude each other from the ranks of the Slavs: Russian scholars have proved that the Poles descend from the non-Slav Sarmatians (and be it said quietly, the Polish nobility thought so too, believing its blood superior to the Slav peasant blood), and the Poles on their part have proved that the Russians are of Mongol origin. . . .

I am very happy that I can proudly say that we Czechs, although insignificant in numbers and power compared to the Russians and Poles, are more highly esteemed by all reasonable and educated men. . . . The Russians are hated everywhere, the Poles are merely pitied everywhere . . . but the world looks on us Czechs with respect seeing . . . how manfully we fight for our preservation, for our life, for nationality! Should we perhaps be afraid of the great and many obstacles, should we perhaps become down-hearted before the hard and unpleasant road which we must tread? Should we perhaps rely in a childish and unmanly way upon others? A Czech is not afraid of hard work and obstacles, he is not downhearted, and he does not rely on others: a Czech sets out to do his work and will overcome everything. For the very reason that people work harder among us, there is no doubt that on the better historical foundation we have, and with our better general education, we Czechs will advance in the arts, in literature, and generally in national happiness beyond the Russians and the Poles. . . .

What I wrote here stems from the reading of almost the whole literature on Pan-Slavism and from personal experiences . . . and everything written here is my full conviction. The plain principles, once more summarized, are: the Slavs are not one nation but four nations as independent and unconnected as any other European nations. Each of these Slav nations stands for itself, and none is responsible for another; they share neither national honor nor national infamy. As the result of the great similarity of the Slav languages, it is useful and necessary for each Slav nation to pay as much attention to the literature of the others as possible, and to profit from their literature and languages and nationality. Only between the Czechs and the Illyrians can there be more far-reaching sympathies, because under present conditions one cannot be dangerous to the other but on the contrary useful. The Austrian monarchy is the best guarantee for the preservation of our and the Illyrian nationality, and the greater the power of the Austrian empire grows, the more secure our nationalities will be. It is impossible then for all Slavs to use one literary language, and therefore all efforts in this direction are meaningless and, as a waste of time, harmful.

V

Russia and the Revolution I

TYUCHEV

Fedor Ivanovich Tyuchev, who belonged to the group of thinkers known in Russian history as Slavophils, was deeply convinced of Russia's Pan-Slav mission. He went beyond Pogodin in two points. In expounding his belief that Russia was the heir of the Eastern Roman Empire, he stressed the need for the conquest of Constantinople; moreover, the European revolutions of 1848 convinced him of the inevitable and fast approaching struggle between Russia and the West.

Tyuchev wrote only a few political articles. His reputation in Russian literature rests upon his poetry, and he is regarded by many critics as Russia's greatest lyric poet after Pushkin. His fervent messianic Russian nationalism, which he expressed not only in his essays but in many of his poems, is especially remarkable in view of the fact that by background and upbringing Tyuchev resembled Chaadayev. Like him, Tyuchev was a member of the aristocracy brought up in a cosmopolitan spirit. He preferred to use the French language for his correspondence and in daily life. He left Russia in 1822, as a young man of nineteen, to serve abroad in diplomatic posts for an unbroken period of more than

twenty years. Both of his wives were German without any
knowledge of Russian. But in spite of this background his
poems and articles proclaimed and glorified the supposedly
inevitable struggle between a triumphant Slavdom led by
Russia and a Western conspiracy determined to crush Moscow, the center of a universal empire based upon universal
faith. He saw the struggle in almost supernatural apocalyptic colors and in a world-wide historical perspective.

Russia was to Tyuchev the true Empire, representing
unity, peace, and faith. These had been undermined by the
West when Charlemagne usurped the empire which rightly
belonged to Constantinople, with the help of the Pope, the
leader of the schismatic revolt against the Universal Church.
In the East, Empire and Church, order and faith, remained
united because they grew out of the same soil of legitimate
tradition. In the West, Empire and Church fought a bitter
struggle which ended in the Protestant Reformation, the
denial of the unity of faith, and in the French Revolution,
the denial of peaceful order. The West was doomed to
permanent strife because it had inherited from Rome the
cult of violence and of power. The Orthodox Church, according to Tyuchev, was "a society of the faithful freely
united in the spirit and the truth under the law of Christ";
the Roman Church on the other hand was "a political
power, a state in the state," addicted to wars and politics.

"The indispensable fulfillment of Russia as the Slavonic
Empire," Tyuchev was convinced, would establish the
unity of Europe under Russia's leadership and the re-union
of the Christian Churches on a Greco-Slavonic foundation.
To that end Tyuchev wished the Russian autocracy to grow
more national, to be more closely united with the masses, to
be supported by a unanimous public opinion. When the
Crimean War approached, Tyuchev was certain of Russian
victory and of the impending capture of Constantinople. In
1853 he wrote to Chaadayev, with whom in spite of their

ideological differences he was on the friendliest terms:
"After many trials and vicissitudes, the last word will belong to Russia, . . . but it will be a Russia very different
from what she is at present. She will have become herself,
and yet she will be associated with so many other elements
which will complement and transform her that her very
name will be changed. She will no longer be an empire but a
world." For Tyuchev, as for so many other Russian thinkers, Russia was something entirely unique. Her problem
was in its essence neither political nor national. As Tyuchev
expressed it in a famous short poem in 1860, it was *the* problem of modern history, a problem of faith.

> One cannot understand Russia by reason
> And measure her by a common yardstick.
> She has a peculiar nature.
> One must simply believe in Russia.

The French Revolution of 1848 shocked Tyuchev deeply.
To the Czech leaders of that year, to Palacký and Havlíček,
the revolution carried the promise of a liberal era for Europe and of the full integration of the Western Slavs into
the new Europe; to Tyuchev the same event signified the
beginning of the very end of Europe and of liberalism, a
catastrophe out of which only Russia would emerge as the
rock of refuge. He wrote on April 12, 1848 an article "Russia and the Revolution," which was published in the following year in Paris in the *Revue des Duex Mondes*. He used
the word "Revolution" as meaning the freedom of modern
Western civilization. Individual liberty seemed to him the
soil for dissolution and anarchy, and he could not see any
middle ground between the chaos of liberty and the absolute order based on unity for which Russia stood. Though
some of the points raised by Tyuchev in the article have
since been settled by history, its fundamental attitude still
explains the continuing East-West conflict in Europe. His
point of view also throws much light on the position of Ger-

many, which from 1813 to 1848 leaned towards Russia.
Tyuchev foresaw for Germany the dangers of nationalism
and racialism, but above all he was afraid lest Germany
might swing into the Western orbit.

Equally relevant to present Russian-Western relations is
the prescription which Tyuchev laid down for Russian foreign policy in a letter to his sister. "I of course am not one
of those who in their gloomy patriotism would like to doom
Russia to permanent isolation," he wrote in 1864. "I am
willing to enter into agreements, but only if they are of a
temporary nature and if their acceptance does not make us
forget the axiomatic truth that there can be no alliance between Russia and the West, either for the sake of interests
or for the sake of principles. There is not a single interest,
not a single trend in the West, which does not conspire
against Russia, especially her future, and does not try to
harm her. Therefore Russia's only natural policy towards
the West must be to seek not an alliance with the Western
powers but their disunion and division. Only then will they
not be hostile to us, not of course out of conviction but out
of impotence." For Russia and the West, according to
Tyuchev, were separated not by politics but by an irreconcilable opposition in philosophical outlook and social system.

RUSSIA, THE ROCK OF REFUGE

[*From "Russia and the Revolution," 1848*]

TO UNDERSTAND the meaning of the supreme crisis
into which Europe is entering, one must tell oneself
that for a long time there have been in Europe only two real
powers: the Revolution and Russia. These two powers face

each other at present, and tomorrow they will perhaps come to grips with each other. Neither treaties nor negotiations are possible between the two. The life of the one means the death of the other. The whole political and religious future of mankind depends for centuries ahead on the outcome of the struggle between the two, the greatest struggle that the world has witnessed.

The fact of this antagonism now becomes clear to everybody, and yet, so much has the intelligence been weakened in this century that the present generation though facing this immense fact is far remote from having understood its true character and appreciated its reasons. So far, one has sought the explanation for it in the realm of purely political ideas; one has tried to understand the difference as based on purely human principles. But certainly the conflict between the Revolution and Russia stems from much deeper reasons; they can be summed up in a few words.

Russia is above all the Christian Empire; the Russian people is Christian not only through the orthodoxy of its beliefs but also by something more intimate than belief. It is Christian by that ability of renunciation and sacrifice which forms the basis of its moral nature. The Revolution is above all anti-Christian. The anti-Christian spirit is the soul of the Revolution, its true and essential character. The forms which the Revolution has adopted successively, as well as its various slogans, all these, down to its violence and crimes, are only accessory or accidental to the anti-Christian principle which animates the Revolution; and, one must confess, this principle has given to the Revolution its terrible power over the world. Whoever does not understand that, witnesses as a blind man the spectacle the world has offered for the last sixty years. The human ego, wishing to depend only on itself without recognizing or accepting any other law but that of its own pleasure, the human ego substituting itself for God, is certainly nothing new among men; but what is new is the absolutism of this human ego proclaimed as a political and social right and aspiring on this ground to take possession of society. This new demand was called in 1789 the French Revolution.

Since then, and through all its changes, the Revolution has remained faithful to its nature, and at no time perhaps has it felt itself more true to its character, more intimately anti-Christian, than at the present moment, when the Revolution has adopted the war-cry of Christianity: Fraternity. For that very reason one can believe that the Revolution approaches its zenith. In fact, if one hears all these naively blasphemous declamations which have become as it were the official language of the period, who would not believe that the new French Republic has come into the world to fulfill the law of the Gospel? The authorities which the Revolution created have solemnly assigned to themselves this mission, with the amendment however that the Revolution substitutes the spirit of pride and superiority for the spirit of humility and self-renunciation which is the basis of Christianity, and enforced charity for free and voluntary charity; and that it wishes to establish in place of a fraternity preached and accepted in the name of God, a fraternity imposed by the fear of the sovereign people. With these differences, the reign of the Revolution promises to be that of Christ. . . .

The explosion of February [1848] has rendered a great service to the world by destroying the façade of illusion which was hiding reality. The least intelligent must now have understood that the history of Europe for the last thirty-three years has been one long mystification. In fact, how relentless was the light that suddenly illuminated this whole recent past which already seems so remote? Who for instance does not understand now the ridiculous pretention of the wisdom of this century which has convinced itself happily that it has succeeded in taming the Revolution by constitutional exorcism, to tie its terrible energy with a formula of legality? Who could still doubt after what has happened that from the moment when the revolutionary principle enters into the blood of a society, all these formulas and transactions are no more than narcotics which can momentarily put the sick man to sleep but cannot hinder the evil from taking its course? . . .

At this juncture, may I be permitted to point out that among all the rulers and statesmen of Europe during these years there has been only one who from the beginning has recognized and drawn attention to the great illusion of 1830? How is it that he alone in Europe, alone perhaps in his environment, has consistently refused to cede? Fortunately there was this time a sovereign on the throne of Russia in whom the Russian thought has found its incarnation, and in the present state of the world the Russian thought is the only one placed sufficiently outside the revolutionary milieu to be able to appreciate sanely the facts which take place there. What the emperor foresaw in 1830, the Revolution has not failed to realize step by step. . . .

One can say that the great task of the [revolutionary] party during these last eighteen years has been to revolutionize Germany from top to bottom, and one can judge now whether this task has been well fulfilled. Germany is certainly the country about which one has formed the longest time the strangest illusions. One thought it to be a country of order because it was tranquil, and one did not wish to see the terrifying anarchy which had penetrated there and undermined the intellects. Sixty years of a destructive philosophy have completely dissolved there all Christian beliefs and, in this void of all faith, have developed the revolutionary sentiment to its highest degree: the pride of the mind, so that at present this wound of the century is perhaps nowhere deeper and more poisonous than in Germany. As a necessary result, the more Germany became revolutionary, the more it felt hatred for Russia. And under the burden of the good deeds done by Russia to Germany, a revolutionary Germany could feel for Russia only an implacable hatred. In the present moment this violent hatred seems to have reached its culmination; for it has triumphed in Germany, not only beyond all reason, but even over the instinct of self-preservation. ˙. . .

One should not say in justification of all these so evidently artificial movements which have just shaken the whole political order of Germany and imperiled the very existence of the social order, that they were inspired by a sincere and generally experienced sentiment, the need for German unity. This sentiment may be sincere; I am willing to concede that it expresses the wish of the great majority; but what does it prove? . . . It is another and most foolish illusion of our era to believe that it is sufficient that something be vividly and ardently desired by the great majority to become for that reason alone necessarily realizable. Moreover, one must recognize that there is in the present society neither wish nor need, however sincere or legitimate, which the Revolution would not pervert and transform into a lie.

If during the last thirty-three years, perhaps the happiest of its whole history, Germany has formed a political body constituted in a hierarchy and functioning in a regular way, what were the conditions that produced and assured such a result? Clearly it was the sincere entente between the two great powers which represent in Germany the two principles which have contended for this land for more than three centuries. But of this accord which was so slow to be established and so difficult to maintain, does anybody think that it would have been possible, that it could have lasted so long, if Austria and Prussia, at the end of the great wars against France, had not closely rallied around Russia and strongly relied upon it? That is the political arrangement which realized for Germany the only system of unity which can be applied there and which brought it that armistice of thirty-three years which has now been broken.

Already by now, the question of German unity has been decided for every intelligent man. One would have to possess that ineptitude characteristic of German ideologies to ask seriously whether this lot of journalists, lawyers, and professors who have met in Frankfurt and have given themselves the mission to rebuild the empire of Charlemagne have any appreciable chance to succeed in their undertaking, whether they will be strong and adroit enough to reerect on the soil which trembles the pyramid turned upside down, to make it stand on its tip.

[The German Republicans hoped to make common cause with the French Republicans for a war against Russia.] That is at least the chance which the revolutionists of all countries contemplate lovingly; but there is one aspect of the question which they do not take into sufficient account, and that omission could oddly disturb their plans. The Revolutionary party, above all in Germany, seems to have convinced itself that because it thought the national issue of so little importance, the same would be the case in all the countries that submitted to its action, and that everywhere and always the question of principle would take precedence over the question of nationality. . . . But the breaking or weakening of all the ancient powers, the shaking to the depth of the whole political order of the country, would produce there the most terrifying complication, the question of life and death for its future—the racial question. The Germans overlooked the fact that in the heart of Germany, of the unity of which they dreamt, there lived in the basin of Bohemia and in the Slav countries which surround it six to seven million men for whom, from generation to generation, the German has never ceased for one moment to be something worse than an alien. . . .

I do not speak of the patriotic literature of some scholars

in Prague; these men have certainly rendered a great service to the cause of their country, and they will continue to
render it; but the life of Bohemia does not consist of it. The
life of a people is never in the books which one prints for it,
unless it be the life of the German people; the life of a
people is in its instincts and in its beliefs, and books, we
must confess, have more power to enervate and dry up than
to strengthen and revive these instincts and beliefs. Everything that remains of true national life in Bohemia is in its
Hussite beliefs, in this ever-alive protest of its oppressed
Slav national feeling against the usurpation of the Roman
Church and against German domination. That is the tie
which united the Czech of Bohemia with his whole past of
struggle and glory, and that is also the link which could
attach him one day to his brothers in the East. We cannot
insist enough on this point. For it was precisely these sympathetic recollections of the Church of the East, these returns to the old faith of which Hussitism in its own time was
only an imperfect and disfigured expression, that established a profound difference between Poland and Bohemia:
between Bohemia, which suffers against its will the yoke of
the Occidental community, and the seditiously Catholic
Poland, a fanatical partisan of the Occident and always a
traitor to its own side.

When the Austrian Empire is dissolved by the loss of
Lombardy and by the now complete emancipation of Hungary, what will Bohemia and the surrounding peoples do,
the Moravians and the Slovaks—that means some seven to
eight million people of the same language and race? To
know which power Bohemia, in spite of the ideas that domi-
nate it today and of the institutions that will govern it tomorrow, will find itself turning to by necessity, I have only
to recall what the most nationalist of the Bohemian patriots
told me in Prague in 1841. "Bohemia," Hanka told me,
"will not be free and independent and really in control of

its destiny until Russia has gained possession of Galicia."
Generally the persistent favor which Russia, its name,
glory, and future, has found among the nationalists in
Prague is noteworthy at the very moment when our faithful
ally, Germany, made itself with more disinterestedness than
justice the understudy of the Polish emigration in order to
stir up the public opinion of the whole of Europe against us.
Every Russian who has visited Prague in the course of these
last years can certify that the only complaint he heard there
against us concerns the caution and lukewarmness with
which we received the national sympathies of Bohemia.
High and generous considerations then imposed this attitude upon us; today it certainly would be an absurdity: for
the sacrifice which we then made for the cause of order, we
would not make hereafter for the profit of the Revolution.

But if it is true that Russia under the present conditions
has fewer rights to discourage the sympathies brought to it,
one has to recognize on the other hand a historical law
which so far has always providentially ruled its destiny: always Russia's bitterest enemies have worked most successfully for the growth of its greatness.

This providential law has just aroused an enemy that will
certainly play a great role in Russia's future and that will
contribute a great deal to hasten its fulfillment. That enemy
is Hungary, the Magyar Hungary. It, among all enemies of
Russia, hates with the most furious hatred. In the Magyar
people the revolutionary ardor combines in the strangest
way with the brutality of an Asiatic power, of which one
could say with as much justice as of the Turks that it is only
encamping in Europe. This people lives surrounded by
Slavs who are all equally contemptible in its eyes. The
Magyar people has for a very long time ruined the destiny
of the Slav peoples and become their personal enemy. Yet
the Magyar people finds itself after centuries of turbulent
agitation still surrounded by these peoples: the Serbs, the

Croats, the Slovaks, the Transylvanians, and even the Ukrainians of the Carpathians, are the links of a chain which the Hungarian people believed forever broken. And now the Hungarian people feels above it a hand which could when it so desired join the links together and tighten the chain again at will. For that reason the Magyars hate the Russians instinctively. On the other hand, if we believe the reports in foreign newspapers, the present leaders of the party are seriously persuaded that the Magyar people has a great mission to carry out in the Orthodox East, that briefly its task is to keep the destinies of Russia in check. . . .

So far the moderating authority of Austria has kept this turbulence and this madness more or less under control; but now . . . the completely emancipated Magyarism will probably give full vent to all its eccentricities and run the most foolish risks. . . . The Hungarian Slavs would probably succumb in the struggle if there were not a circumstance which sooner or later must come to their help: the enemy they have to fight is above all Russia's enemy. Along the whole military frontier, which consists by three-fourths of Orthodox Serbs, there is not one cottage (even according to Austrian travelers) where one would not find side by side with the portrait of the Emperor of Austria the portrait of another emperor whom these faithful races obstinately consider the only legitimate one. Moreover (why conceal it?), it is hardly probable that all these earthquakes which shake the West stop at the border of the East. In this war to the death, in this ungodly crusade which the Revolution, already the mistress of three-fourths of Western Europe, prepares against Russia, the Christian East, the Slav Orthodox East, whose life is indissolubly bound up with ours, will by necessity enter the struggle on our side. Perhaps the war will start in such a way. For all the various agitations at work, the Catholic propaganda, the Revolutionary propaganda, etc., all of them, at cross purposes among themselves but united in common hatred against Russia, will now begin to work with greater fervor than ever. One can be certain that they will not stop at anything whatever to achieve their goal. And what, good heavens! would be the fate of all these peoples, Christians as we are, if, exposed as they are by now to all abominable influences, in such a moment the only authority to which they call in their prayers should fail them? In one word, in what horrible confusion these Eastern lands in close quarters with the Revolution would fall if the legitimate sovereign, if the Orthodox Emperor of the East, should for a long time delay to appear there!

No, that is impossible. The foreboding of one thousand years cannot deceive. Russia, the land of faith, will not be unfaithful in the supreme hour. It will not be frightened by the greatness of its destiny and will not retreat from its mission.

And when has this mission been more indisputable and evident? One can say that God writes it in flaming signs across a sky blackened with storm clouds. The Occident disappears, everything collapses, everything totters in a general conflagration: the Europe of Charlemagne and the Europe of the treaties of 1815, the papacy of Rome and all the kingdoms of the West, Catholicism and Protestantism, faith long lost and reason reduced to absurdity. Order becomes henceforth impossible, freedom becomes henceforth impossible, and Occidental civilization commits suicide on top of all the ruins accumulated by it. . . . And when we see rise above this immense wreck this even more immense Eastern Empire like the Ark of the Covenant, who could doubt its mission, and should we, its children, show ourselves sceptic and pusillanimous?

VI

Slavophil and Orthodox Russia
KHOMYĀKOV and ĀKSĀKOV

The Slavophils were really Russophils believing in the unique history, character, and mission of the Russian people, whom they sharply distinguished from the peoples of Western Europe and from Western Christianity. The center of Slavophil thought was the contrast between Russia and the West and the identification of Russia with the Orthodox faith.

Whereas Chaadayev had declared the Russian past a barren desert and the present life of Russia a waste land, the Slavophils, including Pogodin and Tyuchev, idealized the Russian past and attributed the shortcomings of her present life, which they did not deny, to the acceptance of Western ways. They saw the only hope of salvation, for Russia and ultimately for mankind, in Russia's return to her original character. The Slavophils found Europe's past far inferior in spiritual wealth to that of Russia, and they were convinced that nineteenth-century Europe was in full decay as an inevitable result of the past. Whereas Chaadayev saw in Peter's reforms the dawn of a new and better era for Russia, the Slavophils rejected these reforms on the grounds that they exposed the people to alien influences, estranged the educated classes from the common folk, and established in St. Petersburg a "soulless" government without any real support in the masses. The Slavophils called upon the Russian educated class to return to their people and its faith, to put down deep roots in folk and soil. None voiced this Slavophil appeal with greater power than the novelist Fedor Dostoevsky.

The Slavophils—and Dostoevsky among them—were convinced that the Russians were the true divine people of modern times and that the twentieth century would be the century of Russian, or Slav, leadership. But in order to fulfill her providential mission, Russia must emphasize her folkdom (*narodnost*), her own kind and identity, and develop an original and independent civilization on a strictly national basis. Russia owed it to mankind to bring her creative potentialities to full fruition. She could do it only by turning away from alien ways, from imitating the West, to become herself.

The leaders of the older generation of the Slavophils, which flourished in the 1840's, were Ivan Vasilievich Kireyevsky and Alexei Stepanovich Khomyakov. Both were men of great learning, thoroughly familiar with Western religious traditions, and devout followers of the Orthodox Church. They recognized the greatness of Europe, but they were convinced that the Occident had finished its role, that Russia must take over the torch and become the capital of civilization. The West, Kireyevsky taught, was built on a threefold false foundation: spiritually, on the rationalism of the Roman Church; politically, on Roman and Teuton conquests; socially, on the absolute property rights of Roman law. These foundations doomed Europe to the decay of faith by doubt, to a tragic barrenness of spiritual life, to internal strife, power politics, and social unrest. Russia on the other hand presented an organic unity, a wholeness permeated by the feeling of spiritual integrity and brotherhood, and thereby filled with the promise of a true community.

Khomyakov shared Kireyevsky's convictions. In their love and admiration of the common Russian people which was untouched by Western civilization, the early Slavophils were in no way reactionaries. They advocated the emancipation of the peasants and a just distribution of the land. To a certain degree they could be regarded as forerunners of a national-religious socialism. They found the strength of Russia not in the court but in the people and demanded free scope for its spiritual development. But they were not opposed to a truly benevolent autocracy based upon the broad support of the masses. They strove for social justice and spiritual freedom, not for political rights or constitutional guarantees. With her unity of faith, Khomyakov believed, Russia did not need the legal and formalistic safeguards of European democracy, which were essential in a society divided by multiplicity and conflict of opinions and parties, classes and races. Russia possessed a true democracy based upon a high moral unity. Khomyakov saw in the peasant commune, the *mir,* a peculiarly Russian institution and the best protection against the extreme individualism and materialism of the West.

This first period of Slavophilism came to an end with the outbreak of the Crimean War. Khomyakov welcomed it, not only because Russia was fighting for the Orthodox Balkan Slavs but also because he believed that the war would inaugurate the era of leadership of the Russian spirit and the Orthodox Church. In that vein he wrote his famous "Letter to a Foreign Friend on the Eve of the Crimean War." The younger generation of the Slavophils was deeply impressed by the general sympathy shown by Europe for the Turks in the Crimean War and for the Poles in their uprising against the Russians in 1863. At the same time the growth of the revolutionary movement in Russia, which they regarded as a product of alien Western influences, turned the younger Slavophils more and more to a bitter denunciation of the West. They feared the contagion of the West, the dangers of which Shevyrev, Pogodin's friend, had stressed as early as 1841, and like him they regarded the West as a putrifying corpse. The second generation of Slavophils wrote in a militant tone unknown to the preceding generation. They were encouraged by Alexander II's reforms, the emancipation of the serfs, the alleged solution of the agrarian question in Russia. They fanned the popular enthusiasm for the Russian war against Turkey in 1877, and they welcomed the great era of Russian expansion in Central Asia, which brought Russian power to the gates of India and of Chinese Turkestan. The exploits of General Skobelev, who distinguished himself in the first crossing of the Balkan mountains by Russian troops in 1877 and completed the conquest of Russian Central Asia in 1881, and the writings of General Fadeyev aroused the pride of the Slavophils in the Russian school of military warfare, represented above all by Count Alexander Suvorov. In their praise of this great Tsarist general of the late eighteenth century, the Slavophils of the 1870's were the forerunners of the Communist rulers of Russia in the 1940's.

The most popular spokesmen of the second generation of Slavophils were Dostoevsky, who belonged to the new class of urban intelligentsia and professional writers, and Ivan Aksakov, a minor poet and a leading political publicist. The latter belonged like Khomyakov to the wealthy landowning nobility. He was the son-in-law and biographer of Tyuchev and the son of Sergey Aksakov, who in a famous Russian classic *A Family Chronicle* (1856) described his grandfather's and father's life on their immense estate in the frontier land of the Bashkirian steppe. The older Aksakov's house in Moscow was "a stronghold of pure Russianism." After 1870 the growing revolutionary movement seemed to threaten the foundations of Russian traditionalism, religion, and autocracy. Dostoevsky's novel *The Possessed* and Aksakov's articles combated the revolutionaries, who scored their most resounding success in March 1881, a few weeks after Dostoevsky's death, with the assassination of Alexander II. In a memorable speech after the assassination Aksakov defined that "democratic autocracy," which was Slavophil theory, and which Stalin in a slightly disguised form tried to establish as a reality.

RUSSIA AND WAR

[Khomyakov's "Letter to a Foreign Friend on the Eve of the Crimean War"]

THE year which is just beginning will leave deep traces in history. The forces of all the nations advance and regard each other. A terrible struggle will begin. The public opinion of Europe shows itself in books, pamphlets, and newspapers read and known all over the world. It is impossible that you should not be interested in learning about the silent public opinion of the country against which all the others arm. . . . The Russian people is bound by the ties of blood to the Slav peoples; it is bound to the Greeks by the ties of faith; for their ancestors were, to quote St. Paul, our fathers in Jesus Christ. These are ties which we cannot forget or disregard. We may be ignorant of the fine points of politics, we may be little enlightened about the ideas of conventional duties, but we know our real duties towards our brothers by blood and faith.

The story of our relations with Turkey bears witness to it. Europe was satisfied to push back the dreaded force of the Ottomans. Russia, which had hardly emerged from alien fetters and interior convulsions, has revived peoples who were forgotten by the rest of the world. Protected Montenegro and Greece, called back to life, bear witness to it. Later, Greece was saved with English and French help on the sea at Navarino, and still later that country was consolidated forever by our arms alone on the fields of Roumelia. Moldavia and Wallachia, torn away from the Turkish yoke and purged from the disgrace and tyranny which weighed upon them for centuries; Serbia, saved from slavery and elevated to the rank of an almost independent power; the churches, rebuilt from the ruins in all the parts of the Ottoman Empire—the re-established cult, the reawakened intelligence. All that bears witness to it, as do, above all, the manifestations of charity, of sympathy, of consolation, which we offer every day and from all the parts of our vast fatherland to our brothers who still suffer under the Mohammedan domination. Yes, we have fulfilled one part of our duty; we have not yet fulfilled the whole of it.

Turkey has failed in its obligation towards us; it violated its promises, to the detriment of the rights of our brothers. Russia demanded guarantees; they were refused. Russia demanded at least more solemn promises; they were refused. Public opinion became disturbed; Russia felt that justice must be supported by force against a nation which does not understand justice, or pity, or the sanctity of promises. England and France, under the pretext of supporting the European equilibrium which was not menaced, have upheld Turkey's refusal. Without offering anything to take the place of the guarantees which we demanded, except perhaps some vague promises for the future, without respect for our sympathies, without concern for the simplest duties of humanity, England and France have strengthened Turkey's hopes by their alliance and help; they have aroused the courage of the Mohammedans and fanaticized their passions. . . . As a result, our duty has become more difficult to fulfill; it has also become more urgent, and it shall be fulfilled.

Russia arms herself. I wish, dear and respected friend, that you were in our midst to see the movement in our country at the present moment. It is not the proud armament of England or the bellicose fervor of France; no, it is the calm and considerate movement of a man who has consulted his heart, listened to his conscience, and consulted his duty, and who takes up the arms because he would think himself guilty if he did not. This man—he is a whole people, and, may I be allowed to say it, a great people. Believe me, there is something imposing in such a spectacle. The Russian people does not think of conquests: conquests never had anything alluring for it. The Russian people does not think of glory; that is a sentiment which has never moved its heart. It thinks of its duty, it thinks of a holy war. I shall not call it a crusade, I shall not dishonor it by this name. God has not given us the task of conquering far-off lands, however precious they may be to our religious feelings, but he does give us the task of saving brothers who are blood of our blood and heart of our heart. A war which would be criminal in the first case is holy in the second case. Thus Russia understands the struggle which she is about to enter. That is the reason why she arms with joy, ready, if need be, for the fullest mobilization. . . .

I do not wish to hide it from you; it seems in our eyes hateful and dishonorable when some nations, either to consolidate their own hegemony or to diminish the influence of another people, declare war upon the truest and most natural and most sacred sentiments of the human heart, and protect even temporarily the most infamous tyranny exercised upon defenseless victims by barbarians whose laws are cruel and whose actions are even more cruel. Briefly, there is something unworthy in the attitude of men who call themselves Christians and who draw the sword to deprive Christians of the right to protect their brothers against the arbitrary cruelties of Mohammedans. It is painful to see England the first to rush into this ignominious way, to see this indelible blemish on the brow of a nation to which human intelligence owes so many precious gifts, the human heart so many beautiful and noble enjoyments, the human soul so many high aspirations, and the whole human society so many improvements. . . .

But in the midst of this general ignominy [of nations coming to Turkey's help] there is one state which though passive appears worse than the others, which seems to shout louder though it is silent, and that is Rome. The so-called vicar of Christ, who pretends to be the head of Christendom, who recently has sent forth a polemical blast against the Churches of the East, does not find one voice, one accent of charity, to stop the peoples, his spiritual children, his dear flock, at the moment when they rush to fight against the liberty of Christians. Not one word of intercession, not one word of love, not one tear of compassion. . . .

Whatever happens, Providence has marked out our time to become a decisive era in the destiny of the world. From now on, two great principles are on the rise: The first is the Russian or rather the Slav principle, the principle of the real fraternity of blood and spirit. The second, which is much higher, is that of the [Orthodox] Church—and it is only under its protecting wing that the first principle could preserve itself in the midst of a world of trouble and discord, and only thanks to divine might that it will pass from being almost an instinctive tendency of one race alone to the dignity of a moral law guiding the future steps of mankind. . . .

Thanks should be given to the Western powers. They hasten unwittingly the coming of the moment when two great principles which have so far been kept in the background will enter the great light of history and will rise in

the world; unwittingly they push Russia herself to enter a
new road on which she had been vainly invited for many
years. Blind instruments of God's decrees, the Western generations will march on in a clearer and purer light than the
past generations.

Human blood is precious, war is horrible—but the de-
signs of Providence are inscrutable, and a task must be fulfilled whatever its rigors.

Wave, flags! Sound, trumpets of battle! Nations, forward
into battle! God orders mankind to march on!

RUSSIA AND AUTOCRACY

[*Aksakov's "Address to the St. Petersburg Benevolent Slav
Society after the Assassination of Alexander II"*]

Gentlemen—I came from Moscow to take part in your
meeting, and to join my Moscow voice to yours. I should
greatly like to convey to you what is said and thought in
Moscow, but it is beyond expression by spoken word. How,
indeed, are we to define the impressions which fill our souls
at this moment? It is sorrow, it is grief, it is shame and horror—a kind of solemn foreboding horror. Divine judgment
has now risen up against us. It is God Himself, living in
history, who is sending us His terrible revelations. We are
now standing before Him, and called upon to answer. What
is the answer we give? Is there any answer we could give? Let
everyone appeal to his conscience. Is he not partly to be
blamed for the infamy which has deserved the punishment
of God and stained our country in the eyes of the whole
world? . . .

The Emperor is murdered; the same Emperor who was
the greatest benefactor to his country, who emancipated
tens of millions of Russian peasants, bestowing upon them
human and civil rights. He is murdered; not for personal
vengeance, not for booty, but precisely because he is the

Emperor, the crowned head, the representative, the first man of his country, that vital, single man who personified the very essence, the whole image, the whole strength and power, of Russia. From time immemorial that power has constituted the strength of the country. The attempt directed against the person of the Tsar is always directed against the whole people; but in this case the whole historical principle of the national life has been attacked, the autocratic power bestowed upon the Emperor by the country itself. Who are those who dared to bring that awful shame upon the people, and, as if by mockery, in the name of the people? Who are they? Is it merely a handful of criminals, bloodthirsty blockheads, enslaved by the demon of destruction? Where did they come from?

Let us address that question sternly to ourselves. Are they not the product of our moral treason, of which almost all the so-called liberal press is guilty? Can it be anything else but the logical, extreme expression of that Westernism which, since the time of Peter the Great, has demoralized both our government and our society, and has already marred all the spiritual manifestations of our national life? Not content to profit from all the riches of European thought and knowledge, we borrowed her spirit, which had been developed by a foreign history and a foreign religion. We began idolizing Europe, worshiping her gods and her idols! Who is to be blamed? . . .

Who really are those Anarchists, Social Democrats, and Revolutionists, as they call themselves? Have they the smallest particle of Russian spirit in all their aspirations and aims? Is there in their teachings the slightest shade of a protest against the real shortcomings from which Russia is suffering? Just the opposite; what they despise most is precisely the Russian people. In their servile imitation of foreign teaching and foreign idols, they only borrow what can easily be explained, if not excused, in Western Europe by historical and social conditions. There, results of that kind are the natural protest caused by unequal partition of land, by the unjust reign of the bourgeoisie over the fourth class—a protest, therefore, against the present constitutional forms.

But that injustice is exactly what we do not possess. Thanks to God, and thanks to that martyr-Emperor so brutally murdered, our fourth class, our peasantry, comprising almost 80 per cent of the whole realm, now possesses land, organization, and the most complete self-government. To this very day, that fourth class is the keeper of our historical instinct, of our religion, and of the whole element of our political organism. They, and not the so-called Intelligentsia, are the real supporters of our country. . . .

The reforms of Peter the Great weakened our memory and disabled us from understanding our own history—so very different from that of the West. Conquest is not at the bottom of our historical life, as is the case in all the Western countries. Our history begins with quite a voluntary and rational appeal to power [when the Russians called Rurik's dynasty to rule Russia]. The same appeal was repeated much later, in 1612, and provided the foundation of the present reigning dynasty, empowered with autocracy; and no one, and nothing, could induce the country to alter that shape of government. Such was the will, such was the inspiration of the national spirit.

Our history, therefore, does not possess that fundamental trait which characterizes the political life of the Western powers in Europe, that antagonism between the people and a power imposed by conquest. That antagonism, however, is the very foundation of Western constitutionalism, which is a compromise between two camps hostile to each other, mistrusting each other; a kind of treaty, surrounded by all sorts of conditions. To evade those conditions without contradicting the letter of the agreement constitutes the great talent of the rulers as well as that of the ruled. Struggle for power—that is the real essence of political life in European countries. . . .

Such are the types of freedom promised to Russia by worshipers of European liberal institutions. But the instincts and notions of freedom in the Russian people are higher and broader than in any part of the world, because they are free from the conventional and the formal element and are based on moral truth. They are easily traced in our self-government, the broadest in Europe, and in the largest application of the elective element. There was no antagonism between our Emperor and the people, for his superior power has been voluntarily recognized by the whole country. . . .

It is necessary—it is absolutely necessary—for us to implore our Emperor to allow us, the whole country, the whole nation, to surround his throne and to express fearlessly, openly to the whole world, our horror and indignation at all who dare to make any attempt against what is most sacred to our national feeling, the historical principle of the autocracy, which constitutes the very foundation of our political life. Yes! let us implore that the old union between the Emperor and the country be revived, based upon reciprocal, sincere confidence, love, and union of souls.

VII

Progressive Russia

BELINSKY

The reform movement in Russia in the first three decades of the nineteenth century was fomented by members of the landowning aristocracy, then the only vocal group in the empire, though like all other groups without any possibility of political activity or influence. In the 1840's a different type came to the fore, that of the *raznochintsy* or commoners, the sons of merchants, priests, or former serfs who formed the new middle-class intelligentsia. Their leader was Vissarion Grigoryevich Belinsky, the son of a poor military surgeon. In his short life which was a constant struggle with poverty and ill health he became the foremost Russian literary critic. He and his followers opposed Slavophilism and its glorification of the Russian past, of Orthodoxy and of autocracy. They turned to the West and wished to continue the work of Peter the Great. But unlike Chaadayev they did not look to the conservative and ordered monarchies of Europe. Belinsky and Young Russia found their source of inspiration in the utopian socialism and the generous but vague radicalism of the French opposition to the bourgeois reign of King Louis Philippe.

Belinsky "was the true father of the intelligentsia," Prince

Mirsky wrote of him, "the embodiment of what remained its spirit for more than two generations—of social idealism, of the passion for improving the world, of disrespect for all tradition, and of highly strung, disinterested enthusiasm." Belinsky exercised his influence through the many essays of literary criticism and the annual surveys of Russian literature which he contributed to various magazines after leaving the University of Moscow. In 1839 he moved to Petersburg, where he became the principal critic of *Otechestvennie zapiski* (*Patriotic Notebooks*). In 1846 his friend Nikolai Alexeevich Nekrasov acquired the magazine *Sovremennik* (*The Contemporary*), which had been founded by Pushkin. Nekrasov, whose poetry of social compassion was highly praised by Belinsky, turned the magazine into the chief organ of radical opinion. (It was suppressed by the authorities in 1866.) Criticism of the existing political and social order could not be expounded in nineteenth-century Russia except in indirect form. Thus literature and literary criticism became the chief vehicles for voicing political and social demands. In that respect, Belinsky and his generation set the tone for much of later Russian writing.

For Belinsky art was an instrument of social progress, and he had little feeling for form and esthetic values. He demanded from literature that it be realistically true to life and above all inspired by socially progressive ideas. He not only welcomed Gogol as the great representative of the new realism, but also he praised the French novelist who wrote under the name of George Sand as the true model of the new art. This latter fact indicated the serious limitations of Belinsky's artistic judgment. However, he turned the Russian mind from the prevailing uncritical rhetorical attitude and helped to bring it to maturity.

At the same time his role as a national educator went beyond the realm of literature. Belinsky loved freedom of thought and hated all constraints which limited it. He demanded "heroes to combat society's tyranny." Belinsky was convinced that Russia's malady was rooted "in the lack of personal independence. As a consequence the government did not respect the individual, and the individual did not oppose the government. To the cynicism of the authority corresponded the forebearing of the people. Russia's future will be a great danger to Europe and full of misfortune to herself if there is no emancipation of individual rights. One century more of despotism will destroy all the good qualities of the Russian people."

Belinsky was one of the very few Russian thinkers of his time who insisted on the constructive importance of the middle class for the intellectual and political development of the nation. On the other hand, he expressed the general feeling of Young Russia when he championed the progressive causes of the period, the need for education, the confidence in science, the expectation of a bright future, social reform, and the emancipation of women. In 1847 Gogol, whose work Belinsky had interpreted as an attempt to expose "all that was bad in Russia," published his *Selected Passages from a Correspondence with Friends,* a labored defense of serfdom and autocracy, a moral sermon on behalf of Orthodoxy and mysticism. Belinsky replied in a famous letter which, of course, could not be published in Russia at that time. Against Gogol's idealization of the Russia of Tsar Nikolai I, Belinsky painted the extremely dark picture of the Tsarist régime and of the Orthodox clergy as the progressives saw it. Russia needed, according to Belinsky, not faith or mysticism, but respect for law and individual rights. Herzen printed the letter for the first time in London in 1855, seven years after Belinsky's death, but in the meantime the letter was circulated widely in hand-written copies throughout Russia and became the credo of the progressive circles. When Dostoevsky was arrested in April 1849, as a member of a socialist circle, a copy of the letter was found on him, and he was found guilty "of having circulated the letter of the journalist Belinsky full of insolent expressions against the Orthodox Church and the Supreme Power." Ivan Aksakov wrote to his father on October 9, 1856, that "there is not a single high school teacher in the capital of the Russian provinces who does not know Belinsky's letter to Gogol by heart."

RUSSIA AND THE WEST

[From "Literary Reveries," 1834]

IN THE East of Europe, where the two parts of mankind meet, Providence has settled a nation that differs sharply from its Western neighbors. Its cradle was the radiant South, and the sword of the Asiatic-Russ gave it its name. Moribund Byzantium bequeathed to it the beneficent word of salvation; the chains of the Tartar held together its disunited parts in a strong bond, and the hand of the Khans sealed them with Russian blood. Ivan III taught Russia to fear, love, and obey its Tsar, forced it to look upon the Tsar as Providence, as sovereign fate, meting out punishment and mercy of his own will alone and admitting above himself none but the will of God. And that nation became as cool and calm as the snows of its native land when it lived peacefully in its hut; as swift and terrible as the heavenly thunder of its brief but blazing summer when the hand of the Tsar pointed out the enemy; as reckless and riotous as the blizzards and storms of its winters when it held wassail; as sluggish and lazy as the bear of its primeval forests when it had plenty of bread and home-brew; as intelligent, shrewd, and cunning as the cat, its domestic penate, when necessity becomes the mother of invention. It stood stoutly for the church of God, the faith of its forefathers, and was staunchly true to its royal "little father," the Orthodox Tsar. Its favorite saying was: We all are God's and the Tsar's; God and the Tsar, the grace of God and the grace of the Tsar, were mingled into a single concept. It jealously guarded the crude and simple ways of its ancestors and honestly believed foreign ways to be devilry. Beyond this the poetry of its life did not extend: for its mind was sunk in quiet slumber and had never ventured outside its conventional precincts; for it had never bent one knee to Woman, of whom its proud and savage force demanded slavish submission and not sweet reciprocity; for its life was a monotony, enlivened only by boisterous games and the daring hunt; for war alone stirred the whole power of its cold, iron soul; for only the sanguinary riot of battle gave it unbridled scope and full play. This was an original and characteristic life, but one-sided and isolated. . . .

Yes—much was accomplished that was great, useful, and glorious! Peter was quite right: he could not afford to wait. He knew that he would not live twice, and so he hastened to live, and for him, to live was to create. But the people thought otherwise. It had long been sleeping when suddenly a mighty hand roused the giant from his sleep. He opened his heavy lids with difficulty and was astonished to see what foreign customs had invaded his home, like uninvited guests, without taking off their boots, without bowing before the holy icons or saluting the house. The foreign customs had seized him by the beard, which was dearer to him than his head, and plucked it out. They stripped off his majestic raiment and clad him in motley, marred and mutilated his virginal language, and insolently desecrated the sacred customs of his forefathers, outraged his fondest beliefs and cherished customs. He saw and stood aghast. . . . What was the outcome of it all? The mass of people stubbornly remained what it was before; but the upper classes followed the course along which the strong hand of genius had launched them. . . .

And so, the nation or, better to say, the mass of our people and the upper classes went separate ways. The former retained its pristine, rude, and half-savage mode of life and its melancholy songs in which it poured out its heart in grief and joy. The latter apparently underwent a change if not an improvement, forgot everything Russian; forgot even how to speak Russian; forgot the poetic lore and legends of their native land, those beautiful songs full of a deep sadness, sweet yearning, and boisterous revelry, and begot a literature which faithfully mirrored them. It should be observed that the mass of the people and the upper classes each split up, especially the latter, into a multitude of species and degrees. The former showed certain signs of life among the social strata which had direct relations with the upper classes—townsfolk, artisans, petty tradesmen, and manufacturers. Necessity and the competition of foreigners who had settled in Russia made these townspeople active and enterprising when it was a matter of profit, forced them to shake off old habits of sloth and the supineness induced by the amenities of the old Russian stove, and roused a striving after improvement and the innovations hitherto so odious to their mind; their fanatical dislike of Germans abated from day to day and has now disappeared entirely; they have even managed to obtain a sort of education and cling ever more strongly to the wise maxim bequeathed them by their ancestors: instruction is light, and ignorance is darkness. This promises well for the future, the more so that these estates have preserved their national features.

As for the middle class, it has in turn divided up into many categories, among which the most prominent place numerically is occupied by the so-called commoners. This estate more than any other defeated the hopes of Peter the Great: it always purchased learning with brass farthings

and applied its Russian sagacity and shrewdness to the rep-
rehensible pursuit of interpreting the royal ukases; in
learning how to bow and kiss the hands of ladies it did not
unlearn the performance by noble hands of ignoble corporal chastisement.

The upper classes, on the other hand, plunged headlong
into imitation, or rather mimicking of foreigners. . . .

Yes!—the first essays were all too feeble and ineffectual.
Then suddenly, using the happy expression of one of our
compatriots, Lomonosov shone forth like the aurora bore-
alis on the shores of the Arctic Ocean. Dazzling and beautiful was this appearance! It went to prove that a man is a
man in any condition and any clime, that genius can triumph over all the obstacles that an inimical fate places in its
path, that, finally, the Russian can achieve the great and
beautiful no less than any European. But at the same time,
I say, this gratifying spectacle also corroborated, to our misfortune, the irrefragable truth that the pupil will never
surpass the teacher if he regards him as a model instead of
a rival, that the genius of a nation is always timid and tied
when it does not act originally and independently, that its
productions in such cases will always resemble artificial
flowers: bright, exquisite, resplendent, but inodorous and
lifeless. With Lomonosov our literature takes its rise; he
was its father and mentor; he was its Peter the Great. . . .

But first of all I should like to make the following remark.
Our literature, as I have already mentioned, is still governed
by an abject sense of childish veneration for authorities; in
literature, too, we highly esteem the table of ranks and
classes and are afraid to speak the truth aloud about highly
placed persons. In speaking of an eminent writer we always confine ourselves to empty utterances and turgid eu-
logies; to say the harsh truth about him is sacrilege. . . .
Where is criticism whose object is to cultivate taste; where

is truth, which should be dearer than all the authorities on earth? . . .

Catherine II ascended the throne, and a new, a brighter page was opened in the life of the Russian nation. . . . Then did the Russian people, more or less accustomed to the constraining and unfamiliar forms of its new life, inured and almost reconciled to them, and bowing its head, as it were, to the verdict of an inexorable and inevitable fate— the will of Peter—for the first time breathe freely, smile cheerfully, look proudly, for it was no longer being driven to a great goal but led of its own free will and consent. Then it was that the Russian mind awoke, schools were founded, all the necessary textbooks were published for elementary education, and everything worthy was translated from European languages. The Russian sword was unsheathed, monarchies were shaken to their foundations, kingdoms shattered and merged with Russ! . . .

Karamzin set before himself the aim of developing in the Russian public a reading habit. I ask you: can the vocation of an artist lend itself to a premeditated aim, no matter how splendid that aim may be? More: may an artist debase himself, bend, so to speak, to the public which does not reach above his knees and is therefore incapable of understanding him! Let us presume that it is permissible. Then another question crops up: can he in such a case remain an artist in his creations? Undoubtedly not . . . *The History of the Russian State* is Karamzin's most important achievement; there he is mirrored with all his faults and merits. I do not venture to pass a learned judgment on this work for, I frankly confess, I should by no means be equal to such a task. My opinion (by no means new) will be that of an amateur and not an authority. Considering all that was done for systematic history before Karamzin, one cannot deny that his study was a prodigious feat. Its chief fault consists in his view of things and events, often childish and always, at any rate, unmanly; in vociferous rhetoric and a misplaced desire to be didactic and edifying where the facts speak for themselves; in a partiality for the heroes of his narrative which does credit to the author's heart but not to his intelligence. Its chief merit consists in interesting narrative and skillful presentation of events, not infrequently in artistic delineation of characters, and, above all, in style, in which he decidedly excels. Nothing has yet been written in our country that would resemble it in this last respect. Karamzin's style in *The History of the Russian State* is pre-eminently a Russian style; it can be compared only to the verses of Pushkin's *Boris Godunov*. . . .

And so, the Pushkin period was marked by a movement of life to a supreme degree. During that decade we experienced, re-lived, and re-thought the whole intellectual life of Europe, whose echo reached us by way of the Baltic Sea. We had threshed and argued it all out and mastered it without having reared, nurtured, or created it ourselves. Others had worked for us, and we had merely taken it ready-made and used it; that is the secret of our incredibly swift successes and the reason for their incredible instability. This, I also believe, is one of the reasons why Pushkin is almost the only one who has survived that brisk and active decade so replete with talents and geniuses, and now, forlorn and sad, he sees the names of those who rose with him upon the horizon of our literature disappearing one by one in the waters of oblivion like an unfinished word vanishing into the air. . . .

It will come, you may be sure of that! But for that we first need the education of a society that would express the character of the great Russian people. We need an enlightenment created by our own efforts, cultivated on our own native soil. We have no literature: I reiterate this with joy, with delight, for I see in that truth the guarantee of our future successes. Take a good look at the trend of our society, and you will agree that I am right. See how the new generation, disillusioned in the genius and immortality of our literary works, instead of giving immature creations to the world, is avidly studying the sciences and drinking the life-giving water of education at the fountainhead. The age of childhood is apparently passing! Please God, may it pass quickly. But please God still more that men's minds may quickly be disabused of the illusion that we possess a rich literature! Noble poverty is better than illusory riches! There will come a time, and enlightenment will spread throughout Russia in a broad torrent, the intellectual countenance of the nation will stand out clearly, and our artists and writers will then place on all their creations the stamp of the Russian spirit. But now we must learn, learn, learn! . . .

Can we fail to achieve that end when the government represents such a unique, such an unprecedented model of solicitude for the dissemination of education, when it expends such vast sums on the maintenance of schools, encourages teachers and students with magnificent awards, and has thrown open the door of opportunity for the educated mind and talent! Does a year ever pass but an indefatigable government accomplishes new deeds for the benefit of education, or bestows new favors and new bounties upon men of science? . . .

Yes! The seed of the future is ripening today! And it will sprout and blossom, blossom forth in full splendor at the behest of affectionate monarchs! Then shall we have our own literature, then shall we be the rivals and not the imitators of Europe. . . .

THE MIRACLE OF PETER THE GREAT

[From a review of The Acts of Peter the Great, *1841]*

Russia was cut off from the West at the very beginning of her existence, and Byzantium, as regards civic education, had nothing to offer her other than the custom of blackening the teeth and whiting the face, and gouging the eyes of enemies and malefactors. . . . Then came the Tartar irruption which forged the scattered parts of Russia into unity. This was the great boon of the two centuries of the Tartar yoke; but how great was the mischief it caused Russia, how many were the incidental vices it engrafted? Seclusion of women, slavery in notions and sentiments, the knout, the habit of burying money in the ground and going about in tatters for fear of showing one's self a rich man, corruption in the affairs of justice, Asiatism in ways of life, mental sloth, ignorance, despising of self—in a word, everything that Peter the Great had been eradicating, everything in Russia that was directly opposed to Europeanism. All these ways were not our native characteristics, but engrafted on us by the Tartars. The Russians' very intolerance of foreigners generally was a consequence of the Tartar yoke and not at all of religious fanaticism: the Tartar made everyone who was not a Russian repugnant to the Russian mind—and the word *bosurman* [infidel] came to be extended from the Tartars to the Germans. Thus the principal faults of our *narodnost* [nationality] are acquired and not inherent faults; therefore, we can cast them off, and already we are beginning to do it. . . .

In pre-Petrine Russia there was no trade, no industry, no police, no civil security, no diversity of wants and demands, no military organization, for all was poor and insignificant, since it was not law but custom. And morals? What a sad spectacle! How much there was that was Asiatic, barbaric. How many rites degrading to human dignity there were, e.g., in marriage, and practiced not only by the common people but by the highest personages in the realm! How much there was that was vulgar and coarse in feasting! Compare those heavy repasts, those incredible beverages, those gross kissings, those frequent knockings of the forehead on the floor, those grovelings on the ground, those Chinese ceremonies—compare them with the tournaments of the Middle Ages, the European fêtes of the seventeenth century! . . . Remember what our long-bearded knights and chevaliers were like! Think of our gay ladies lapping up vodka! Men married they knew not whom! Deluded, they beat and tormented their wives in order to raise them by brute force to an angelic status—and if that did not work, they poisoned them with philters. They ate Homerically, drank almost in tubfuls, and kept their wives out of sight, and only when flushed after having eaten several scores of peppery dishes and drunk several buckets of wine and mead would they call them out for a kiss. . . . But, for all that, this has not the slightest bearing on a nation's degradation either morally or philosophically: for it was all the result of our isolation and of Tartar influence. No sooner did Peter open his nation's door to the light of the world than the darkness of ignorance was gradually dispersed—the nation did not degenerate, did not yield its native soil to another people, but became something it had not been before. . . . Yes, gentlemen, defenders of ancient custom, say what you will, but the equestrian statue to Peter the Great on St. Isaac's Square is not enough; altars should be put up to him in all the squares and streets of the great kingdom of Russia! . . .

The point is not whether Peter made us half Europeans and half Russians, consequently neither Europeans nor Russians. The point is are we always to remain in this characterless condition? If not, if we are destined to become European Russians and Russian Europeans, we should not reproach Peter, but rather wonder how he could have accomplished such a gigantic, such an unprecedented task! And so the crux of the matter consists in the words, "shall we"—and we can answer firmly and explicitly that we not only shall become but we are already becoming a people with a character of our own since the reign of Catherine II, and we are making progress therein day by day. We are today the pupils and no longer the zealots of Europeanism; we no longer wish to be either Frenchmen, or Englishmen, or Germans; we want to be Russians in the European spirit. This consciousness is permeating all spheres of our activity and made itself strikingly manifest in our literature with the advent of Pushkin, that great independent and national talent. The fact that the final great act—the utter permeation of our *narodnost* by Europe—has still not been accomplished and will not be accomplished for a long time merely goes to prove that Peter carried out in thirty years a task that needs centuries. That is why he is a giant among giants, a genius among geniuses, a king among kings. Napoleon himself had a rival in antiquity—Julius Caesar. Our Peter has neither rivals nor models since the beginning of the world; he is akin and equal to no one but himself. . . .

THE REFORM OF SOCIETY THROUGH WESTERNIZATION

[From letters to V. P. Botkin and a review of Markevich's History of Little Russia, *1841 and 1842]*

Sociality, sociality—or death! That is my motto. What care I for the existence of the universal when individuality is suffering? What care I if genius on earth lives in heaven when the crowd is wallowing in the dirt? What care I if I conceive the idea, if the world of ideas is open to me in art, religion, and history when I cannot share it with all those who should be my brothers in mankind, my neighbors in

Christ, but who are strangers and enemies to me in their ignorance? What is it to me that there is delight for the elect when the majority does not even suspect the possibility? Away then delight, if it is given to me alone out of a thousand! I will not have it if I cannot have it in common with my lesser brethren! My heart bleeds and shudders when I view the crowd and its representatives. Grief, poignant grief, overcomes me at the sight of the barefooted little boys playing in the street, of the tattered beggars, of the drunken cab-driver, of the soldier returning from sentinel duty, of the official hurrying along with a portfolio under his arm, of the complacent officer, and of the haughty grandee. I all but cry when I give the soldier a farthing, I run from the beggar to whom I have given a farthing as though I have committed an evil deed and would fain be deaf to the sounds of my own footsteps. And that is life: to sit in the street in rags with an idiotic expression on one's face collecting farthings in the daytime to be spent on booze in the evening—and men see it and no one cares about it.

I don't know what is happening to me, but at times I can gaze for several minutes with unutterable anguish at a harlot in the street, and her vacuous smile, the seal of arrant depravity, lacerates my soul, especially if she be good-looking. Next door to me lives a fairly well-to-do civil servant who has become so Europeanized that when his wife goes to the baths he hires a carriage for her. I recently learned that he smashed her teeth and lips, dragged her over the floor by her hair, and kicked her for not having prepared good cream for the coffee; and she had borne him six children. And whenever I met her, I always fled distressed at the sight of her pale, worn face stamped with the sufferings of tyranny. On hearing this story I gnashed my teeth—to burn the scoundrel on a slow fire seemed to me too lenient a punishment, and I cursed my impotence at not being able to go to kill him like a dog. And that is society, existing on ra-

tional principles, a fact of reality! And how many such husbands, such families, are there! How many beautiful women
there are, thrown by the hands of fond parents to the rape
of a brute, through calculation or unintelligence! Has a
man after that the right to bury himself in art, in knowledge?

I am inflamed against all the principles which bind the
ill of men to a creed! My God is negation! In history my
heroes are the destroyers of the old—Luther, Voltaire, the
Encyclopedists, the Terrorists, Byron (*Cain*), and so on.
Sense with me now stands higher (in its immediacy, of
course), and that is why I prefer the blasphemies of Voltaire
to acknowledging the authority of religion, society, or anything or anybody! I know that the Middle Ages were a great
epoch. I understand the sanctity, the poesy, the grandeur of
medieval religion, but I prefer the eighteenth century—
the epoch of religion's decline. In the Middle Ages, heretics,
free thinkers, and witches were burnt at the stake; in the
eighteenth century, the guillotine chopped off the heads of
aristocrats, priests, and other enemies of God, Reason, and
Humanity. There will come a time—I fervently believe it
—when no one will be burnt, no one will be decapitated,
when criminals will plead for death as a mercy and salvation, and death will be denied them, but life will serve as
their punishment as death does not, when there will be no
senseless forms and rites, no contracts and stipulations on
feeling, no duties and obligations. Then we shall not yield
to will but to love alone. There will be no husbands and
wives, but lovers and mistresses, and when the mistress
comes to the lover saying: "I love another," the lover will
answer: "I cannot be happy without you, I shall suffer all
my life, but go to him whom you love." Should she wish,
through generosity, to remain with him, he will not accept
her sacrifice, but like God will say to her: "I want blessings,
not sacrifices." . . .

Woman will not be the slave of society and man. She will, like man, freely follow her inclinations without losing her good name, that monstrosity of conventional ideas. There will be neither rich nor poor, neither kings nor subjects. There will only be brethren, there will only be man. According to the words of the apostle Paul, Christ will pass his power to the Father, and Father-Reason will hold sway once more, but this time in a new heaven and above a new earth. . . .

The very idea that states are obliged to watch one another jealously and have the right to restrict one another, this very idea contains the principle, albeit misinterpreted, of unity. This unity is now interpreted differently; it consists in the subordination of the great idea of national individuality to a still greater idea of humanity. The nations are beginning to realize that they are members of the great family of mankind. They are beginning to share with each other in the spirit of brotherhood the spiritual treasures of their nationality. Every success of a nation is being rapidly assimilated by the other nations. Every nation adopts from another, especially what is alien to its own nationality, and gives in return what constitutes the exclusive possession of its own historical life and what is alien to the historical life of the other. Today only weak and narrow minds can think that the successes of humanity can harm the successes of nationality and that we need Chinese walls to safeguard nationality. Strong and clear minds understand . . . that the national spirit can no more disappear or degenerate through intercourse with foreigners and the invasion of new ideas and new customs than a man's face or nature can disappear or become transformed through science and intercourse with other people.

The day is not far off when the petty, egoistic calculations of so-called politics will disappear and the nations will fraternally embrace amid the triumphant sunshine of reason, and paeans of reconciliations between jubilant earth and conciliated heaven will resound! Though the present historical situation contrasts sharply with this picture and makes it appear an unrealizable dream of the heated imagination, nevertheless to thinking minds capable of grasping the gist of things, the present situation of mankind in all its inauspicious character presents all the elements and data, on the basis of which the most daring dreams of today will become the most positive reality tomorrow.

Our haters of Europeanism reproach their countrymen for their passion for traveling abroad and for the ease and zest with which they adopt Western ways, that means, the ways of enlightened and educated men. In their benighted fanaticism, these would-be patriots go to such length that they look upon the educated (Westernized) members of Russian society almost as renegades, almost as degenerates who have nothing Russian in them. They hold up to them the unkempt, dirty masses as an example of unspoiled Russian nationality worthy of imitation! . . .

In England the middle class stands for something. It is represented by the House of Commons, and in the proceedings of that House there is much that is dignified, and there is plenty of patriotism. But in England the middle class is counter-balanced by the aristocracy, and this fact makes the English government as statesmanly, dignified, and reputable as the French government is mean, vulgar, and disreputable. When the aristocracy in England will have had its day, the people will counterbalance the middle class; otherwise, England will offer perhaps a still more disgusting spectacle than France does today. I am not one of those who decree that the bourgeoisie is an evil, that it must be destroyed, and that only then things will go well. (That is what the socialists think.) I could agree to it only when I should see in practice a state prospering without a middle class. So far I have seen only that states without a middle class are doomed to perpetual futility. I shall not attempt to solve a priori a problem that only experience can solve. As long as the bourgeoisie exists and as long as it is strong, I know that it must be and cannot but be. I know that industry is a source of great evil, but I also know that it is the source of great blessings for society. It is only the least of evils in the rule of capital and its tyranny over labor. I agree that even the reprobate breed of capitalists should have their share of influence on public affairs, but woe to the state where this class stands alone at the helm!

RUSSIA AND THE SLAVOPHILS

[From "A View on Russian Literature in 1846"]

The influence of Karamzin through his *History of the Russian State* is still very conspicuous. This is best evidenced by the so-called Slavophil party. We know that in Karamzin's eyes Ivan III stood higher than Peter the Great, and pre-Petrine Russ was better than the new Russia. Here you have the origin of the so-called Slavophil movement, which, by the way, we regard in many respects as a very important phenomenon. It proves that the adult and mature period of our literature is close at hand. During the infancy of literature all men are engaged with problems which, though they may be important in themselves, have no practical bearing on life. Slavophilism without doubt has a vital bearing on the most important aspects of our public life.

Slavophilism is first of all a conviction. Like all convictions, it merits our utmost respect, even though we may entirely disagree with it. We have many Slavophils, and their number is steadily growing.

The positive side of their doctrine consists of some sort of nebulous, mystical presentiment of the victory of the East over the West. The Slavophil fallacy is all too clearly exposed by the facts of reality. The negative side of the Slavophil creed, however, deserves much more attention, not in that it falls foul of the allegedly decaying West—the Slavophils are absolutely unable to understand the West because they measure it with an Eastern yardstick—but in that it falls foul of Russian Europeanism. They have a good deal to say of it, which is pertinent. One cannot help at least half-agreeing with some of their contentions, for instance that there is a sort of duality in Russian life and consequently a lack of moral unity; that this deprives us of a clearly defined national character such as distinguishes, to their credit, all the European nations; that this makes a kind of nonesuch out of us, well able to think in French, German, and English, but unable to think in Russian; and that the cause for all this lies in the reforms of Peter the Great.

To some extent, all this is correct. We must not, however, confine ourselves to such an admission; we must investigate the causes in the hope of discovering, within the evil itself, a way out of it. This the Slavophils have not done; but this is what they have made their opponents, if not accomplish, then at least attempt to do. Herein lies the true service which they have rendered. It is equally fruitless and harmful to fall asleep in ambitious dreams, whether of our national glory or of our Europeanism. Sleep is not life, but merely a realm of fancies, and we cannot but be grateful to him who breaks such a sleep. Indeed, never before has the study of Russian history assumed such a serious character as lately. We probe and question the past for an explanation of our present and a hint as to our future. We seem to have taken alarm for our life, for our significance, for our past and future, and are in a hurry to solve the great problem of to be or not to be. . . .

Russia should not be compared to the old states of Europe. Their history followed a course diametrically opposed to ours, and has long since yielded both its blossom and its fruit. Without doubt it is easier for a Russian to adopt the view of a Frenchman, Englishman, or German than to think independently in Russian, for the first way presents a ready-made view the acquaintance with which is rendered easy both by science and by present-day realities. To think in Russian is much more difficult, because the Russian to himself is still a riddle, and the significance and destiny of his native land, where everything is embryonic and incipient and nothing is determinate, fully evolved, and formed, are likewise a riddle to him. To be sure, there is something sad in it, but still more something that is comforting. The oak grows slowly, but then it lives for centuries. It is natural for man to wish the speedy fulfillment of his desires, but precocity is unreliable: we more than anybody else should have convinced ourselves of this truth. . . .

We Russians need have no doubts as to our . . . political significance: we alone, of all the Slav peoples, have formed a strong and powerful state, and have, both before and ever since the time of Peter the Great, come through many a severe ordeal with flying colors. We often stood on the brink of ruin, and yet we invariably rode out the storm to reappear on its crest in new and greater vigor and strength. A nation incapable of internal growth could not possess such strength and vigor. Yes, we have the national life in us, we are destined to give our message and our thought to the world; but it is too early yet to conjecture what that message or thought will be. Our grandchildren or great-grandchildren will learn it without any effort at hard guessing, because that message and that thought will be uttered by them. . . .

AGAINST GOGOL'S ORTHODOXY

[From a letter to Nikolai Gogol of 1847]

Russia sees her salvation not in mysticism, asceticism, or pietism, but in the success of civilization, enlightenment, and humanity. She needs no sermons—she has heard enough of them!—or prayers—she has repeated them too often! She needs the awakening in the people of a sense of their human dignity, lost for so many centuries amidst the dirt and refuse. She needs rights and laws conforming not with the preaching of the Church but with common sense and justice, and she needs their strictest possible observance. Instead of which, Russia presents the dire spectacle of a country where men traffic in men, without even having the excuse so insidiously exploited by the American plantation owners who claim that the Negro is not a man. Russia is a country where there are not only no guarantees for individual rights, honor, and property, but even no police order. There is nothing but vast corporations of official thieves and robbers of various descriptions. The most vital national problems in Russia today are the abolition of serfdom and corporal punishment, and the strictest possible observance of at least those laws which already exist. . . .

Proponent of the knout, apostle of ignorance, champion of obscurantism . . . that you base such teaching on the Orthodox Church, I can understand. It has always served as the servant of despotism. But why have you mixed Christ up in this? What did you find in common between Him and any church, least of all the Orthodox Church? . . . How can it be that you, the author of *Revizor* and *Dead Souls*, have in all sincerity, from the bottom of your heart, sung a hymn to the nefarious Russian clergy which you rank immeasurably higher than the Catholic clergy? Let us assume that you did not know the latter had once been something, while the former had never been anything but a servant of the secular powers; but do you really mean to say that you do not know that our clergy is held in universal contempt by Russian society and by the Russian people? Of whom do the Russian people tell obscene stories? Of the priest, the priest's wife, the priest's daughter, and the priest's farm

hand. Does not the priest in Russia represent for all Russians the embodiment of gluttony, avarice, servility, and
shamelessness? Do you mean to say that you do not know
all this? Strange! According to you the Russian people is the
most religious in the world. That is a lie! The basis of religiousness is pietism, reverence, fear of God, whereas the
Russian utters the name of the Lord by scratching himself
somewhere. He says of the icon: If it is not good for praying,
it is good for covering the pots.

Take a close look at the Russian people, and you will see
that by nature it is profoundly atheistic. It still retains a
good deal of superstition, but not a trace of religiousness.
Superstition passes with the advances of civilization, but
religiousness often keeps company with them. We see that
clearly in France, where even today there are many sincere
Catholics among enlightened and educated men, and where
many people who have rejected Christianity still cling stubbornly to the idea of God. The Russian people is different.
Mystic exaltation is not in its nature. It has too much common sense, a too lucid and positive mind, and therein, perhaps, lies the vast scope of its historical destinies in the future. . . .

When a European, especially a Catholic, is seized with a
religious ardor, he denounces iniquitous authority, like the
Hebrew prophets who denounce the iniquities of those in
power. With us, on the contrary, no sooner is a person, even
a reputable person, afflicted with the malady which psychia-
trists know as religious mania than he begins to burn more
incense to the earthly god than to the heavenly one, and so
overshoots the mark in doing so, that the former would fain
reward him for his slavish zeal, did he not perceive that he
would thereby compromise himself in the eyes of society.
. . . What a rogue our fellow the Russian is!

VIII

Radical Russia

CHERNYSHEVSKY

Russian literature in the sixties, following the lead given by Belinsky, became a chief instrument for enlightening the Russian about his place in society and for discussing the ways of reforming society. This was a time of heightened social and political expectation due to the emancipation of the serfs and the accompanying administrative and judicial reforms. The educated youth of the country began to organize itself in secret societies (public political life and the formation of parties remained forbidden in Russia until 1905) and to ask itself "what to do." From abroad the new generation whole-heartedly accepted the materialism of Ludwig Feuerbach and Ludwig Büchner and the positivism of Auguste Comte and the English Utilitarians. The German idealist philosophy which had exercised such potent influence on the preceding generation was rejected as "rubbish." The new youth no longer drew their inspiration from poetry and art, which appeared to them conducive to an aristocratic life of futile leisure. To them science became the new idol. They regarded it as an impregnable foundation of a democratic and progressive society. "Facts" alone counted.

The recognized leader of this youth was Nikolai Gavrilovich Chernyshevsky. He was the son of a priest and was educated for the priesthood in the seminary in his native city of Saratov. With the consent of his father, however, he left the seminary to enter the University of St. Petersburg. Like Belinsky, he came from the lower classes and lacked the esthetic culture of the nobility. In the fifties he wrote many articles on economic problems. He was especially concerned with the position of the Russian peasant. For his revolutionary activities he was imprisoned in the St. Petersburg fortress from 1862 to 1864. There he wrote a novel *What to Do?* which became the bible of the young generation. In 1864 Chernyshevsky was sentenced to hard labor in Siberia. By the time he returned in 1883, he was broken in mind and body.

Chernyshevsky exercised an immense influence upon the youth of the period by his moral earnestness. But as a writer he was far surpassed by two younger men, Nikolai Dobroliubov and Dmitri Pisarev, both of whom died in their twenties. Dobroliubov, like Chernyshevsky, was the son of a priest. In 1858, he published in the *Sovremennik* (the periodical for which Belinsky had written and on which Chernyshevsky collaborated) a famous essay on Oblomovism. Through this essay, Oblomovism became the term generally used to characterize the typical "superfluous man" and his attitude. The new youth thought of themselves as the very opposite of Oblomov and of all the other superfluous men who played such a great role in nineteenth-century Russian literature and life. The conflict between the two generations, the old cultured aristocracy and the militant materialist youth, was well portrayed by Turgenev in his novel *Fathers and Children* (1861). He coined for his youthful hero, the medical student Bazarov, the term "nihilist." The stagnant conditions of Russian life led this youth, ardent for action, to a total rejection of the existing society and its values.

Their attitude was best expressed by Pisarev, the son of an impoverished nobleman. In his essay "The Annihilation of Aesthetics" he wished, like Tolstoy in his later years, to discard all art that did not directly contribute to the improvement of mankind. A good cobbler seemed to him preferable to a Raphael. In May 1861 Pisarev wrote as a spokesman of the new revolutionary attitude: "What can be smashed must be smashed. Whatever will stand the blow is fit to survive. What flies into pieces is rubbish. In any case, hit right and left; from that no harm can or will come." Referring to Pushkin's word "Long live reason!", Pisarev bitterly decried "decrepit despotism, decrepit religion, and the decayed timbers of contemporary official morality."

The question which the youth faced was: what to do. Chernyshevsky tried to answer it in his novel, to which he gave the subtitle *Tales about the New People*. (Five excerpts from the novel are given in this chapter.) He was devoid of all artistic talent. For the modern reader, his prose with its effusive sentimentality makes difficult reading. Yet several generations of Russian youth were educated by it, and it occupied an important place in Lenin's library. Readers of contemporary Soviet literature will feel more at home with Chernyshevsky's novel than will those who are familiar with the art of Russia's great age. Not without justice, Professor Barghoorn pointed out that Russian Marxism absorbed the emotional quality of the nihilism of the sixties.

The "new people" whom Chernyshevsky introduces fight the lies and conventions of society and strive for a life of emotional sincerity and truthfulness. The eternal triangle is not missing here, but it is "purified" according to the dreams of the new morality. Vera Pavlovna is rescued from an unbearable domestic situation by a student of medicine, Dmitri Lopukhov, who marries her, but she later falls in love with his best friend, Alexander Kirsonov. Very nobly,

Lopukhov removes himself from the scene, and Vera with the help of her new husband can truly start the life of the new woman, becoming a useful member of society, founding an industrial cooperative to save poor girls, becoming herself by hard work the first woman physician in the country. In addition to these "new people," whom the author regards as ordinary representatives of the radical youth, is presented another type, Rakhmetov, an extraordinary man with unusual strength of character and purity of purpose, a dedicated professional revolutionary, who became the ideal hero of the young generation. In the 1870's, the "new people" became "populists" who went out to preach the new gospel to the peasantry, or terrorists who wished to force the government into establishing the new society. In both of them, the nihilism of the 1860's continued, and they looked to Chernyshevsky and Rakhmetov as their guides.

THE NEW YOUTH IN LOVE

WHAT! So quickly, and against all expectation!" thought Vera, on finding herself alone in her room after the guests had gone. "We have talked only once. Half an hour ago we did not know each other, and already we are so intimate! How strange!"

No, it is not strange at all, Verotchka.

Men like Lopukhov have magic words which attract to them every injured and outraged being. Their sweetheart whispers to them these magic words. What is strange indeed, Verotchka, is that you should be so calm. Love is thought to be an exciting feeling. Yet you will sleep as calmly and peacefully as a little child, and no painful dreams will trouble your slumber.

To others it is strange, to me it is not. Trouble in love is not love itself; if there is trouble, that means that something is wrong, for love itself is gay and careless.

"Yes, it is very strange," still thought Vera; "what he told me about the poor, about women, about love, was what I had already thought myself. Where did I find it? In books? No, for everything in them is expressed with so much doubt and reserve that one thinks he is reading only dreams.

"To me these things seem to be so simple and inevitable, and life is impossible without them. Yet the best books present them as incapable of realization. Take George Sand, for instance. What goodness! What morality! But only dreams. Why do our novelists not see that life cannot continue without this new justice, which will tolerate neither poverty nor wretchedness, and that it is towards such justice that we must march? They deplore the present, but they believe that it will go on forever or for a very long time. If they had said what I thought, I should have known then that good and wise people think so too, whereas I thought myself a poor, dreamy, and inexperienced young girl, alone in thinking and hoping for a better order.

"Lopukhov told me that his sweetheart inspires all who know her with these ideas and urges everyone to work for their realization. The sweetheart is quite right, but who is she? I must know her; yes, I must get to know her.

"Certainly, it will be very fine when there are no more poor people, when there is no more servitude, and when everybody is gay, good, learned, and happy."

Amid these thoughts Vera fell into profound and dreamless sleep. No, it is not strange that you have conceived and cherished these sublime thoughts, good and inexperienced Verotchka, although you have never even heard the names of the men who first taught justice and proved that it must be realized and inevitably will be. If books have not presented these ideas with clarity, it is because they were written by men who caught glimpses of these thoughts when they were only marvelous utopias. Now it has been demonstrated that they can be realized, and other books are being written by other men who show that these thoughts are good, with nothing of the marvelous about them. These thoughts float in the air, they penetrate everywhere.

It is not difficult, Verotchka, to share your ideas. But others have not taken them to heart as you have. Your ideas are not at all strange. What can there be strange, indeed, in your wish to be free and happy? The desire is not an extraordinary discovery; it is natural. What is strange, is that there are men who have no such desire and who would regard as strange the thoughts with which you fall asleep on the first evening of your love. They would think it strange that after questioning yourself as to him whom you love and as to your love itself, you think that all men should be happy and that we should aid them to become so as fast as possible. Nevertheless, it is very natural and human. . . .

As yet, very few people have felt that the charm which love gives to everything should be more than a passing phenomenon in man's life. This intense gleam of life should not light simply the period of desire, of courting, of seeking in marriage; no, this period should be only the enchanting dawn of a day more enchanting yet. During the course of life, love and its delight ought to increase. Among people of the old society such is not the case. With them the poetry of love does not survive satisfaction. The contrary is the rule among the people of the new generation whose life I am describing. The longer they live together, the more they are lighted and warmed by the poetry of love, until the time when the care of their growing children absorbs them. Then this care, sweeter than personal enjoyment, becomes uppermost; but until then, love grows incessantly. That which the men of former times enjoyed for only a few short months the new men keep for many years.

And why so? It is a secret that I will unveil to you. One need have but a pure heart, an upright soul, and that new and just conception of the human being which prompts respect for the liberty of one's life companion. Look upon your wife as you looked upon your sweetheart. Remember that she at any moment has the right to say to you: "I am dissatisfied with you, leave me." Do this, and ten years after your marriage she will inspire in you the same enthusiasm that she did when she was your sweetheart, and she will have as much charm for you as then and even more. Recognize her liberty as openly and with as little reserve as you recognize the liberty of your friends to be your friends or not, and ten years, twenty years, after marriage you will be as dear to her as when you were her sweetheart. This is the way in which the people of our new generation live. Among them, husbands and wives are loyal and sincere, and love each other ever more and more.

THE NEW WOMAN

"It is already the end of April. At the beginning of July, I shall have finished my studies. I must finish them so that we may live," Lopukhov told Vera. "I will obtain employment in my profession, though it will not pay me much. But there will be time left to attend to patients, and taking all things together, we shall be able to live."

"Yes, dear friend," Vera replied, "we shall need so little; but I do not wish to live by your labor. I have piano lessons, which I shall lose, for Mamma will go about telling everybody that I am a wretch. But I shall find other pupils, and I, too, will live by my work. Is that not just? I shall not live at your expense."

"Who told you that, dear Verotchka?"

"Oh! He asks who told me! Have you not yourself stressed

such ideas, you and your books? For your books are full of such thoughts."

"My books? At any rate, I never said such a thing to you. When, then, did I say so?"

"When? Have you not always told me that everything rests on money?"

"Well?"

"And you really think me, then, so stupid that I cannot understand books and draw conclusions from premises?"

"But again I ask you what conclusions. Really, my dear Verotchka, I do not understand you."

"Oh! The strategist! He, too, wants to be a despot and make me dependent upon him! No, that shall not be. Do you understand me now?"

"Speak, and I will try to understand."

"Everything rests on money; consequently, whoever has money, has power and freedom. Thus, as long as woman lives at man's expense, she will be dependent on him, will she not? You thought that I could not understand that and would be your slave? No, I will not suffer your despotism. I know that you intend to be a good and benevolent despot, but I do not intend that you shall be a despot at all. Now this is what we shall do. You shall cut off arms and legs and administer drugs; I, on the other hand, will give lessons on the piano."

"Perfect, Verotchka. What further plans do you propose for our life? I am sure that I shall have only congratulations to offer."

"What! Now you pay me compliments! You wish to be agreeable? You flatter yourself that you are going to rule, while appearing to submit? I know that trick, and I beg you to speak more plainly. You praise me too highly. I am confused. Don't do it or I shall grow too proud."

"Very well, I will be rude, if you prefer. Your nature has

so little of the feminine element that you are undoubtedly about to put forth utterly masculine ideas."

"Will you tell me, dear friend, what a feminine nature is? Just because woman's voice is generally clearer than man's, is it necessary to discuss the respective merits of the contralto and the baritone? We are always told to remain women. Is that not stupidity? I am going to throw off this femininity and express utterly masculine ideas as to the way in which we shall live. We will be friends. Only I wish to be your first friend. . . ."

"You asked me," Vera told Kirsonov, "why I wanted an occupation upon which I should look as seriously as you do on yours, which should be as engaging as yours, and which should require as much attention as yours requires. I want this occupation, my dear friend, because I am very proud. I wish to be as strong as you, your equal in everything. You may be very anxious about me, my dear friend, but how happy we shall be if I prove capable of success in what I wish to undertake." Vera Pavlovna had just thought of an occupation which, under Kirsonov's guidance and her hand in his, she could engage in successfully. As for her thoughts, this is the order in which they came to her:

"Almost all the professions are formally closed to us, and those which are not closed by formal obstacles are by practical difficulties. Only the family is left to us. What occupation can we engage in, outside of the family? That of a governess is almost the only one, and thus we all rush into the single vocation and stifle there. We are too numerous to find independence in it. There are so many women to choose from that no one needs us. When anyone wants a governess, he is besieged by ten, a hundred, even more applicants, each trying to get the place at the expense of the others.

"No, until women launch out into a greater number of careers, they will not enjoy independence. It is difficult, to be sure, to open a new road. But I occupy an especially favorable position for doing it. I should be ashamed not to profit by it. Public prejudice has closed to us such paths of independent activity as the law has not forbidden us to enter. But I can enter whichever of these I choose, provided I am willing to brave the usual gossip. Which shall I choose? My husband is a doctor; he devotes all his leisure time to me. With such a man it would be easy for me to attempt to follow the medical profession.

"It is most important that there should be women physicians. How much easier it is for a woman to talk to another woman than to a man. How much distress could thus be averted! The experiment must be tried!"

THE NEW PEOPLE

It has been my purpose to present to the reader ordinary upright people of the new generation, people whom I meet by the hundreds. I have taken three of them: Vera Pavlovna, Lopukhov, and Kirsonov. I consider them ordinary people, they consider themselves such, and are considered such by all their acquaintances who resemble them. Have I told any extraordinary things about them? It is true, I have presented them with affectionate esteem, but that is because every upright man is worthy of such esteem. But when have I bowed before them? Where have you seen in me the slightest tendency to adoration, or a hint that nothing superior to them can be imagined and that they are ideal characters? What do they do that is remarkably lofty? They have honest but ordinary convictions and try to act accordingly; that is all. Where is their heroism? No upright man in the place of the people pictured by me would have considered it heroic to do as they did; but he would do likewise under similar circumstances. And the friends of such a man, who resemble him (for these people form friendships only with those who act and think as they do), consider him an estimable man, but never dream for a moment of dropping on their knees before him. They say to themselves: we, too, are like him.

I hope that I have succeeded in making every upright man of the new generation identify his friends with my three characters. But those who are able to think of Vera Pavlovna, Kirsonov, and Lopukhov as "our friends, people like ourselves," are yet only a minority of the public. The majority are still much below this type. A man who has never seen anything but dirty huts might take an engraving of a very ordinary house for the picture of a palace. How can the house be made to appear a house and not a palace to such a man? Only by showing in the same picture a wing of the palace. He will then see from this wing that the palace must be quite a different thing from the house. If I had not shown the figure of Rakhmetov, the majority of my readers would have had a false idea of the principal characters of my story. These characters might have appeared to the majority of the public as heroes, as individuals of a superior nature, persons impossible in real life by reason of their very noble conduct. But in this thought you would be wrong, my friends. The characters in my story are not too high and lofty; you are too low. To the height on which they stand all men should and can reach.

Heroic natures, such as neither you nor I can equal, are not like these. I have shown you, in Rakhmetov, a faint outline of the profile of one of them. The features are different, as you clearly see. It is possible for you to become entirely the equals of the ordinary upright people I presented to you provided that you work for your intellectual and moral development. Come up from your caves, my friends, ascend! It is not so difficult. Try: development! development!

Observe, think, read, those who tell you of the pure enjoyment of life, of the possible goodness and happiness of man. Read them, their books delight the heart. Observe life, it is interesting. Think: it is a pleasant occupation. And that is all. Sacrifices are unnecessary, privations are unnecessary. Desire to be happy: this desire alone is indispensable. With this end in view, you will work with pleasure for your development, for there lies happiness. Oh! How great is the pleasure of a man of developed mind! Try it, and you will see how good it is.

THE NEW HERO

The reader sees perhaps that I know more about Rakhmetov than I say. It may be so. But I really do not know where Rakhmetov is now, what has become of him, and whether I shall ever see him again. About these matters I know no more than his other friends. Three or four months after his disappearance from Moscow, we supposed, though we had heard nothing from him, that he was traveling in Europe. This conjecture seemed to have been correct. At least, it is confirmed by some evidence. A year after Rakhmetov's disappearance, one of Kirsonov's acquaintances met in a railway carriage between Vienna and Munich a young Russian who said that he had traveled through all the Slav countries, meeting all classes of society, and had stayed in each country only so long as it was necessary in order to form a true conception of its ideas, its customs, its manner of life, its local institutions, its material condition, and the various branches of its population. He said that with this view he lived in cities and villages, going on foot from one village to another. He had studied the Rumanians and the Hungarians in the same way. He had traveled, now on foot and now by rail, through northern Germany, and had visited in detail southern Germany and the German provinces of Austria. Now he was going to Bavaria, and thence to Switzerland by way of Württemberg and Baden. Afterwards, he would go to France and England in the same way. He counted on doing this in a year; if there was enough of the year left, he would see also Spain and Italy; if not, he would not go there. Why? Because in a year it was absolutely necessary that he be in the United States, a country which he must study more than any other. There he would remain a long time, perhaps more than a year, and perhaps forever, should he find occupation there; but it was more likely that in three years he would return to Russia, as it seemed to him that at that time it would be necessary to be back.

All this is much like Rakhmetov, including the "it is necessary" impressed upon the memory of the narrator. The age, the voice, and the features of the traveler were also confirmatory indices, but the narrator had not paid much attention to his fellow traveler, who, moreover, had left him two hours later, descending from the train at a little village. Consequently, the narrator gave only a vague description of his external appearance, and the authenticity is not complete.

It is also said that a young Russian, an ex-seigneur, once presented himself to one of the greatest European thinkers of our century, the father of the new German philosophy, and said to him: "I have thirty thousand thalers; I need but five thousand; the remainder I beg you to accept."

The philosopher, who was living in great poverty, asked: "What for?"

"For the publication of your work."

The philosopher did not accept, but the Russian nevertheless deposited the money at a banker in the name of the philosopher and wrote him a note which read as follows: "Do with this money as you will; throw it into the river, if you like; but you cannot send it back to me, for you will not find me." The money is reported to be still at the bank.

If this report be true, it was Rakhmetov and none other who called on the philosopher. . . .

Yes, people like Rakhmetov are very droll. I tell them that they are very droll, I tell them so because I pity them.

I say to the noble hearts who are charmed by them: "Do not imitate them. The way in which they lead you is poor in personal joys." But, instead of listening to me, they say: "The way is not poor at all; on the contrary, it is very rich. Though it be poor in some particular spot, it can never long continue so, and we shall have strength enough to scale the difficult points in order to enter the immense prairies so fertile in all sort of joys." Men like Rakhmetov are few in number, but through them the life of all mankind expands; without them it would have been stifled. They are few in number, but they put others in a position to breathe, others who without these few would have been suffocated. Great is the number of good and honest men, but the Rakhmetovs are rare. They are like the bouquet in fine wine, its strength and aroma. They are the best among the best, they are the movers of the movers, they are the salt of the salt of the earth.

NO MORE SUPERFLUOUS PEOPLE

"One may be gay or not, according to circumstances," said Mr. Beaumont, an American of Russian descent, to his Russian hosts, "but to suffer from ennui is, in my opinion, unpardonable. Ennui is a fashion among our English cousins, but we Americans know nothing about it. We have no time for it, we are too busy. It seems to me that the same should be true of the Russian people also. In my opinion, we have too much to do. But I notice in the Russians just the opposite: they are strongly disposed to spleen. Even the English are not to be compared with them in this respect. English society, looked upon by all Europe as the most tiresome in the world, is more talkative, lively, and gay than Russian society. Russian travelers talk of English spleen; I do not know where their eyes are when they are in their own country."

"But the Russians have good reasons to feel ennui," said Katerina, the host's daughter. "What can they busy themselves about? They have nothing to do. They must sit with folded arms. Name me one occupation, and my ennui probably will vanish."

"You wish to find an occupation? Oh! That is not so difficult: you see around you such ignorance! Pardon me for speaking to you in this way of your country, but I was born here myself and grew up here, and I consider it as my own, and so I do not stand on ceremony. You see here in Russia an ignorance like that in Turkey or Japan. I hate your native country, since I love it as my own country—may I say, in imitation of your poet. Why, there are so many things here to be done."

"Yes, but what can one man do, to say nothing of one woman?"

"Why, you are doing something already, Katia," said her father. "I will unveil her secret to you, Karl Yakovlich. To drive away ennui she teaches little girls. Every day she receives such pupils, and she devotes three hours to them and sometimes even more."

Beaumont looked at the young girl with esteem: "That is American. By America I mean only the free States of the North. The Southern States are worse than all possible Mexicos, are almost as abominable as Brazil. (As you see, Beaumont was a fervent abolitionist.) It is like us Americans to teach children, but then why do you suffer from ennui?"

"Do you consider that a serious occupation, Mr. Beaumont? It is but a distraction; at least, so it seems to me. Perhaps I am mistaken, and you will call me materialistic."

"Do you expect such a reproach from a man belonging to

a nation which everybody reproaches with having no other thought, no other ideal, than dollars?"

"You jest, but I am seriously afraid. I fear to state an opinion on this subject before you. My views might seem to you like those preached by the obscurantists concerning the uselessness of instruction."

"I am an obscurantist myself," replied Beaumont. "I am for the unlettered blacks against their civilized owners in the Southern States. But pardon me, my American hatred has diverted me. It would be very agreeable to me to hear your opinion."

"It is very prosaic, Mr. Beaumont, but I have been led to it by life. It seems to me that the matter with which I occupy myself is but one side of the whole and, moreover, not the side upon which the attention of those who wish to serve the people should be first fixed. This is what I think: give people bread, and they will learn to read themselves. It is necessary to begin with the bread. Otherwise, the time will be wasted."

"Then why don't you begin with the necessary?" said Beaumont. "It is possible. I know examples, with us in America."

"I have already told you why. What can I do alone? I do not know how to go to work; and, even if I knew, could I do it? A young girl is so hampered in every direction. I am free in my own room. But what can I do there? Put a book on the table and teach people to read it. Where can I go? What can I do alone?"

"Are you trying to make me out a despot, Katia?" said her father.

"I blush at the thought, Papa. No, you are good, you do not thwart me. It is society that thwarts me. Is it true, Mr. Beaumont, that in America a young girl is much less hampered?"

"Yes, we may be proud of it, although we are far from

where we ought to be. But what a comparison with Europeans! All that you hear about the liberty of women in our country is really the truth."

"Papa, let us go to America, after Mr. Beaumont has bought the factory," said Katerina jokingly. "There I will do something. Ah! How happy I should be!"

"One may find an occupation in St. Petersburg also," said Beaumont.

"How?"

Beaumont hesitated two or three seconds. "But why, then, did I come here? And who could better inform me?" said he to himself. And then he continued, turning to Katia: "Have you not heard of it? There is an attempt in progress here to apply the principles lately deduced by economic science. Are you familiar with them?"

"Yes, I have read a little about that. It must be very interesting and very useful. And could I take part in it? Where shall I find it?"

"In the cooperative shop founded by Madame Kirsonov."

"Is she the doctor's wife?"

"You know him? And has he said nothing to you about this matter?"

"I met him a long time ago. Then he was not yet married. I was sick, and he came several times to treat me and saved my life. Ah! What a man! Does she resemble him?"

IX

The Education to Liberty
HERZEN

Belinsky and Chernyshevsky expressed and directed the revolutionary ferment in Russian thought and society; Alexander Herzen, who spent the major part of his mature life abroad, made it known to Europe. He belonged to Belinsky's generation. Herzen was a man of independent means, the son of a rich landowner, and in his youth participated actively in the passionate discussions among the students and young intellectuals of Moscow, who found themselves confronted with the bewildering currents of European thought. He belonged to the revolutionary and rationalist wing of the young intelligentsia, which looked westward for guidance. At the same time he maintained friendly relations with the Slavophils and shared their faith in the archaic Russian village community, the *mir*. But he did not follow them in finding the hope for Russia's future in the virtues of her past. To Herzen, Russia's very lack of a past made her the potential heir of Europe's achievements and aspirations. He had no illusions about her backwardness and her need of learning from Europe; but he believed that semibarbaric Russia might, in her youthful approach, avoid some of the failures of older Europe.

Herzen left Russia in 1847 with eager visions of the won-
ders of Europe. Yet the West did not live up to his utopian
hopes. He was deeply disappointed by the defeat of the
French and Italian Revolutions of 1848. He had then little
understanding of the evolutionary process of democracy
and of the temporary character of the popular autocracy
of Napoleon III. Bourgeois mediocrity and moderation
seemed to triumph over social justice. What Herzen saw in
Europe enhanced his confidence in Russia. His famous
autobiography *My Past and Thoughts* is a moving and revealing document of the Russian mind of the 1840's and
1850's.

In 1852 Herzen settled in London. There he started the
newspaper *Kolokol* (*The Bell*), the first free and uncen-
sored voice raised in Russian against the Russian autocracy. It appeared for ten years, from 1857 to 1867, and
many copies were smuggled into Russia, where they were
widely and eagerly read, even in the ruling circles. Herzen
was a brilliant publicist and a courageous independent
thinker. It was this independence that caused his paper to
lose its influence in later years, for he and the new generation drifted apart. Through the sixties, the youth in Russia
became more and more radical and utopian, while Herzen,
in England, developed into a true liberal.

Like John Stuart Mill or Henrik Ibsen, Herzen was a
frontiersman of human liberty. "Since the age of thirteen,"
he wrote to Giuseppe Mazzini, "I have served an idea,
marched under one banner—war against all imposed authority, against every kind of deprivation of freedom, in the
name of the absolute independence of the individual. I
should like to go on with my little guerrilla war, like a real
Cossack, *auf eigene Faust,* as the Germans say." Herzen believed in the absolute value of individual liberty and opposed its sacrifice to any abstraction, History or Progress,
Revolution or Nation. The masses, he suspected, care only
for bread. "They are indifferent to individual liberty and

freedom of speech. They love authority. They interpret equality as an equality of oppression. . . . Individual liberty is the supreme good; on this basis alone the true will of the people can express itself. . . . The subordination of the individual to society, to the people, to humanity, to an idea, is a new form of human sacrifice, the crucifixion of the innocent for the sake of the guilty."

The rift between Herzen and his compatriots was widened by his espousal of the cause of Polish and Ukrainian freedom from Russian domination. Herzen knew that Russia's desire for military power and aggrandizement had suffocated the liberty not only of neighboring peoples but of the Russians themselves. He and his friend Mikhail Bakunin were in fact among the very few Russian progressive thinkers who recognized the Polish and Ukrainian claims for national independence. His love of Russia never degenerated into a narrow patriotism. In this he resembled Chaadayev. Like the latter, Herzen did not welcome the Crimean War as a struggle against the West which must end in Russian victory and in her conquest of Constantinople. He never doubted that the Russians, not the Turks, were the aggressors and responsible for the war. At the outbreak of the war, he appealed to the Russian soldiers garrisoned in Poland not to quell expected Polish uprisings.

When Alexander II, in 1855, followed his father Nikolai and promised the emancipation of the serfs, Herzen advised patience and the acceptance of evolutionary reforms. He did not believe that Russia needed hatchets; he pleaded for brooms. As his comprehension of human and national realities grew, Herzen became increasingly averse to violence and bloodshed. Herzen's liberal voice did not reach the hearts of the new generation of nihilists, populists, and terrorists. He died in Paris, a lonely and disappointed man. But his thought survives today as one of the potential springs of a new freedom in Russia.

Herzen gained a friendly understanding of the strength

in the liberal Anglo-American tradition. When the first transatlantic cable was laid between England and North America in 1858, Herzen foresaw the Atlantic Union, the deep unity of the two English-speaking nations: "What can a country which feels the beat of an uninterrupted pulse with America not do, for the ocean will become an internal cistern! In truth, there are not two states but two different shores, belonging to the Anglo-Saxons." Herzen saw individual liberty and creative diversity equally threatened by "the senile barbarism of the scepter and the wild barbarism of communism, by a blood-stained saber and by the red flag." The invocation of the *salus populi* seemed to him as disastrous as the worship of *lèse majesté*. In 1869, one year before his death, Herzen wrote his "Letter to an old Friend" (Bakunin) warning against revolutionary violence: "What thinking persons will forgive Attila, the Committee of Public Safety, even Peter the Great—they will not forgive us. We have heard no voice commanding us from above to fulfill a destiny, we have heard no call from below to direct us. For us there is only one voice, one guide; the power of reason and understanding. In rejecting it we become renegades to civilization."

THE DEVELOPMENT OF REVOLUTIONARY
IDEAS IN RUSSIA

[From Herzen's book written in 1851]

WHAT a painful epoch is ours! Everything around us is in a state of dissolution, of an agitation which recalls a dizzy spell or a malignant fever. The darkest forebodings are materializing with a frightening speed. . . . A free man who refuses to bow before force will soon have no other refuge in Europe but the deck of a boat sailing for America.

Should we not commit suicide as Cato did, because our Rome succumbs and because we see nothing or do not wish to see anything outside Rome? . . . We know what the Roman thinker who deeply felt the bitterness of his time did; crushed by sadness and despair, realizing that the world to which he belonged was collapsing, he turned his eyes beyond the national horizon and wrote a book: *De moribus Germanorum*. He was right, for the future belonged to these barbarian peoples. We do not predict anything, but neither do we believe that the destiny of mankind is tied up with Western Europe. If Europe does not succeed in recovering through social transformation, other countries will transform themselves. Some are ready for it, others prepare themselves for the task. One is well known: the United States of America; another, full of vigor but also full of savagery, is little or badly known. . . . Caesar knew the Gauls better than modern Europe knows Russia.

If it is horrible to live in Russia, it is as horrible to live in Europe. Why did I leave Russia? To answer this question, I shall quote some words of the farewell letter to my [Russian] friends: "Don't be mistaken! I have found here neither joy nor rest. I can't even imagine anybody finding rest or joy in Europe today. Sadness breathed in every word of my letters. Life here is very painful. I believe in nothing but the movement; I regret nothing but the victims; I love only the persecuted, I esteem only the tortured, and yet I stay. I stay to suffer twice: our own pain and that which I find here, perhaps to sink in the general dissolution. But I stay because here the struggle is wide open, because here it has a voice. Woe to the defeated here! But here he does not succumb without making his voice heard and without having tried his strength in the struggle. For the sake of this voice, for the sake of this open struggle, for the sake of this publicity, I stay!" This I wrote on March 1, 1849. . . . But if in Europe also they succeed in gagging us and if oppression no longer permits us to curse our oppressors openly, then we shall leave for America, sacrificing everything to the dignity of man and to the freedom of expression. . . .

One thought only united the Petersburg period of Russian history with that of Moscow, the thought of the aggrandizement of the state. Everything was sacrificed to it, the dignity of the rulers, the blood of the subjects, justice towards one's neighbors, and the welfare of the whole country.

Pushkin had an instinctive faith in the future of Russia; the shouts of triumph and victory of 1813 and 1814 which he heard as a child reverberated in his soul; for a time he was even carried away by St. Petersburg patriotism, which boasts of the number of its bayonets and leans upon cannons. It is painful to say, but even Pushkin had an exclusive patriotism. Great poets like Goethe or Racine were courtiers; Pushkin was neither a courtier nor a member of the government; the brutal force of the state pleased him out of patriotic instinct, so that he shared the barbaric wish to answer reasoning by bullets. One of the causes for Russia's enslavement is the fact that she finds poetry in material force, and glory in frightening people. . . .

This discontent of which we speak cannot be easily seen. Russia always seems so tranquil that one has difficulty in believing that something is happening there. Few people know what happens beneath the shroud with which the government covers the corpses, the stains of blood, the military executions, while maintaining hypocritically and arrogantly that there is neither blood nor corpse beneath the shroud. . . .

Not to demand anything from the government, but to try to remain independent: that suffices under a despotic régime to incur the charge of active opposition. . . . One will easily understand that I cannot say everything and that in many cases I cannot name the persons involved. To be able to speak of a Russian freely one must know that he is either under the ground or in Siberia. I have decided upon this publication only after much thought, but to remain mute meant to support the despotism. The things which one does not dare to speak about do not fully exist. . . .

The publication of Chaadayev's Letter ["Philosophical Letter on Russian history"] was one of the greatest events. It was a challenge, a sign of awakening. It broke the ice which had covered everything after the fourteenth of December [1825]. Finally a man appeared who found terrible words with which to express all the bitterness accumulated during ten years in the heart of a civilized Russian. Severe and cold, the author took Russia to account for all the sufferings which she inflicted on a man who dared to be more than a brute. He wished to know what we were buying at this price and why we had deserved this situation. He analyzed it from the inexorable depth of despair, and after this vivisection he turned away in horror and cursed the country, its past, present, and future. His somber voice made itself heard only to say that Russia had never existed on the human level, that she represented only a void in human intelligence, a warning for Europe. He told Russia that her past was useless, that her present was superfluous, and that she had no future. . . . One has accused the author of being harsh, but that perhaps is his greatest merit. We should not be spared; we forget too quickly our real situation, and we are too accustomed to amuse ourselves within the walls of a prison. . . .

The Ukraine maintained her savage and warlike but republican and democratic independence through the centuries until Peter I. The Little Russians [Ukrainians], harassed by the Poles, the Turks, and the Muscovites, never yielded. When Little Russia voluntarily joined Great Russia [1654], she stipulated far-reaching rights in her favor. Tsar Alexis swore to abide by them. Peter I left only a semblance of these privileges. Elizabeth and Catherine introduced serfdom in the Ukraine. The poor country protested, but how could it resist this fatal avalanche, which rolled from the North to the Black Sea and covered everything that carried the Russian name with the same shroud of a uniform and icy slavery. The Ukraine underwent the fate of Novgorod and Pskov, but at a much later date. Thus one century of slavery was not able to destroy every trace of freedom in this courageous people. There we find more individual development and local color than with us; with us an unfortunate uniformity covers all of popular life. Our people are born to bow before an unjust fatality and die without leaving a trace, survived by children who repeat the same life of despair. . . .

Belinsky was one of the freest of men. He was bound neither by beliefs nor by tradition. He did not depend on public opinion, and he accepted no authority. He was not afraid either to anger his friends or to shock the good souls. He was always ready to denounce everything he believed to be vile. How could he have left the Orthodox and ultra-patriotic Slavophils in peace, he who regarded everything that they accepted as the most sacred ties, as heavy chains? . . . Belinsky and his friends did not oppose the doctrine of the Slavophils with a system of their own but with a lively sympathy for everything that agitated their contemporaries, with a limitless love for liberty of thought, and with a strong hatred for everything that curtailed liberty: authority, force, or faith. . . . It seemed to them that the lack of individual freedom engendered the complete absence of respect for the individual, the cynicism of the government, the inexhaustible patience of the people. Russia's future will be a great danger for Europe and a great misfortune for Russia if there is no emancipation of the individual. One more century of the present despotism will destroy all the good qualities of the Russian people.

Can one really believe that servitude, passive obedience, and a despotic government can develop the abilities of the Russian people? A long servitude cannot be an accident, it must correspond to some national trait. This trait can be absorbed and overcome by other traits, but it can also remain victorious; if Russia accommodates herself to the existing order, she will not have the future which we wish for her. If she continues the period of St. Petersburg, or if she returns to the period of Moscow, she will have no future but to throw herself upon Europe, like a semibarbarian and semicorrupted horde devastating the civilized countries and perishing in the midst of general destruction. Was it not necessary therefore to call upon the Russian people to recognize its tragic condition? . . . Instead, the Slavophils preached submission. . . . They preached the contempt of the West, and yet the West alone could enlighten the dark gulf of Russian life; they glorified the past, instead of emphasizing the need of liberation from this past in favor of a future common to Russia and the West. . . .

One has remarked that an opposition which leads a frontal attack upon a government always has itself, in an inverted sense, something of the character of the government attacked. I believe that there is some justification for the fear of communism which the Russian government begins to feel: Communism is the Russian autocracy turned upside down. . . .

Where in Russia can a free man act without making mournful concessions? The despotism grows; the thought, fettered by a twofold censorship, can no longer move freely. Men must be silent or feign; they must speak through insinuations or whisper at a time when a trumpet would hardly suffice to awaken the sleepers. . . . At this moment emigration is the most significant act of opposition which Russians can make. The government understood that well.

[Therefore] it answered by the promulgation of the incredible decree regarding passports.

TO THE RUSSIAN SOLDIERS IN POLAND

[From Herzen's appeal at the start of the Crimean War]

So the Tsar has finally brought war upon Russia. . . . The whole world feels sorry for the Turks, not because they are near or dear to anyone but because they are fighting for their own land; they were attacked, and so they must defend themselves. But our own poor brothers are shedding their blood, fighting bravely, leaving their bodies on many fields, and no one except ourselves cares about them; nobody values their courage, for their cause is unjust. The Tsar says he is defending the Orthodox Church. . . . "Orthodox Christians are being ground down by the Turks," he adds. We haven't heard that they are any more oppressed than our own peasants, especially our serfs whom the Tsar holds in bondage. Wouldn't it be better to begin by freeing one's own bond servants—after all, they are Orthodox like us, fellow believers, and Russians into the bargain. . . .

Look at Poland. No sooner had the news of war reached her than she raised her head, and now she is waiting for a chance to rise once more for her rights, for her freedom. What will you do when the Polish nation takes up arms? Yours will be the worst lot of all. Your comrades in Turkey are soldiers; you in Poland will be hangmen. . . . We know that you are not going to march against the Poles of your own free will, but this is just the point: the time has come for you to show some will of your own. . . .

Great times are in the making. Let it not be said that at such a solemn and dreadful moment you were left without brotherly counsel. . . . Through our mouth speaks the Russia that is being born, a Russia free, young, and alive—in hiding at home, but outspoken in exile. Through our mouth speaks the Russia of martyrs, the Russia of dungeons and Siberian mines . . . the Russia whose witnesses we are before the world and for whose good name we have up-rooted ourselves from our homeland. . . .

Poland has suffered enough at the hands of Russians. If there were faults on her side, she made amends for them long ago. Her small children have been taken from her, her women thrown into prison, her defenders have perished in Siberia, her friends are roaming all over the world, her trophies have been carried off to Petersburg, her legends distorted . . . not even her past has been left to her!

No, for Russian soldiers there grow no laurels on Polish soil; it has been drenched by too many women's tears, by too much blood of men shed through your fathers' fault, maybe through your own. On the banks of the Vistula, near the cemetery of Praga, this graveyard of freedom, there is no warrior's glory for you. But another kind of glory awaits you there—the glory of reconciliation and alliance!

When the time comes, you will learn what to do and how to do it. We will not leave you without brotherly counsel. Meanwhile, be assured that our words are true, and swear by all that is holy to you not to take up arms against Poland.

This oath of yours is not wanted by the Tsar; it is your repentant nation and its conscience that demand it; and should death await you for it, it will be a sacred death. You will fall as victims of redemption and will seal with your martyr's blood a free and indissoluble alliance of Poland and Russia—the beginning of a free union of all Slavs into one commonwealth.

EVOLUTION AGAINST REVOLUTION

[*From* The Bell, *1859*]

It was with close attention and with a sense of gratitude that I read your article about me and the Free Russian

Press in London. There is a Slavic heart, a kindred heart beating within you, and that is why you understand what I am saying; that, too, is why I want so much to answer you. Naturally, I have paid special attention to those points where you express your doubts or disagree. One may at times overlook the criticisms, even the accusations, made by one's opponents and enemies, but the criticism offered by a friend must lead either to an explanation or to the admission that it is justified. I am glad that your article gives me occasion to account for the reasons why I proceed thus and not otherwise, and to touch upon the principal foundations of my beliefs, for I am convinced that I proceed in complete accordance with them. . . .

There was a time—how well I remember it—when the mere word "Republic" would set hearts abeating; but now, after 1849, 1850, 1851, this word raises as many doubts as hopes. Have we not seen for ourselves that a republic with governmental initiative, with despotic centralization, with a huge army, will do far less to promote free progress than does the English monarchy without initiative, without centralization? Have we not seen that the French form of democracy, i.e., equality in slavery, is the form nearest to absolutism?

Out of some filial piety, we have shrunk from these bitter truths until now; and in concealing them from ourselves we were led by understandable feelings of loyalty. But even these must not be allowed to stand in the way of truth or to prevent a frank, conscientious examination. Paraphrasing the famous Latin proverb, I freely say: I am a friend of the republic, I am a friend of democracy, but an even greater friend of liberty, independence, and progress.

If anyone should object: "Can there be any liberty and independence without a republic and a democracy?"—I answer that even with these there can be none if the people are not yet ready for them.

Every monarchy moves towards a republic and towards a higher social structure, i.e., an intelligent and free economic order—unless it is to move towards dissolution and death. In those places where a republic and democracy are consistent with the people's development, where they are not only words but facts, as in the United States or Switzerland, there, without any doubt, is the maximum of individual independence and liberty. The results will be entirely different in countries where these political forms are too advanced for their present state. Take, for example, a nation that is ignorant and soldierly at its bottom, corrupt and utterly acquisitive at its top: there a republic [Second French Republic of February 1848] will, within four months, turn into a Cavaignac, within nine, into a Napoleon. The granting of universal suffrage has turned France into a house of correction.

Does it follow from what I have said that I prefer a constitutional monarchy to a republic, and an electoral tax to universal suffrage? Not in the least. I am stating a fact—no more. Looking at it, I cannot, in all conscience, say: Since universal suffrage is more than just voting qualifications, next time—that is to say, after passing through yet another era of slavery and corruption—France will have better elections under universal than under limited suffrage. I do not believe it, just as I do not believe that the Turks, while clinging to Mohammedanism and the fatalistic teachings of their Koran, would stand to gain much if they were to proclaim a republic.

It is our aim to work and strive within our own time, within contemporary Russia: this leads us, not to introduce new problems, but to try to master such problems as have already arisen. The men of distant ideals, the prophets of reason, and the prognosticators of things to come do not bother much with practical difficulties. They point out the rational principles towards which society is moving; they

give society's laws and some general formula governing its
motion, and leave it to future generations to work out these
principles in the daily struggle of jostling interests and
parties.

A month and a half ago, one of these men was lowered
into Scottish soil by a small group of friends; and I am most
thankful to my fate for having met him while he was still
among the living, for having been allowed to clasp the hon-
ored and work-worn hand of Robert Owen. Owen was right,
and England will appreciate him, but, of course, not in the
nineteenth century. Great and indispensable are the men
like him who establish the rights of reason within the fitful
and fanciful tale of history, and all these forerunners of a
new world, men like Saint Simon or Fourier, will take a
mighty place in the growth of human consciousness, in the
self-knowledge of the body politic. But they have almost no
part in current affairs; this lot falls to us, the everyday workers.

The heavier the dead hand of the present upon us, the
stronger our desire to break away from it and to rise to the
algebraic heights of theory. Germany in her civic insignificance surpassed all countries in the philosophy of law, and
lacking a history of her own, came forth as the aroused conscience of other nations. The reign of Nikolai I produced
a similar effect upon two Russian generations. Under his
direction, the coach of government got stuck in the snow
up to its axle, the ice-covered wheels stopped turning; no
matter how hard he whipped his horses, the coach wouldn't
move. He thought terror might help matters. Writing was
forbidden, traveling was forbidden. Thinking was still possible, so people began to think. Russian thought developed
amazingly in that dark hour. . . . But when the old coach,
slightly the worse for wear, was starting on its way once
more, clearly a different time began, a different breeze was
blowing. Now the task of those who want to take part in the

new movement is becoming different: it is becoming more specific. It is not much use knowing the station towards which we are driving; what we must determine is which mile of our road we are now passing over and what ravines and bridges there are in this particular mile. . . .

I am convinced that since the beginning of the Crimean War, Russia has entered upon a new era in her development, that she is leaving behind her the rocky road of her harsh upbringing and is entering now the broad channel of adult life. I know I differ with many in my internal estimate of the Russian people. Whoever fails to distinguish between the Russian government and the Russian people will understand nothing. They do not know Russia who want to measure her in yards and meters. Those standards which a study of Western civilization has set up in our minds can find neither room nor substitutes for the peculiar and individual properties of Russia's national life. The deceptive resemblance of her governmental forms to those of the West will be the final obstacle in the way of understanding. Behind the Tsarist screen, behind the trappings of St. Petersburg, it has been impossible to see or hear the people. One could hear only drum rolls and official speeches; one could see only bayonets and office clerks. To be sure, it had dawned on some that behind familiar forms there lurked some unknown content; they had begun to guess that these forms had been forcibly clamped on like a prisoner's stocks, yet they would not proceed to study the character of the poor prisoner, but turned away, saying: Since he is suffering, he obviously deserves no better.

In order to understand the Russian people without being a Russian (and a Russian, at that, who has not been cowed since his childhood by a sense of his own insignificance and the greatness of the West), one would have to be either a European socialist or a citizen of North America. This may sound strange to you, ridiculous to others, but so it is! All

those things that other nations hold so dear have been held
as nothing in the case of Russia, or, worse, they have served
to malign her: the fact that she survived whole under the
Tartar yoke; that she grew quietly and consolidated herself
into a tremendous state; that she broke away from all her
neighbors and kept her independence; that she had her 1612
and her 1812. The fire of Moscow is spoken of only because
too many foreigners were there who could confirm the fact.
There may be some question whether Russia has redeemed
Europe from the harshness of military rule or has substi-
tuted another kind of rule; but there can be no question
whatever that Russia has saved Germany from the French
yoke. Open the pages of Stein, Arndt, and their contemporaries, and see how in that dark hour for Germany they
were looking towards Alexander I and Russia. What has
become of it all? The utmost hatred—not of the Russian
government (who wouldn't hate it?), not of Russian intervention, but of the Russian people, of any success of ours, of
any of our human impulses. Looming behind the contemporary German journalists, may well be recognized the
shades of the Livonian brotherhoods of the sixteenth century, those knights who would refuse to let physicians enter
Russia. Isn't all this strange?

Take another example: England, bursting with abundance and excess of strength, sets out from her shores, sails
over all the oceans, and founds new worlds. She is admired
and deserves admiration. But how do people look at the
exploit of colonizing Siberia? Here a handful of Cossacks
and a few hundred homeless muzhiks trekked at their own
risk across oceans of ice and snow, and wherever the weary
little bands settled on these frozen steppes which nature had
forgotten, there life welled up, fields and stables covered
the country. . . . And of colossal happenings like these,
history has hardly taken notice, or if so, it was only to strike

the imagination with a Dantesque picture of an icy prison extending for thousands of miles. . . .

At last a new trial has come. Having gone through all sorts of reforms and revolutions, saddled with masses of troops and up to her knees in blood, Europe has been stopped by a terrible, unfathomable sphinx: it is landed property and the proletariat, capital and the worker. Neither the French practice of atomic subdivision of the land nor the parasitic life of the English farmer can prevent or forestall anything. There is less and less land, the proprietor ruins the ploughman, capital ruins the worker, and rising ever stronger from factories, shops, and fields, is heard the chorus of proletarians singing the refrain: "Live working or die fighting!"

A people is said to live nearby, where altogether different relations prevail with regard to landed property, where forms of communistic landholding, having come down through the centuries, exist now in actual practice and range from annual partition of fields among members to full ownership. Whether this is true or not, you will agree that the present economic problem should make it imperative to investigate such an important fact. May not a study of it furnish us with as many data as do the microscopic experiments of the Phalanx and the Icarians [French Utopian Socialist experiments]?

Do you think people paid any attention to these facts? Did they study them, refute or confirm them? They did not. They laughed at whoever mentioned them as they have been laughing until now at everything I said during the war: about the Ukraine's having been a Cossack republic founded on democratic and benevolent principles; about the Zaporozhian Sech [Ukrainian Cossacks], who presented the amazing phenomenon of plebeian knights, of chivalrous peasants. As a Pole, you know your own history too well for

me to have to harp on the paltry kind of ignorance that not
only doesn't know, but scoffs as well.

The superficial custom of keeping one's eyes exclusively
on the political life of states without any regard to the life
of the people or the economic order has led, in the case of
Russia, to several wrong judgments, for in Russia only the
government lives a political life. Even in Poland, as little is
known about the life of the Russian people as in the rest of
Europe. Without exaggerating, I say that the internal condition of Russia is known only to those of your countrymen
who have been sent to Siberia or to the distant northeastern
provinces. How amazing is all this! On observing the Great
Russian peasant with his free, intelligent countenance, his
manly, handsome features, his rugged build, didn't it ever
enter your mind that within him there might be hidden
another kind of strength than that of mere long-suffering,
submissiveness, and perseverance? On reading Pushkin,
Lermontov, Gogol, didn't it enter your thoughts that outside the official, governmental Russia there is another one;
that over and above the Muravyev [suppressor of Polish up-
rising] who hanged there are Muravyevs [participants in
Decembrist uprising] who were hanged? Just think—if
there had not been another kind of strength and another
Russia outside the official one, would a few reverses in the
Crimea and the death of Nikolai really have been sufficient
to plunge the whole immense empire into this activity, this
forward surge that is taking place before our very eyes? Yes,
the Leviathan of the north has passed through her docks;
she shook a little, steadied herself, and is now afloat. To
prove this would be pointless for me, just as I would not
try to predict the future: she may run aground tomorrow—
that will depend on her pilots. Once the fact is granted, it is
most important to find out what is the issue under whose
aegis this new voyage is getting under way; which gateway
will the ship pass through to gain the sea; what is written on

her flag: Constitution, Republic, Parliament, Municipal Freedom, War with Austria, Conquest of Turkey? No—her ensign bears the words Liberation of the Peasants with their Land, i.e., once more a social rather than a political issue.

Seeing this, we have left everything else and fastened upon this question so vital to Russia. And here lies the reason for our success. People will listen only to that *Bell* which summons them where they must go. . . .

There is still one thing left to say before I pass to the second question in the article before us. You say—and I can hear some reproach in your voice—that my relationship to Alexander II differs from my relationship to Nikolai. You think I have changed: No, it is not I, it is Nikolai who has changed—by dying, to be exact. Alexander II has executed nobody, has sent no people off to forced labor for their opinions; he has not taken Warsaw or revenged himself on Poland for dozens of years; he has not destroyed Russian universities and Russian literature; so how can I behave towards him as I behaved towards Nikolai? Such stubborn inflexibility is not to be expected of any living man whose brain is not blighted with monomania.

And that is not all. It was Alexander II and no one else who first raised the cry of Liberation of the Peasants, and I repeat once more: if he does nothing—if the whole problem and its solution slip from his clumsy grasp—even then history will remember his name as one of the reformers that wore a crown.

Is he sincere in wanting emancipation? I don't know, and what is more, I don't care. It may be of interest for a psychological study of his personality, but for no more than that. The speeches of Alexander II, especially the address to the Moscow nobility, prove that he understands the urgent necessity of this measure; and should Alexander free the peasants against his will, as Nikolai (so they now say) wanted to free them all his life and never did—why, then I prefer this

kind of disingenuousness. To understand the necessity of
reform and not to oppose it is all one may ask of a government; the rest we must do ourselves, if we want it to be done
well. . . .

I know it is not consistent with the religion of democracy
to speak anything but evil about crowned heads. . . . The
man who does not place truth—whatever it may be like—
above all other things, who does not consult it and his conscience to get his standards of behavior, that man is not free.

FOR A FREE FEDERAL UNION
[*From* The Bell, *1859*]

Like Italy or Hungary, Poland has a complete, inalienable right to political existence independent of Russia. A
different question is whether we wish that a free Poland
should break away from a free Russia. No, we do not wish
it—and who could wish it at a time when national exclusiveness and international conflicts constitute one of the bar-
riers holding up the free progress of all mankind? In my
deep hatred for any sort of centralization, I am yet convinced that federations of related peoples make for an incomparably more ample political life than does the splitting
of one ethnic group into its separate parts. A federal union
must be a free gift. Russia has no right to Poland; she must
deserve that which she has taken by force; she must make
amends for that which has been committed through her
fault; and if Poland does not want this alliance, we may feel
hurt, we may disagree with her, but we cannot refuse her
freedom, unless we are to repudiate our basic convictions.
This I believe is clear.

But if it is clear that we acknowledge this right, we ought
to explain also why we do not wish for a complete severance
of the two nations. We believe that Russia and Poland, arm

in arm, may march along the same road towards a new life of freedom and social justice. . . .

Except for her borderlands, Russia represents a compact unit, similar in blood, language, and spirit. Every Russian is conscious of being part of the whole state; he is conscious of his kinship with the whole population, who have all been reared in the same village life with its communal order and its divisions of fields. It is for this reason that every Russian, wherever he may live in this immensity between the Baltic and the Pacific, will be on the alert when an enemy crosses the Russian border, and will be ready to come to the aid of Moscow, as he did in 1612 and in 1812.

But what does he consider his border to be? You seem to be greatly interested in this question. If I have never actually talked about it, it has certainly not been for fear of Russian patriots. Of them I am no more afraid than of patriots in general, and if I fear patriots in general, it is because their greedy tribal egotism is always eager for unjust gain, and because their love for their own too often turns into hatred for all others. A mature man may love his country with his heart and soul, he may love it from habit, he may serve it and die for it, but a patriot he cannot be. Eighteen centuries ago, Christianity first began to do away with this heathen virtue, but accomplished nothing because it turned people's minds to another country that did not exist at all, i.e., existed only in heaven. Now socialism will do away with patriotism, by removing all territorial frontiers. We have still a long way to go to reach that point, if people like you and us still have to wrangle over demarcation. . . .

If the Ukraine recalls, on the one hand, all the Muscovite oppression, the serfdom, recruiting, absence of rights, the corruption and the knout; if, on the other hand, she does not forget how she fared under the Polish Rzeczpospolita with her soldiers, gentlemen, and crown officials—what, then, if she wants to be neither Polish nor Russian. In my opinion, this question is easily settled. In such an event the Ukraine should be recognized as a free and independent country. Among us exiles, who have been sorrowful witnesses of so many unsuccessful unions and dissolutions, there cannot, there must not be, any question as to the ownership of this or the other piece of settled land. In Ukraine there live people—people who may have been smothered with serfdom, but who have not been broken so completely by their government and their landowners that they have lost all national feeling. Quite on the contrary, their ethnic consciousness is highly developed. . . . Would it be a step towards their liberation, if after taking off their Muscovite chains, one were to tell them that they must belong to Poland?

Let us untie their hands and loosen their tongues, that their speech may be altogether free, and that they may speak their mind, and either join us, despite the knout, or join you, despite the pope; or, if they are wise, they will offer us their hand as brotherly allies, independent of both of us.

This is why I have such a high opinion of the federal system. There the federated parts are joined together in a common cause, and no one belongs to anybody else, neither Berne to Geneva nor Geneva to Berne.

If Russia, after freeing the peasants and giving them their lands, were really to enter that new phase of which we spoke, I do not think that the Ukraine would want to separate from her. She would not then have those motives she had in the mid-seventeenth century to throw herself into the arms of the Tartars and of Moscow to escape the aristocratic-Catholic yoke of the [Polish] Rzeczpospolita, or the motives she had under Peter I to desert to the Swedes. If Russia, faltering after her first step, were to remain without rights, administered by clerks and orderlies—if this whole movement should prove too feeble and we were to return to the days of Nikolai, unable to break away—why then neither Poland nor the Ukraine should remain with Russia, but rather they should unite, march on Moscow, and shatter this whole gigantic edifice of slavery.

Here you have our whole point of view; and nothing that Russian or Polish patriots may say will make us change it or make us betray it, for we are convinced in heart and soul that it is the right one. . . .

ON RUSSIAN FREEDOM

[From The Bell, 1860]

In speaking of a future Slav federation, I fully agree with you that this problem cannot be solved on the spur of the moment, and that in solving it time enters as a very important element. I do not believe the Slav peoples would be ready at once to enter into that alliance of which I spoke. But if it has to be reached by way of a series of independent bodies and combinations, I still fail to see why one should not have a future alliance in mind, as an ideal, as a secure and spacious anchorage?

You think it would be better and more natural if the Slav world divided into two distinct parts, i.e., on one side Russia, "Slavs mixed with Finnish and Turanian races," and on the other Poland and the "old Slavs." The mission and sphere of the former would lie in the immense areas of Asia as far as the Pacific; the task of the latter would be "resistance to German hegemony and the conquest of Turkey."

I tell you frankly that, speaking for myself, I have little against this. Russia's chief business does lie at home and in Asia, and, as you say, she has no need of any alliance to protect her own borders. Russia ought rather to set her border regions free instead of tying them more closely with the center—an idea which we have already stated in speaking of the Ukraine. But I believe nonetheless that you might more

easily prove the possibility of a complete political estrange-
ment of Poland from the non-Polish Slavs than the possibility of her alliance with the non-Russian Slavs. . . .

Poland has been keeping herself rather aloof from the
Western Slavs; she has been looking at them with indifference and from above. Thus, when the idea of Pan-Slavism
first arose, the sympathies of the Western Slavs turned
towards Russia. There is no doubt that the Russian government exploited these sympathies most greedily and sense-
lessly. But there is even less doubt—as an eyewitness can
tell you—that they found the warmest response among
those groups which have nothing in common with the government.

It does not follow that the Western Slavs must necessarily
unite with Russia, but whether, in the reverse case, they
will enter into a federal union with Poland alone is not at
all a settled question. Besides, they have all they need—
mountains, seas, rivers, and boundaries—to make up a
Danubian and Carpathian federation of their own; and if
they so choose, let them remain independent. . . .

The importance that I attach to a future Slav federation
has a special meaning which I think has escaped you. You
take me for a "patriot" wishing for a Slav federation under
Russian hegemony, for the sake of Russia's glory, for her
might and European importance. Since this would have
sufficed for any patriot, you looked no further; but you are
altogether mistaken: I am even less of a patriot than a liberal. . . .

Well then, I will not hesitate to tell you what I think. If
I wanted with all my heart that the non-Russian Slav world
should enter into a brotherly alliance with Russia, it was
only with this thought: that when that storm which no
earthly power can arrest breaks loose, the Slavs not be
taken by surprise.

Russia is not only a Slav world "with an admixture of

Finnish and Turanian elements," but also, in contrast to
the aristocratic, the burgher, the urbanized states, she is a
poor, peasant state. We have nothing—we are the beggars
of this world—nothing except aspirations, nothing but
faith in ourselves. Even our proximity and kinship with the
"Finnish and Turanian races" have helped us to a humble
recognition of the Jew, the Finn, the Tartar, and the Kal-
muk as our equals: for are we not all alike in serving as
caryatids to prop up the Tsar's Winter Palace? Why should
we look on them from the heights of Western civilization?

What do you think? Is it not easier for such a people to
shove its boat off the old shores?

You may say: shoving off isn't hard, but what are they
going to carry over to the other side? This is a question of
the first importance.

You do not know the Russian people; for this I don't
blame you. After all, how long has it been since we few who
suffered because of their slavery have begun to know them?
Living foreign lives, we understood them with foreign
minds; thus of most things at home we understood nothing
at all, and didn't care. Instead, we took something foreign
and made it our own.

Our first approach towards national self-knowledge came
in the dark days of Nikolai I. His bitter oppression sobered
our minds. Like a policeman barring everyone's way, he
beat us down to the level of peasants. Insulted in our human dignity, we were foreigners in our own home; feeling
our strength, we were forced to concentrate all our activity
within our hearts and minds—and our minds grew bold
and intrepid. We hated everything Petersburg stood for;
our education was completed by Europe's fiasco following
1848; we watched it all with the same pitiless gaze, and it
was only then we fully realized what a hideous state the
Russian Empire was, and how lucky it was for us to be such
a hideous state!

Don't think that I am playing on words.

I am about to explain to you what I mean. Russia has not yet found a civic form that would fit her, a form that would give her sufficient room to exercise all or most of her inner forces; i.e., she has not yet reached an organic political form, as have England or Switzerland, for example. Even in her past Russia has never known such a condition—except possibly in her Kievan teething period. This meaningless, makeshift jumble of institutions has kept an abundance of strength idle, ill-used, or dormant through the centuries; it is a proof of the Russian people's immaturity. Immaturity of long standing does not necessarily give a right to maturity; one must therefore define the Russian body politic. Is it a house of correction for an old madman or a house of education for the young? We believe neither in the mission nor in the predestination of nations; we believe that the destiny of nations may undergo changes along the road, like the destiny of any man. But within the theory of probability, we may properly take the present elements of these nations as our basis for conclusions about their future. . . .

The most hideous government in the world, alien in spirit, took the withered Muscovite state and made it into a close-knit empire reaching from the Baltic to the Pacific—an empire purely Russian, much more Russian than its government. . . .

And there, gradually, a third force grew up, something quite unknown among you—our literature of opposition. During recent times, Russian literature has been consistently either trivial or highly critical of our government and life—given either to a slavish flattery or to a merciless criticism that stops at nothing. . . .

Just think what Russian thought had to grow on, what its cradle song was, what it has seen and remembered—and you will see where it got such characteristics. It was formed next to the redoubt of Alexis [Son of Peter I], where a drunken father was reveling with his henchmen a few hours after strangling his rack-worn son—and it was unable to make a martyr of one so weak and inconsequential; it was formed at Ropsha, where a dissolute wife [Catherine II] poisoned her husband [Peter III]—and it was unable to deny the necessity to get rid of him; it was formed at Mikhailov Castle, where a son [Alexander I] had his mad father [Paul I] executed—and it was unable to withhold its blessing from his decision.

What an upbringing!

But this is not the end of it. It goes on with the sight of the gallows [of the Decembrists] on which [Nikolai I] hanged the five noblest representatives of a civic virtue which was young but maturing in Russia; it goes on with troikas hurrying towards penal servitude, past a people that had nothing to do with them but was simply plowing away in serfdom and under the lash; it goes on, finally, with the sight of a whole society, i.e., the brothers, sisters, and fathers of the hanged and the exiled—dancing till they dropped on coronation days, before the bodies of the former had decomposed and before the latter had reached Siberia.

Warsaw rose up, and a whole army of Poles fought in a transport of inspiration and covered themselves with glory in defeat, while the Russian army was ashamed of its own dark victories. Then silence fell! We grew accustomed to the hatred of all Europe; we justified it; we felt it was merited. . . .

In that twelfth hour, in the midst of an oppression that has reached the ultimate in tyranny, at a time when the Pecherins, the Gagarins, the Golitsyns [members of Russian noble families] were escaping into Catholicism to keep from asphyxiating, we cast one more look into our soul and ceased believing—in what do you think? In the strength of our chains. From the depth of our hearts arose a cry repudiating the present order, a cry of protest. On this lowest

rung of humiliation, something within us said: This is all
wrong: we have not deserved this, because we are morally
free and of sound mind! . . .

ON RUSSIA'S FUTURE

[From The Bell, 1860]

You have given an excellent characterization of the general setting, the atmosphere, in which we are developing.
Here are your words:

"Actually, it is through no fault of his own that the Russian has been accustomed from his infancy to prodigious,
far-reaching dimensions and goals, and that therefore even
his dreams tend involuntarily towards outward greatness.
Everything surrounding him is in fact gigantic: the space,
the population, the uniformity even of language, the
unheard-of despotism and its hidden impotence, the savage
slavery and terrible obstinacy, the barbarous gloom and the
fierce boldness of plans, pretensions, and hopes! Hence his
whole mind turns towards spacious vistas, towards outward
hugeness, and in his mental flights he involuntarily loses
himself in this hugeness. Thus, for instance, his Russia of
the future must be democratic and socially just; and if a
federation, then on a scale the like of which the world has
not seen and before which it would shudder with fright.
Brought up with a gigantic world before his eyes, with his
mental powers fresh, and his mind not yet matured, he de-
velops every idea into prodigious dimensions and has no
presentiment of some other, inward greatness. This is childish enthusiasm, not manly thoughtfulness."

You will agree, being born under such a constellation is
no laughing matter. I do not know what you mean by the
words "inward greatness," but I should like to point out
that a desire that the "Russia of the future should be democratic and socially just," though it may well be proof of a

"fierce boldness of plans, pretensions, and hopes," cannot, of course, be called an "outward" one. As far as that "boldness of plans and hopes" is concerned, it is, in its own way, a tremendous strength and bears no resemblance whatever to the quietistic self-deification of Eastern peoples, who think they have attained to the highest state; nay, on the contrary, it is a mainspring of forward movement. They only achieve great things who have even greater ones in mind and instinctively believe in their possibility.

Among the old Western nations, the tradition and the present are equally alive. They hold their inheritance on condition that they transmit it safely. Of their fatherlands as great a portion lies in the past as in the present—among the English perhaps a greater one. We, on the contrary, are quite as independent of time as of space. We have no ties of remembrance, we are not bound by legacies. We have forgotten our distant past and are trying to slough off yesterday's; our history lies ahead. . . .

Why were forces piled on forces? What did Petersburg expect to squeeze with its autocratic press from its sixth part of the globe? Why did it extend its borders? Why did it lock the people in chains? It would know as little how to answer as a whale would if asked why it swallowed a thousand fishes a day to feed its body—its hunger and its natural conformation required it.

At length Petersburg found its limits. It had collided with the West and seen that it could not break it. Internally it had maneuvered itself into such an absurd position that it stood like an ox at the mountain—as the Germans put it—and had nowhere to march. And this was all very well—it had done all it could do: it had roped off a huge arena, prepared a platform, and set up a police system in it. When the building was ready to collapse, Petersburg had to stay it: the stage was set and the actors were going to work now. Entered Alexander II and announced that the Russian Imperial Officials with a supporting cast of the High-born Russian Nobility were to perform a new piece in Peter's theatre: The Liberation of the Peasants with their Lands.

Nothing has been done yet, the spectacle was merely announced, and already Russia is changed. . . . The words "liberation of the peasants" sounded like a trumpet at dawn. The peasant, the dissenter, the liberal official, and the official's official, the educated nobleman, and the nobleman with a stick—all of them awoke from their heavy slumber and in a kind of nervous irritation they hastened to pack their things and be on their way. They are taking measures against some threatening mishap: the government feels itself weaker. They all seem to have more red blood in their veins now; it alone has less of it—and in the meantime the fetters remain as they were. . . .

Now think of the result when this sixth part of the globe with its social instincts, bound no longer by its German chains and stripped of memories and heritage, can shout across to the Western workers, and they will realize that their cause is really the same. Who can foresee all the clashes and conflicts those days will bring? No one can doubt that they will be terrible. Before the conflict begins, we should like to see the Slavs join hands in a brotherly alliance, to prevent their remaining on the side of the past or from becoming bloody theaters of a terrible conflict. . . .

FOR SOBRIETY IN POLITICS

[From The Bell, 1867]

You are inviting us to form a Russian department of the European Republican Alliance. Are we to do so as a profession of faith or in order to work together?

As to the profession of faith, we are prepared once more to proclaim who we are. We are republicans, consistent republicans, that is to say, socialists. That is what we are and what we have been since we started out activity. Being primarily socialists, we are firmly convinced that social development is possible only under complete republican liberty and with complete democratic equality. A republic that would not lead to socialism seems absurd to us, a transition mistaken for an end. A socialism without political liberty, without equal rights, would quickly degenerate into authoritarian communism.

The matter of working together is more complicated. The Universal Alliance is vast, and we fear that many of its component parts may remain empty spaces or may exist only in illusion. Let us consider merely that part of the universe which we know best. What sort of republican work can be done in present-day Europe, unless it be historical, retrospective work? . . . Surely, the republican idea has no chance in the Old World within any measurable future. If there is in Europe a country with a certain republican element, it is England. And you will agree, in this connection one thinks of her least of all. . . .

People are fond of strong power, they worship glory, they like their state in a threatening attitude, admire royal splendor and military reviews—and feel a definite aversion to democratic simplicity and republican austerity. Political feeling has changed into national feeling. A narrow and exclusive patriotism is the one political passion that has not died.

To this end all is sacrificed: the people's well-being, their hard-won rights, the liberties that used to be. The individual, whose sovereign autonomy the revolutions were to achieve, is now dissolving and disappearing in these alluvial empires that bayonets fence in. Thus the road ahead is all marked.

We are not speaking against the republican principle. Intelligence, truth, morality, are obviously on the side of the republicans and the missionaries of peace. But neither

truth nor morality is compulsory, intelligence even less so:
they cannot be imposed by violence. They can lay no claim
to forced obedience, nor take possession against the will of
nations.

We have constructed and reconstructed human society;
we have wanted to re-create it a priori, according to reason.
This was a necessary step to emancipate it from divine right,
that otherworldly authority which imposed obedience from
on high. Once sovereignty has been transported from
heaven to human reason, it is very necessary to examine
more closely what we want here below. There is a universal
suffrage which can be neither repudiated nor falsified. It
votes through events; its protocol is history. Well, in Europe
this vote has gone against the republicans. A vote of ignorance, a vote of corruption, of decadence—we admit all that
—but all the same, a vote against us.

They strive, not to emancipate themselves, but to ag-
grandize and consolidate themselves, to seize ethnic frontiers, to arm and assert themselves against their neighbors,
i.e., their enemies. Fraternity is being achieved in a strange
manner. One does not disarm Cain, the killer, but gives a
club to Abel, the killed—so there will always be two Cains
facing each other; and, to tell the truth, this is not to the
disadvantage of poor Abel. . . .

We believe that the republic and socialism are great
dreams . . . saintly, transcendental dreams, conjured up
by a minority who forge ahead and, abandoned by their own
generation, bequeath their ideals to those who will come
after them.

The republic is being realized across the ocean.

America, strong, rugged, energetic, persistent, without
ruins of the past to encumber her present journey, America
farà da se. Let us leave her to the Americans.

The socialist elements that have long been misunderstood, buried and trodden underfoot amidst the Slavs, are

now fermenting in Russia. The Slav world is beginning to emerge from the fog. Only some lighted points, some blurred outlines, are as yet to be seen; all is shapeless and feeble, except the possibilities and potentialities. The harvest may be great, but it is not guaranteed by the number of sprouts: one must cultivate the crop if one expects to harvest it.

Let us then leave the old and venerable to their venerable age, the strong to their strength, and as to ourselves, the Slavs, let us devote our efforts and our labor to our sprouting fields.

I have long been in doubt whether to print your letter or not, and have finally decided to do so but think it imperative that I should say a few words about it first. You remark that I have already printed letters from my enemies—so why shouldn't I print a friend's letter, which, as you add in an enclosed note, is "not in complete agreement with my opinion?" . . .

We disagree with you, not on ideas, but about means, not on principles, but on the course of action. You represent one of the extreme expressions of our own tendency; we can understand your one-sidedness; it is close to our heart. Our indignation is just as youthful as yours, and our love for the Russian people is as strong now as it was when we were youths.

But to the hatchet, that last resort of the oppressed, we will summon no one, so long as there remains a single, reasonable hope for a solution without the hatchet.

The longer we peer at the Western world and the closer we investigate the scene around us and the chain of events that has brought Europe to us, the stronger grows our aversion to bloody upheavals. They may at times be necessary; by their means the social organism may cut itself loose from old diseases, from choking tumors. They are always a consequence of centuries-old errors that finally work themselves out in vengeance and flaming hatred. This element is lacking in our case; in this respect our situation is without precedent.

From the times of Peter I, the imperial régime has trampled underfoot the earlier political order and wiped it out to an extent that not even the years 1792 and 1793 managed to do in France—to such an extent that nothing is left of it among the living and one must rediscover it in dusty scrolls and chronicles; to us it is more foreign than the France of Louis XIV. And this has not been a wholly negative accomplishment. What is perhaps more serious is the failure of the imperial régime to substitute for the old order something organically sound, something that might have sunk deep roots and grown up as a bulwark for the future. Quite on the contrary, the state of siege which was the imperial régime constituted also one perpetual reform. . . .

Russia's nobility is an artificial imitation, and therefore it is without strength as an aristocracy. A hundred years ago, a grateful Russian nobility resolved to cast a statue of Peter III in pure gold because he had forbidden the knouting of noblemen. It takes a long time before a flogged back can be made into an aristocratic one; the stripes are passed on as an inheritance to whole generations. A Tsar who does not believe in divine unction is a dictator. A nobility that does not believe in its own independent self-existence and in its own rights inherent in its blood and marrow is a band of domestics.

For this reason these high lordly freedmen are no Western aristocrats, but Byzantine eunuchs, Oriental satraps, German lackeys, favorites, and so on. They are not on their own, but according to the obvious logic of slavery, they are more independent the farther away they are from the throne, and more dependent and lacking in personality the

nearer to it they are. Our nobility can achieve political significance only by passing from the governing caste into that
undetermined class which is called educated. There is one
way to do this: by going even farther than the government
in the liberation of the peasants with their lands.

Where among us are those spots that must be hacked out
with a hatchet? Our lack of faith in our own strength—there
lies our trouble, and, most remarkable of all, this lack of
faith prevails equally among the government, the nobility,
and the people. . . .

"Brooms!" ought to be the cry—not "Hatchets!"

You are indignant because the work of liberation has
been held up; but do you really think that this is all owing
to the dullness of one side and the obstinacy of the other? I
do not think so. . . .

Polemics on a fundamental question must not be taken
into the market place. In 1789 all were carried away—that is
what gave that year its irresistible power. At that time there
were minutes when the hearts of Mirabeau and Robes-
pierre, Sieyès and Lafayette, beat in unison; afterwards, as
controversy developed, there followed a change of heart and
desperate struggle.

In the pitiful upheaval of 1848 you saw something altogether different. The single, indivisible faith was not there;
there was not even a single flag. The socialists were convinced that they were ushering in the social republic; the
political democrats thought that they were proving the fallacy of socialism and the childishness of its problems.

You know what followed, and I have seen it with my own
eyes, and it may be that this fact makes the great difference
between us. The blood shed that June [1848] has entered
into my brain and nerves; since that time, I have fostered
an aversion to any blood that is shed without a definite, extreme necessity.

But even then, in an extreme case, it seems to me that the

summons to the hatchet is a last, not a first, resort. Uprisings are conceived and grow, like any fetus, in the quiet secrecy of the maternal womb; they need many forces and powers in order to come into the world and loudly issue their call. . . .

You may offer one objection: What are we going to do if the people, seeing themselves cheated of their liberation, themselves fly to the hatchets? This would be a great tragedy, but it is still a possibility, owing to the spinelessness of the government and the backbone of the landowners. At such a time deliberation will be impossible, and then everyone will have to do as his conscience bids him, as his love bids him. . . . But even then London is not the place from which to issue the summons to the hatchet. Let us rather take care with all our might that this does not happen!

This is all I wanted to tell you.

X

Russia and the West I
DĀNILEVSKY

To Belinsky, Chernyshevsky, and Herzen, who aspired to reform Russian society along Western lines, the problem of Russia's relations with Europe seemed solvable with the progress of liberty under law and the advance of education and social reform in the Eastern Empire. In any event, Russia's Westernization seemed more urgent than the inquiry into the nature of Russia and the West. But many of their contemporaries were preoccupied with this very inquiry, and the debate over Russia's relations with Europe determined their entire outlook. One of these thinkers, and the most systematic among them, was Nikolai Danilevsky.

Danilevsky's book *Russia and Europe, An Inquiry Into the Cultural and Political Relations of the Slav World and of the Germano-Latin World* was published in 1869. It was enthusiastically acclaimed by Dostoevsky. Nikolai Strakhov, a friend of Dostoevsky's and Danilevsky's, called it "the most complete catechism of Slavophilism." Danilevsky was convinced that Europe and Russia were separated by a deep and nonrational historical instinct. Otherwise, how could one explain the fact that Europe was always united in opposing Russia, although that country was neither aggressive

nor hostile to liberty? What was at the bottom of Europe's
deep fear of Russia? Danilevsky answered these questions
by maintaining that Europe and Russia represented two
fundamentally different civilizations, and that the one was
inescapably declining as the other rose.

The Europeans and the Russian Westernizers apparently
believed that Western civilization was a universally valid
and final form of civilization. Danilevsky rejected this position. According to him, all civilizations were subject to a
historical law of growth and decay. European civilization,
the civilization of the Latin and Germanic peoples, had
reached its climax, he believed, in the sixteenth and seventeenth centuries. In the nineteenth century it had entered
the stage of decay. It was now faced with a new historical
civilization, that of the Slavs, whom Danilevsky, like so
many Russians, simply identified with the Russians. Thus
he maintained that the West felt an instinctive hostility
towards its heir and successor.

Europe, besides declining according to historical laws
which he, Danilevsky, had ascertained and proclaimed infallible, was also beset by intrinsic weaknesses. The West,
heir to the Roman tradition of domination and violence,
manifested this spirit in all its great enterprises: in the
spread of Western Christianity, in the discovery and colonization of new worlds, in the struggle for emancipation
and liberty, and finally in the scramble for commercial
profit. Slav civilization, on the other hand, Danilevsky believed, had known neither force nor intolerance as a dominant trait. It proceeded not by ways of conflict but by ways
of peace. The acceptance of Christianity, the introduction
of state organization and of a dynasty which ruled undisputed for centuries, the colonization and cultivation of vast
tracts of land, the emancipation of the serfs, and the introduction of great liberal reforms all happened in Russia

without the violent conflicts which had characterized similar great events in the West. Nor had the Slavs succumbed in modern times to capitalistic greed. Danilevsky was as deeply convinced as Stalin was seventy-five years later that the Russian people pursued ideals opposite to the warlike and plutocratic spirit of the West.

Danilevsky and Stalin had one more fundamental belief in common: they looked upon Russia as the embodiment of democracy and social justice. European history, Danilevsky explained, was propelled by the interests of conflicting groups, parties, and classes; Russian history moved by the growth of the people's moral consciousness. Therefore, Russia had no need for parties or for the existence of an opposition. True, Russia was not in good circumstances in the nineteenth century, but this was due to the attempt to superimpose Western patterns of thought and social organization upon her life; an attempt which was contributing to the destruction of the true foundations of Russia's civilization and the chances of her great future.

Danilevsky predicted an inevitable struggle between Europe and the Slav world. He believed it would start over the Eastern question and would decide the future not only of Constantinople and Turkey but of world civilization. Russia's victory would establish world order and lasting peace. Like Tyuchev, Danilevsky rejected the idea of Russia as one of the great powers of Europe. Russia was too immense for that; she contained too much of the world's future. Unfortunately, after the Napoleonic Wars, Russia seemed to have renounced the fulfillment of her own historical destiny and had been satisfied to be a part of Europe. Danilevsky called Russia to the realization of her destiny. To that end she must secure the cooperation of all the other Slav peoples. "The Pan-Slav union is the only firm foundation on which an original Slav civilization can grow. It is the indispensable requisite of this cultural development. This is the general sense and the main conclusion of our whole inquiry."

Danilevsky worked out the composition of this Pan-Slav union in detail: it would unite all Europe east of a line running from Stettin on the Baltic Sea to Trieste on the Adriatic Sea under Russia's leadership. The continuous struggle with Europe would have a beneficial effect on all the Slavs. It would alienate them from Western influence and from their subservience to alien models, and it would kindle in them an ever growing love for everything Russian. The inevitable and protracted war with the West would undoubtedly end in Russian victory. Europe was doomed because she was impeded in action by conflicting moneyed interests and class struggle. Russia on the other hand embodied unity without such division, a unity summoned to the will of its beloved leader who controlled all the moral and material forces of his people. Russia must accept all the innovations of Western technology and science without hesitation and surpass them. In Russia, however, they would bring infinitely more beneficial results. For the Slavs with their different mentality and their different social system would use these instruments of progress in a different spirit.

For historical reasons Danilevsky believed that the expansion of the Western nations and Russian expansion had little in common; in fact they represented opposite trends. Western plutocratic imperialism enslaved peoples and numbed their cultural growth. Russian expansion was a mission of peace. It liberated peoples and helped them to fulfill their destiny. Thus the expansion of Russian influence was beneficial to mankind. Danilevsky sounded like a modern Russian Marxist when he wrote: "It is as impossible to fight the historical cause of events as it is impossible to fight superior force. From these general considerations we gain the certitude that the Russian and Slav sacred cause, which is in truth the universal and pan-human cause, cannot fail."

THE SLAV ROLE IN WORLD CIVILIZATION

[*From* Russia and Europe, *1869*]

IN THE preceding chapters, strictly speaking, I finished my self-appointed task. A special case—the course of the Schleswig-Holstein question as compared with the [Middle] Eastern question before the Crimean War—gave me the opportunity to discuss the hostility of Europe towards Russia and the Slav world. . . . This investigation led me to the conclusion that this hostility lies in the deep gulf separating the world of the Slavs and the Germano-Roman world—a gulf which reaches down to the very origins of the general stream of universal history.

Only a false concept of the general development of the relationship of the national to the pan-human, a concept incompatible with the real principles of the systematization of scientific-natural phenomena, as well as with so-called progress, could lead to the confusion of European or Germano-Roman civilization with universal civilization. Only such a concept could produce the pernicious delusion of Westernism, which fails to admit the close affinity between Russia and the Slav world, or the historical meaning of the latter, and assigns to us and our brothers the pitiful, insignificant role of imitators of the West. Such a delusion deprives us of the hope for any cultural signifiance, i.e., for a great historical future.

I attempted to develop this theoretical approach and to

supplement it with indications about the main differences between the Slavs and the Germano-Roman cultural-historical types, and about the fatal predicament to which this Westernization or Europeanization has led us, and the extent to which it is the cause of the disease from which Russia's social body suffers, a disease which is the source of all our social ills. Only historical events can remedy this disease and raise the spirit of our society, suffering from spiritual decay and abasement. The cure is possible and probable, because so far the disease has luckily penetrated only the surface of the social structure. We can see such an event, or rather a whole series of events, endowed with a healthy dynamism, in the latest phase of the struggle known as the [Middle] Eastern question, whose origins are rooted in the general course of universal historical development. This struggle must shortly stamp its imprint upon an entire historical period. The importance of this inevitably approaching struggle forces us to try to understand the objections raised against the only decision useful to the Slav world— the full political liberation of all the Slav peoples and the formation of a Pan-Slav union under the hegemony of Russia. The Pan-Slav union will guarantee our success in this struggle.

In one of the previous chapters we said that those who do not believe in the "originality" of Slav culture object by asking, in what, precisely, will this new civilization consist; and what will be the character of its science, of its arts, of its civic and social structure? I rejected the query in this form as absurd, because a satisfactory answer would make the very development of this civilization entirely superfluous. I promised, nonetheless, to describe its broad characteristics, comparing the essential character of past civilizations with the rudiments discernible so far of the Slav cultural-historical type. Now I have to fulfill this promise, and this forces me to turn again to the area of general historical considerations.

Religion singled itself out as something special and at the same time of a higher type, only in the Jewish civilization; there was religion's perceptible beginning, there it existed in a pure form, and it was the only one that left its imprint upon all the others. Outside of religion, the Jews created nothing worthy of the attention of their contemporaries or of posterity. . . . But the religious aspect of their life and activity was so exalted and so perfect that this people is justly called the people chosen by God; and it is among them that there developed a religious *Weltanschauung* which spread to the highest, most developed civilizations and became the religion of all the peoples, unique, eternal, and unchanging in form. Such a conclusion is not altered in the least, whether we hold to the opinion that the lessons of the Old and the New Testament were a *Weltanschauung* gradually elaborated by this people, or to the opinion that they were a revelation communicated, little by little, from above.

Therefore, we may call the Jewish cultural-historical type not only mainly but even exclusively religious.

In the same way as Jewish culture was exclusively religious, the Hellenic type was primarily artistic-cultural. All other aspects of development lagged behind this one and remained in the background. This people so richly endowed culturally lacked all economic, political, and religious sense. There is nothing much to be said about the socio-political aspect of its development. A people for which slavery was not only an accidental and temporary phenomenon but a fundamental fact, on which rested all its political and spiritual life with all its philosophical humanism and aesthetic luxury, could not contribute to the development of socio-economic ideas. Politically speaking, the Greeks could not even rise to the consciousness of the political unity of their race, though they looked upon themselves as a particular cultural unit in contradistinction to all the barbarian nations. . . . Similarly, the religious doctrines of the Greeks fail to display any real religious sense and feeling. Their religious outlook was most insignificant and pitiful and completely unworthy of a people occupying such a high niche in philosophical thinking. . . .

The Roman type—a cultural-historical type just as one-sided as the Greek or the Jewish—developed and realized successfully only one aspect of activity, the political side of human endeavor. In the political sense the Romans have no equal. A small core crystallized around itself the races of Latium and subjected, little by little, gradually, systematically—and by non-aggressive advances—the whole basin of the Mediterranean and all the Western approaches of the Atlantic. Along with the growth of the state, they altered the form of their government, transforming the republic into an empire which became a popular institution, maintaining itself not by external force (there were very many weak, insignificant emperors) but by popular consent. The people realized instinctively the necessity of the empire in difficult and dangerous times. During the existence of Rome as a state the mutual relationships of the citizens were regulated by the most precise and the most perfect code of civil laws.

But in Rome, as in Greece, slavery represented a basic facet of the social structure. Rome's cultural activity was completely insignificant in science, in philosophical thinking, as well as in the arts; with the exception of architecture, it did not produce anything original. Was the reason for this sterility to be found in the moral and spiritual conditions of the Latin race, or in the imitativeness of the Romans, in their dependence upon the Greeks in the sphere of science and art? What was said about the religion of the Greeks applies in all respects also to the Romans. . . .

In this way the civilizations that followed the primitive autochthonous cultures each unfolded only one aspect of cultural activity in the broad sense of this phrase; the Jews: the religious aspect; the Greeks: the strictly cultural; and the Romans: the political. Therefore, we must characterize the Jewish, Greek, and Roman cultural-historical types by the name of one-sided types. Historical progress beyond this point may and must proceed in two directions: the development of the fourth aspect of cultural activity—the socio-economic—and the attainment of a great many-sidedness through the integration in one and the same cultural type of the four aspects of cultural activity, which have so far manifested themselves only singly. Such a synthesis was first realized by the European cultural type after the fall of the Western Roman Empire.

The circumstances at the time were favorable for the realization of such a synthesis. Religious truth, in the eternal form of Christianity, was discovered and adopted with humility and exaltation by new peoples, who were rich in gifts of a spiritual nature, among which one has to include ardent religious feelings. In this same religious doctrine there was, as its central tenet, the need to do away with slavery; and in reality, slavery appeared only as a transitory phase in the life of the Germano-Roman peoples. These peoples also revealed themselves richly endowed with political sense and an ability for cultural development: scientific, artistic, and industrial. They were not fated, however, to have these great gifts fully realized, due to the violence of their character. With them Roman love for power and Roman state structure fell upon a receptive soil. In this way, Christian truth was distorted, and the Church was transformed into the religiously political despotism of Catholicism. This church despotism in conjunction with feudal despotism, which took root in the violence of the German character, and with the despotism of scholasticism, which

had taken its origin in a slavish attitude to the forms of ancient science, oriented all the history of Europe towards a
severe struggle, ending in a threefold anarchy. It comprised
a religious anarchy, that is, Protestantism with the idea of
basing religious truth upon personal authority; a philosophical anarchy, or an all-embracing materialism, which
began to take on the character of a faith and little by
little replaced religious conviction; and a socio-political anarchy, a contradiction between an ever growing political
democratism and economic feudalism. As these anarchies
are substantially the forerunners and instruments of decay,
they cannot, of course, be considered viable investments in
the treasury of mankind; and the Germano-Roman cultural-
historical type cannot be considered a successful representative of the religious, or of the socio-economic aspect of
cultural activity.

On the other hand, from the political and from the
strictly cultural viewpoints, the achievements of the historical life of Europe are staggering. The nations of Europe
not only founded mighty states that spread their power to
the four corners of the earth but also set up abstract and
equal relationships between the citizens themselves and between the citizens and the state.

In other words, they succeeded in combining the political
power of the state with domestic freedom. If this freedom in
practice has not yet produced the expected results, then this
is due to the incorrect solution of another problem, i.e., the
problem of the socio-economic order. . . .

And now let us turn to the Slav world, and chiefly to Russia, its only independent representative, in order to examine the results and the promises of this world, a world still
only at the beginning of its cultural-historical life. We must
examine it from the viewpoint of the above four foci of
reference: religion, culture, politics, and socio-economic
structure, in order to elucidate what we rightfully expect

as well as hope from the Slav cultural-historical type.

Religion constituted the most essential element of ancient Russian life, and at the present time, the overwhelming spiritual interest of the ordinary Russian is also involved in it; in truth, one cannot but wonder at the ignorance and the impertinence of these people who could insist (to gratify their fantasies) on the religious indifference of the Russian people.

From an objective, factual viewpoint, the Russian and the majority of Slav peoples became, with the Greeks, the chief guardians of the living tradition of religious truth, Orthodoxy, and in this way they continued the high calling, which was the destiny of Israel and Byzantium: to be the chosen people. . . .

We have already pointed to the special character of the acceptance of Christianity by Russia, not through subjection to a culturally higher Christian nation, nor through political supremacy over a nation, nor by way of an active religious propaganda—but out of an inner discontent, a dissatisfaction with paganism, and out of the unfettered search for truth. . . . The religious aspect of the cultural activity belongs to the Slav cultural type and to Russia in particular; it is its inalienable achievement, founded on the psychology of its people and on its guardianship of religious truth.

If we turn to the political aspect and to the extent to which the Slav peoples have manifested their ability to set up their body politic, we find the situation at first sight discouraging, because all the Slav peoples, with the exception of Russia, either did not succeed in establishing independent states, or were incapable of preserving their independence. The Slavophobes conclude from this that the Slav peoples are politically incapable. Such a conclusion cannot stand up if we face the facts as they are. These facts tell us that the vast majority of the Slav tribes (at least two-thirds of them, if not more) have built a huge, continuous state, which has already had an existence of a thousand years and is all the time growing in strength and power in spite of the storms which it has had to weather during its long historical life. This one fact of the first magnitude demonstrates the political sense of the Slavs or at least of a significant majority of them.

If the German Empire [of the Middle Ages], after a relatively short period of glory and power, turned into a political *monstrum*, are we then entitled to conclude that the German race is incapable of political life? Of course not, because the German race also has created the powerful British Empire, and therefore we must ascribe the political situation of Germany exclusively to unfavorable domestic and foreign circumstances, and not to a deep-rooted incapacity. This is confirmed by Prussia's actions which reveal political sense of a fairly long standing (at least since the Great Elector) and led to Bismarck's success.

In judging the political incapacity of the Slavs one also hears of the alleged lack of unity of the Russian state, because there are in it, maybe, about a hundred peoples of different nationalities. But it is forgotten that all this diversity disappears before the preponderance of the Russian race—qualitatively and quantitatively. Even if all the Western and Southwestern Slav peoples were really incapable of political life, nonetheless one must recognize the high political sense of the Slav race as a whole, in view of the Russian state alone.

The example of the Ukraine, which for a long time was torn from the rest of Russia but voluntarily united with her after gaining her independence, furnishes the proof that there is more than one Slav people gifted with deep political insight; therefore, we may hope that when the opportunity arises, other Slavs will display the same insight, voluntarily recognizing the hegemony of Russia after having gained their independence, and realizing that the circumstances in which the Ukraine found itself at the time of Bogdan Khmelnitsky and in which the Western Slavs find themselves now are essentially similar. Popular enthusiasm, favorable circumstances, and the genius of a leader placed at the head of a popular movement can achieve independence for them. But preservation of their independence and of the Slav character of life and culture will be impossible without a close mutual union with Russia.

Whatever the future may bring we are entitled, on the evidence of the past alone, to consider the Slavs among the most gifted families of the human race in political ability. Here we may turn our attention to the special character of this political ability and show how it manifested itself during the growth of the Russian state. The Russians do not send out colonists to create new political societies, as the Greeks did in antiquity or the English in modern times. Russia does not have colonial possessions, like Rome or like England. The Russian state from early Muscovite times on has been Russia herself, gradually, irresistibly spreading on all sides, settling neighboring nonsettled territories, and assimilating into herself and into her national boundaries foreign populations. This basic character of Russian expansion was misunderstood because of the distortion of the original Russian point of view through Europeanization, the origin of every evil in Russia. . . .

But the expansion of the state, its attainment of stability, strength, and power, constitutes only one aspect of political activity. It has still another one, consisting of the establishment of equal relationships between the citizens themselves and between them and the state, i.e., in the establishment of civil and political freedom. A people not endowed with this freedom cannot be said to possess a healthy political sense. Is the Russian people capable of freedom?

Naturally our "well-wishers" give a negative answer: some

regard slavery as a natural element of the Russians, and others are afraid, or pretend to be afraid, that freedom in Russian hands must lead to all sorts of excesses and abuses. But on the basis of Russian history and with knowledge of the views and traits of the Russian people, one can only form an opinion diametrically opposed to this view— namely, that there hardly ever has existed or exists a people so capable of enduring such a large share of freedom as the Russians and so little inclined to abuse it, due to their ability and habit to obey, their respect and trust in the authorities, their lack of love for power, and their loathing of interference in matters where they do not consider themselves competent. If we look into the causes of all political troubles, we shall find their root not in the striving after freedom, but in the love for power and the vain cravings of human beings to interfere in affairs that are beyond their comprehension. . . .

This nature of the Russian people is the true reason why Russia is the only state which never had (and in all probability never will have) a political revolution, i.e., a revolution having as its aim the limitation of the power of the ruler. . . . All the troubles in Russian history were popular rebellions without political character, in the strict meaning of the word; their causes were doubt in the legitimacy of the ruling person, dissatisfaction with the serfdom that was oppressing the people to an ever greater extent than had been foreseen by the laws, and finally high-handedness and violence, which necessarily develop in Russia's borderlands, in the unceasing struggle of the Cossacks with the Tartars and other nomads. . . .

With legality in the succession of the throne secured, with civil order introduced among the Cossacks, and finally with the liberation of the peasants, all the reasons which in former times had agitated the people disappeared; and even an ordinary rebellion, going beyond the limits of a regrettable misunderstanding, has become impossible in Russia so long as the moral character of the Russian people does not change. . . .

To what degree moderation, an easy-going nature, and common sense characterize both the Russian people and Russian society has been clearly demonstrated by the events of the last years. As far as the historical memory of mankind can go back, one can scarcely find faster, more sudden changes, within the general social conditions of popular life than those that took place before our eyes. . . . The change from oppressive servitude to full freedom was sudden. . . . Even when the new authority of the communal organization was not yet established, and the people existed in critical moments without any direct close authority, public order was nowhere disturbed, and no incitements could swerve the population from giving full confidence to the government either then or later. . . . It thus became clear to all, even to those who were ill-disposed to the reform and almost expected it to result in the fall of the hated colossus, that here (as always) Russia could lean on her broad, unshakable foundations. . . .

And so, what do we see? The abuses and the oppression from which Russia suffered before the reforms of the present reign were not smaller, but in many respects they were even more severe than the ones from which France suffered until the Revolution; the transformation was more radical than the one carried out by the French National Assembly. Yet, whereas the broken dam in France released a general flood of harmful antisocial instincts and passions, in Russia it could not disturb the peace, respect, and trust towards the authorities, but even emphasized them and strengthened all the foundations of the state. Are we not then entitled to assert that the Russian people and Russian society, in all social classes, are capable of accepting and enduring any amount of freedom, and that to advise its restriction can

only be done by a distorted belief in self-created dangers or
(what is even worse) under the influence of certain secret
motives, unfair and hostile to Russian aspirations? Thus we
may conclude that the Russian people, by their attitude
towards the power of the state, by their ability to sacrifice to
it their own personal interests, and by their attitude towards
the use of political and civil freedom, are gifted with wonderful political sense.

In the socio-economic sphere, Russia is the only large
state which has solid ground under its feet, in which there
are no landless masses, and in which, consequently, the
social edifice does not rest on the misery of the majority of
the citizens and on the insecurity of their situation. In
Russia, only, there cannot and does not exist any contradiction between political and economic ideals. This contradiction threatens disaster to European life, a life which has
embarked on its historical voyage in the dangerous seas between the Charybdis of Caesarism or military despotism
and the Scylla of social revolution. The factors that give
such superiority to the Russian social structure over the
European, and give it an unshakable stability, are the
peasant's land and its common ownership. On this health of
Russia's socio-economic structure we found our hope for
the great socio-economic significance of the Slav cultural-
historical type. This type has been able for the first time to
create a just and normal system of human activity, which
embraces not only human relations in the moral and political sphere, but also man's mastery of nature, which is a
means of satisfying human needs and requirements. Thus it
establishes not only formal equality in the relations between citizens, but a real and concrete equality.

However, as regards the prominent place of the Slav
cultural-historical type in the field of culture proper, one
must admit that so far the Russian and other Slav achievements in the sciences and in the arts are insignificant in

comparison with the accomplishments of the two great cultural types, the Greek and the European. . . . Let us concentrate all our attention upon Russia, the only independent Slav state. The establishment of a state, we said, is the first historical activity of a people emerging through circumstances from a purely ethnographic existence, and such a people must progress to a certain point before it can become culturally productive. The difficulty of the political task which was the lot of the Russian people was such that it is no wonder that it took one thousand years and demanded all the national energy; yet the incomparably easier task of the Western peoples took the same length of time to be fulfilled. I have already mentioned the special obstacles that geography presented to the establishment and the consolidation of the Russian state. The large forests and steppes gave to a sparse population, still living at the ethnographic stage of its development, the possibility of escape from the burdens imposed by the state, the choice of refusing them without active opposition. When such a fate befalls a population already accustomed, from an earlier time, to living in a state and already possessed of some measure of education (as happened in the United States of America), and when security from outside attacks is assured without the necessity of a strong union or political centralization, then national activity is directed in a struggle against nature, in the acquisition of wealth, whose value the population has already learned to understand. This is what gave American culture a primarily technical and industrial character. In Russia, on the contrary, where foreign enemies threatened on all sides, at first primarily from the East and later from the West, a lack of the governmental centralization needed to repel the enemies would inevitably have entailed the irrevocable loss of national independence.

Thus arose the need for the utmost concentration of governmental power, i.e., for an autocratic and monolithic government which would with unlimited strength drive and direct individual activity towards general goals. The conditions of American life, on the other hand, led to technical activity, under the weakest possible federative-democratic direction. In both cases, scientific and artistic activities receded into the background; their time had not yet come. The intense governmental activity of the Muscovite State was still further intensified by the Petrine reforms, the essential character of which was purely political and governmental, and not at all cultural. In principle everything was sacrificed to the state. . . . From the time of Peter, according to an expression adopted quite aptly in our country, all the people were harnessed into state service. The nobility were harnessed directly and the other classes indirectly; the merchant class by the fiscal character given to industry; the peasantry by its attachment either to the state or to the nobility. The necessity for such an enslavement of all the national forces for political goals could be explained by the fact that the European states, with which Russia had, *volens nolens,* to come into close political contact, had in the course of their existence become thickly populated, had achieved a harmonious order, and had accumulated a large scientific and industrial capital. Armies, which in the Middle Ages had not numbered more than a few tens of thousands, began from the time of Louis XIV on to number hundreds of thousands of soldiers, equipped with expensive armaments, the manufacture of which required a significant technological development in the country. This applied to an even greater degree to the navy. . . .

Scientific and artistic activity can thrive only under conditions of leisure, of an overflow of forces that remain free from daily toil. Could much leisure be left over among Russians and Slavs? . . . All these considerations fully answer, it seems to me, the question why until now Russia and the other Slav countries could not occupy a respected position in purely cultural activities. . . . But indications of these aptitudes, of these spiritual forces, which are necessary for brilliant achievements in the fields of science and art are now indisputably present among the Slav peoples in spite of all the unfavorable conditions of their life; and, consequently, we are justified in expecting that with a change in these conditions, these peoples will bring forth remarkable creations. . . .

The Slav cultural type has already produced enough examples of artistic and, to a lesser degree, scientific achievements to allow us to conclude that it has attained a significant degree of development in these fields. The relative youth of the race and the concentration of all its forces upon other, more urgent types of activity have not, until now, given the Slavs the opportunity of acquiring cultural significance, in the exact meaning of the phrase. This should not embarrass us; rather, it points to the right path in our development. As long as there is no strong foundation, we cannot and we must not think of the erection of a durable edifice; we can only set up temporary buildings, which cannot be expected to display the talents of the builder in every respect. The political independence of the race is the indispensable foundation of culture, and consequently all the Slav forces must be directed towards this goal. Independence is indispensable in two respects: without the consciousness of Slav racial unity, as distinct from other races, an independent culture is impossible; and without fruitful interaction between the Slav peoples, liberated from foreign powers and from their national divisions, diversity and richness of culture are impossible. A well-known example of the beneficial influence of unity is the relationship and interaction between the spiritual developments of Great Russia and the Ukraine.

The requisite preliminary achievement of political in-

dependence has still another importance in the cultural
as well as in all other spheres: the struggle against the
Germano-Roman world (without which Slav independence
is impossible) will help to eradicate the cancer of imitativeness and the servile attitude towards the West, which
through unfavorable conditions has eaten its way into the
Slav body and soul. Only now has the historical moment for
this cultural development arrived: only with the emancipation of the peasantry can the period of Russian cultural life
begin, and her purely state period of life (which consisted in
leading the people from tribal will to civil liberty) end. But
first, as a *sine qua non* condition of success, strong and
powerful Russia has to face the difficult task of liberating
her racial brothers; for this struggle, she must steel them
and herself in the spirit of independence and Pan-Slav consciousness.

Thus, on the basis of our analysis of the preceding cultural-historical types and of the peculiarities of the Slav
world, we can maintain the fundamental hope that the Slav
cultural-historical type will, for the first time in history,
accomplish a synthesis of all aspects of cultural activity—
aspects which were elaborated by its precursors on the
historical scene, either in isolation or in incomplete union.
We may hope that the Slav type will be the first to embody
all four basic cultural activities, the religious, the political,
the esthetic-scientific, and the socio-economic. . . .

Two sources on the banks of the ancient Nile begin the
main flow of universal history. One, heavenly and divine,
has reached Kiev and Moscow with unsullied purity by way
of Palestine and Tsargrad [Constantinople]; the other,
earthly and human, divided itself into two main streams,
that of esthetic-scientific culture and that of politics, which
flowed through Athens, Alexandria, and Rome into Europe, drying up temporarily, then enriching themselves
with new and ever more abundant waters. On Russian soil

a new fountainhead, a fourth river, originates, providing the popular masses with a just socio-economic structure. These four streams will unite on the wide plains of Slavdom into a mighty sea.

XI

Russia and the West II

SOLOVEV

Danilevsky's influence reached its climax in the late 1870's, when Russia fought against Turkey for the liberation of the Balkan Slavs and Russian armies approached the gates of coveted Constantinople. Within another decade the opposition to Slavophilism and Pan-Slavism gained the upper hand in Russian intellectual society. At the same time an idealistic reaction set in against the materialist positivism of the sixties.

The leading spokesman of this new movement was Vladimir Solovev, son of the famous Russian historian Sergei Solovev. In the seventies, while a youth, Solovev was an admirer of Dostoevsky's Christian Slavophilism, and it is generally thought that he was the model for Dostoevsky's Alyosha Karamazov, the spiritual disciple and heir of Father Zossima. Solovev later turned away from Slavophilism and became the advocate of an extensive Russian rapprochement with the West. Most Westernizers were materialists and radicals, disciples of Belinsky and Chernyshevsky. But Solovev, like Chaadayev, remained an Orthodox Christian. The Orthodox faith was meaningful to him not because it was the religion of the Russian people—as was the case with Dostoevsky—but because it was part of the univeral Christian Church. Solovev strove for the unity of the Christian churches, especially for a unity with Rome. In his political views, however, Solovev sided with the agnostic Westernizers in a common effort to liberalize Russian government and society.

With a conviction much like that of Tolstoy, Solovev opposed all nationalism and all idolization of the state; but he was more realistic than Tolstoy and did not share the latter's Rousseauan adoration of the Russian peasant masses or his doctrine of nonresistance to evil. Solovev strove to overcome the hatred and misunderstandings which separated Russia and Europe, and he sought a universalism which would recognize and respect the value of human diversity.

Solovev's chief interest was philosophy, and though his significance in this field is not world-wide, he is nevertheless the greatest philosopher so far produced by Russia. His academic career was brief. He was an enemy of capital punishment, and while a lecturer at St. Petersburg University in 1881, he protested against the execution of the assassins of Alexander II and was forced to resign.

Besides his career as philosopher and religious thinker, Solovev was "the best poet of his generation," and the brilliant array of Russian poets in the first decade of the twentieth century owed a great deal to him. He was a mystic and an ascetic. Yet he possessed an extraordinary sense of humor and wrote some of the finest nonsense poems in Russian literature.

Solovev's great concern was freedom. He rejected all kinds of subjugation, in politics as well as in religion. "We shall not regard transitory forms and instruments of the historical activity of Providence as the core and goal of this activity. . . . As long as the state means everything, an ordering of human existence becomes meaningless." He accused the Church of having failed to carry out "Christ's chief commandment—to make the active love for one's neighbor the basis of social life. This commandment, however, inspires unbelievers to champion freedom and social justice, and such champions must therefore, in spite of their unbelief, be recognized as true disciples of Christ."

Solovev, who died in 1900, is the exponent of Russia's most fruitful encounter with Europe during the nineteenth century. In the last years of his life Solovev lived under the foreboding of an approaching world crisis. He saw the need for Western unity—and he included Russia in the West— against the storms which he felt approaching from the Asian steppes. He predicted the threat to Western civilization of the rising Pan-Mongolism. His last work, *Three Conversations on War, Progress, and the End of History,* concludes with "A Short Story of the Anti-Christ," a vision of an approaching apocalyptic struggle and the coming unity of mankind. As Solovev had foreseen, Western civilization was challenged. But this challenge, which came two decades after his death, did not give reality to Solovev's dream of Russo-European integration and mutual enrichment. Instead, it found Russia organizing Asia for the struggle with the West.

AGAINST THE SLAVOPHILS

[*From a criticism of books by Danilevsky and Strakhov, 1888*]

THE admirers of Danilevsky's *Russia and Europe* regard it as the catechism or codex of Slavophilism. Danilevsky set himself the task of explaining and justifying the discord among peoples through a historical-philosophical system and of drawing from this system some practical conclusions for that part of mankind to which he himself belonged. The division of mankind into tribes and nations, which was mitigated by the influence of the great universal religions and replaced by wider and more flexible units, has been resuscitated since the beginning of the nineteenth century with renewed vigor in Europe and has exercised a potent influence as a conscious and systematic idea. . . .

Although Russian science and scholarship, whose serious beginnings we can date from Lomonosov, had less time for its development than Western European science, it had on the other hand the great advantage that the Russian scholars found a soil well prepared for them by their European colleagues and could thus build on secure foundations. The Russians have certainly proved their qualifications for every scholarly or scientific activity. These qualifications, together with the excellent training which the Russian scholars received, aroused the hope among the Slavophils, that the Russian nation would accomplish real miracles in the scientific field, in view of the extraordinarily fast intellectual development of our time. Reality has not fulfilled these hopes. Born under unusually favorable circumstances, Russian scholarship has not been able to make any startlingly new contributions. In mathematics, chemistry, and biology we can, it is true, find some Russian scholars who occupy a considerable and honorable position in the European world of scholarship. Yet their work bears no stamp of a specifically Russian science. It has no sharply defined national character. Moreover, the scientific works of our greatest scholars, in spite of their excellent qualities, are not so profoundly significant as to influence definitively the general course of scientific development. None is of epoch-making importance in the history of even one of the various fields of scientific endeavor.

In speaking of the scientists of the coming Slav-Russian cultural type, Danilevsky refers among others to Copernicus. If it were necessary to prove that the Slavs have the ability to produce a great scholar from time to time, Copernicus would certainly prove it. But this aptitude has never been questioned by anyone. However, this famous Pole can in no way be invoked to prove Danilevsky's Slavophil theory. For Copernicus' work is indissolubly linked with that of the German Kepler, the Italian Galileo, and the English Newton. It belongs, therefore, only to the European or Roman-Germanic world of scholarship and in no way to the future Slav-Russian type.

It is characteristic that our Slavophils accept the Poles as true Slavs if a great man of Polish descent is under discussion. Then the differences between Poles and Russians are almost entirely overlooked, and their glory is also our glory. But if on the other hand the Slavophils wish to stress the existing abnormal relationship between Russia and Poland, then the Poles are called renegades and traitors to Slavdom, deserters to the hostile Roman-Germanic camp who will perish with it, having lost all right to participate in the future greatness of the Slavs.

Let us repeat that there is no proof that Russian and Slav scholarship constitutes a special cultural-historical type which is destined to create a unique Slav-Russian science different from that of Europe. Nor does Danilevsky succeed in supplying such a proof. He cannot present even one case of Russian scholarship that is independent of European influence. He names a few Russian and Slav scientists (and we could add some other names), but all belong to the European scholarly world as Copernicus did—with the difference that Copernicus is the only one who marked a turning point in the history of science.

Until Russia appeared on the scene as a cultural factor, none of the Slav peoples, who participated to a varying degree in European intellectual life, claimed to embody a peculiarly anti-Western character in its thought. All such claims have originated in Russia alone. But even the most prejudiced researchers in this field can find nothing that corresponds even remotely to these claims. If we disregard all prejudices and arbitrary fantastic prophecies, then we can conclude on the basis of an experience of 140 years, that the Russians are capable of participating in European scholarship to about the same degree as the Swedes and the Dutch. . . .

German idealistic philosophy in its final Hegelian form has nowhere in Europe aroused the interest and understanding that it awakened in our educated circles in the thirties and forties. Yet in spite of the enthusiasm that it aroused among so many excellent minds, this philosophic movement bore no fruit. A prominent thinker, Ivan Kireyevsky, came to the conclusion that true wisdom and real science could be found only in the ascetic writers of the Orthodox East. His friends hoped that he would draw from this deep well the living waters of a new Eastern philosophy; and that he would oppose it triumphantly to the desiccated intellectual life of the rotting West. But Kireyevsky failed to produce anything beyond a few general remarks. The entire Russian philosophical movement of that period left nothing but a few essays, which were partly inspired by the outlook of Western philosophers and partly directed against that outlook. These essays, however, contained no positive foundations of an independent and original philosophical system.

In the following twenty-five years, Russian literary life mirrored in an exaggerated and caricatured way the reaction then prevalent in Europe against philosophic idealism. Everyone remembers the fervent enthusiasm with which the new German materialism and French positivism were received among us. I do not believe that we Russians have accepted the various European intellectual currents simply out of a desire to imitate the West, as Danilevsky supposes.

That author forgets to mention that Slavophil scholars too have found all their leading philosophic and theological ideas in French and German authors. I wish to emphasize one fact, namely that in this second period, also, there was no sign of an independent, characteristically Russian philosophical system.

Russian intellectual life oscillates between two points of view, an extreme scepticism, and mysticism. It is evident that both points of view preclude a real philosophy. It is true that every profound philosophical system contains a sceptical and a mystical element. Philosophical scepticism is directed against all arbitrary authority and against all apparent reality. Philosophical mysticism is the consciousness of the inner and indestructible connection of the thinking mind with the absolute. But the attitude which underlies Russian thought has no relation to this kind of scepticism or mysticism. Russian scepticism has little in common with the legitimate doubts of Descartes or Kant who wished to find the limits of cognition. Russian scepticism wishes to destroy the idea of truth itself and to undermine the interest in cognition. In a similar way our national mysticism leads to the subordination of our spiritual individuality to an absolute object recognized as something superior. This irretrievable loss of self in a higher entity expresses itself sometimes in an unshakable indifference and passivity and sometimes in a suicidal fanaticism. Under these conditions there can be no foundation for a great and independent Russian future in the field of thought and knowledge.

This conclusion was not so evident when Danilevsky wrote his book; nevertheless, he anticipated it, opposing to it an odd consideration. He said that the intellectual development of each nation reaches its peak only when the nation has achieved its greatest political power. History, however, shows us that the opposite can happen. For Greeks and Germans certainly belong to the culturally prominent nations.

Yet the intellectual flowering of Greece preceded its political triumphs; the century of Pericles preceded the century of Alexander. Similarly in Germany, Lessing and Kant, Goethe and Hegel, Mozart and Beethoven, lived long before Bismarck and Moltke.

Without doubt the best examples of Russian creative writing have a specific character and intrinsic value. However, this is also true of German, Spanish, and English literature; and yet these qualities do not imply a special cultural-historical type for these nations. Why should it do so for Russia? Nobody contests the existence of a Russian national character which manifests itself, among other things, in literature. The Russian and the English novel certainly differ, but not more than the English and Spanish. The Russian novel represents one type among the many types of European novels. And as Russian literature can be regarded only as a form of European literature, so Russia, in spite of her distinctive character, is only a European state among the other European states. Danilevsky's contrary position cannot adduce a single proof for its point of view.

In periods of national egoism and isolation from the rest of the Christian world, Russia has not been able to produce anything great or significant. Only through the closest internal and external ties with Europe can Russia become great. . . .

Danilevsky opens his book *Russia and Europe* with the question, "Why doesn't Europe love Russia?" His answer is well known. Europe, he thinks, fears us as a new and higher cultural-historical type which is destined to replace the obsolescent Roman-Germanic civilization. However, the contents of his book and his own confessions suggest another answer. Europe views Russia with hostility and anxiety, for she recognizes the dark and enigmatic elemental forces alive in the Russian people, and, together with Russia's spiritual and cultural poverty, that country's vast and well defined ambition. Europe fears above all the voice of our "nationalism," a nationalism which desires to destroy Turkey and Austria, to divide Germany, to annex Constantinople, and, should an opportunity arise, even India. If, however, we are asked what we have to offer mankind as compensation for what we take and destroy, what spiritual and cultural principles we have contributed to world history, then we must either be silent or indulge in meaningless phrases.

If Danilevsky's bitter confession that Russia is a "sick and enfeebled colossus," is true, then the question "Why doesn't Europe love us?" must be replaced by a more obvious and important one, namely, "What is the nature and cause of our malady?" Physically Russia is strong enough, as the last Russian war in the East has demonstrated. Our illness must therefore be of a moral nature. We carry the burden, as an old writer says, of our people's sins, which we do not wish to acknowledge. That is a fact which must be foremost in our minds. As long as we remain morally crippled, our elemental energies can only harm us. Therefore the most important, nay, the only important question for a true, clear-sighted Russian patriot, is not the question of our power or of our mission, but the question of "Russia's sins."

ON DOSTOEVSKY

[From a lecture, 1891]

Some people believe that Dostoevsky is the true representative both of the Russian national conscience and of the Russian concept of Christianity. It is true that in his inspired moments this man of genius has comprehended the universalist ideal of our people. Under solemn circumstances [in an address delivered on June 8, 1880, at the unveiling of a monument for Pushkin] Dostoevsky announced the formula of a Russian and Christian ideal which was intended to be universal, and to bring about unity and peace. But it was not enough to proclaim the ideal. Dostoevsky would have had to indicate the means to its realization. He would have had to apply his ideal as a standard by which to regulate all the practical questions of our collective life. But even in the literary field alone, such a labor would have demanded Dostoevsky's renunciation of his many deeply rooted prejudices, preconceived ideas, and elemental nationalist instincts. These he revealed in his works without being aware of their conflict with the universalist ideal which he proclaimed. Russian life was soon to underline this conflict, and Dostoevsky would have had to revise all his personal opinions in the light of the formula announced in the course of an inspired address. It would have been cruel to demand from the sixty-year-old man, who had undergone a life of suffering, such an intellectual and emotional feat. Moreover, Dostoevsky was a seer and an artist rather than a master of logic.

Of all the ideas recently proposed by Tolstoy, the most striking, at least for those who believe in Providence, is the theory according to which every man necessarily dies at the moment most providential for him. To every mortal, a just measure of trying experiences is granted, and death prevents any excess of this measure. Death freed Dostoevsky from an internal conflict which would have been beyond his strength. But though the memory of this great seer and martyr has not been blemished by the clash between his best ideal and his triste reality, there remains the serious contradiction between Dostoevsky's ideal and the many nationalist passages in his work. Thus none among us can assume his entire spiritual heritage.

If we admit with Dostoevsky that the true Russian national character, its dignity and value, consists in its capacity to understand and love all alien elements and to

reincarnate itself in them, and if we believe that the mission
of the Russian people consists in the realization of the ideal
of a unified mankind through a brotherly union with the
other peoples, then we cannot accept the numerous attacks
of the same Dostoevsky on the Jews, the Poles, the French,
the Germans, on the whole of Europe, on the other Christian creeds. And too, if the opponents of universality can
justifiably find a support in these passages of Dostoevsky,
they must limit their solidarity with him strictly to these
attacks. For they cannot espouse his ideal and his prophetic
view. If the incontestable ambiguity of Dostoevsky's concepts allows even the enemies of his best ideals to claim him,
then the true disciple of his ideal cannot remain in his camp
without reservation.

Everyone is entitled to wish for a Russia that will be the
salt of the earth and the kingdom of the saints. But it is not
permissible to make this wish merely a patriotic dream, as
we tend to do. We must struggle to free Russia from social
injustices and from conditions which negate Christianity.
Thirty years ago one of these injustices was abolished [serf-
dom]. Are there no others? Russia's true national ideal im-
poses the task of finding a Christian solution to all the national and religious questions before us. Only thus can the
national ideal be justified. Otherwise it will remain a vain
and mendacious pretense. Russia must not allow herself to
be seduced by those who call her saintly merely to prevent
her from becoming just.

AGAINST EXTREME NATIONALISM

[From an essay written in 1889]

The three successive stages of our nationalism appear as,
first, the cult of our people as the privileged bearers of
universal truth, then, the veneration of this people as an
elemental force irrespective of all truth, and finally, the cult

of its exclusive cultural and historical character—a negation of the very idea of universal truth. These three stages are faithfully represented by the Slavophils, by Katkov, and by the new obscurantists. The first were pure fantasts; the second was a realist, not devoid of fantasy; the obscurantists are realists without fantasy and without scruples.

In its most recent stages, our nationalism has established itself on the firm ground of forces and facts. The more it loses intellectual content, the more insensitive it becomes to every rational objection. Every discussion of principles presupposes the jurisdiction of general ideas and a universal system of laws established by reason. How can one argue with a man who declares that he can respect only facts and that he can esteem only force, being totally indifferent to the moral character and ethical quality of that force.

It is impossible to enter into direct discussions with the supporters of this extreme nationalism because the most violent contradiction between their views and human reason or conscience is to them a matter of pride rather than something problematical. Nevertheless, there is an indirect way to convince them. Since our obscurantists recognize the opposition of their national values to the national values of others as the only criterion of all ethical and social judgments, they must admit that the Russian people accept their concepts and that their nationalism expresses the Russian mind. It is therefore of supreme importance to them to know whether the Russian people really think as they do.

One cannot solve this problem by questioning the Russian masses directly. But one can search Russian history and literature. The greatest representatives of Russian literature have shown themselves to be free of all national exclusivism. They were deeply affected by all that was good among other peoples, and they condemned all that was bad among us, i.e., the very aspects of Russian life which so enchant our obscurantists. However, the obscurantists can dispute our claim that the great figures of Russian history and literature did not adhere to an exclusive nationalism. They can say, for example, that St. Vladimir and Vladimir Monomach did not follow the true Russian path and that Peter the Great deliberately forsook the Russian path to our greatest detriment. They can find certain passages in our writers which seem to coincide with their views, and thus they can claim for themselves the greatest Russian authors. In Zhukovsky, instead of praising the charming sweetness of his poetry which transplanted "alien gods to our savage shores," they can appreciate only the reactionary romanticism of certain of his prose passages.

As to Pushkin, nobody can prevent our nationalists from closing their eyes to the Byronism of his youth and the great universalism of his maturity, and from regarding, instead, his poem "To the Slanderers of Russia" [which fiercely denounced the West for its sympathy towards the Polish uprising of 1830] as his supreme achievement. Gogol's great Russian satire, the last judgment on Russia before Sevastopol [Crimean War], is abandoned in favor of the superficial and abstract sermons of that author's *Correspondence*. The nationalists prefer certain general passages of Goncharov about nihilism to his Oblomov, an essential type of Russian impotence, masterfully represented and denounced. As regards the European liberal Turgenev, and Saltykov, the nationalists ignore them and declare their work devoid of all interest. They discover in Dostoevsky a former nihilist who never fully repented and who compensated for his Western-inspired universal Christian ideas only by his close ties with certain Slavophil periodicals. Finally, while bowing to Tolstoy's popularity, they simultaneously praise the artistic value of his novels and obscure the humanitarian principles which inspired them (they come partly from Rousseau) and which smothered all incipient nationalism.

All these uninspired evasions have been used by our nationalists to deny the tremendous influence of the West in the formation of a Russian universalist awareness. However, suppose we admit that the only important truths in the life and work of the Russian people are those of exclusively national origin, and that all the elements borrowed from foreign nations are empty and insignificant. How then should we judge the doctrine of these "independent" nationalists when it becomes clear that our "Russian" principles are borrowed entirely and directly from foreign pamphlets? In that case, their point of view becomes untenable even for themselves. For us, it is inadmissible because it is false and immoral; and for them, it must be rejected because it is alien, non-Russian, and slavishly borrowed from foreign sources. This latter fact can be unequivocally demonstrated.

PETER'S REFORMS

[From an essay written in 1888]

The period of reforms, closely linked with the name of Peter the Great, represents for us the core of Russian history. I speak not of Peter's personality but rather of his work. If his work is condemned, Russian history loses its meaning. For how could one justifiably assert that one man alone turned Russia forever from the right path? But if we defend Peter's work, then we defend the meaning of Russian history and the true significance of the Russian state. For that reason we consider this defense important and useful.

In its general orientation and its profound meaning, Peter's reform was nothing entirely new for the Russian people. He again took up the tradition of Kievan Russia which had been interrupted by the Tartar invasion and the tortuous labor of national unification. Whatever Peter's personal character was, his historical work turned Russia once again to the Christian path in which St. Vladimir had formerly led her. By rejecting national idolatry and accepting a universal faith according to which there is "neither Greek nor Jew," Russia renounced pagan isolation and acknowledged herself as part of all mankind. She thereby became conscious of her true interests, and she began to broaden herself by acquiring a universal view.

The principal sins of Muscovite Russia were essentially involuntary, provoked by the course of external events. Forced to withdraw into the northeastern corner of Europe and to use all their strength there in the difficult labor of national unification, the Russian people found themselves, from the thirteenth century on, physically separated from the rest of the Christian world. This situation contributed greatly to the spiritual isolation of the Russians and to the development of their national egoism and pride. The lively relations between Kievan Russia and the other Christian nations obliged our people to consider themselves a part of European mankind and to maintain a certain feeling of universal solidarity. Moscow, however, did not have this beneficial opportunity, but had to accommodate herself to humiliating relations with the Tartar horde. The influence of the latter was doubly unfortunate. Subordination to an inferior race and the permanent contacts with it exercised an assimilative influence upon the Russians, who were then completely cut off from Europe. And the cultural and spiritual level of the Russian people sank. But in spite of their degradation, the Russians felt the privilege of being a historical and Christian nation, and from their contacts with the Mongols developed a permanent sense of national pride as Muscovites. The Russian people were like a man who has contact only with inferior people and thereby gains an exaggerated opinion of himself.

The Muscovite national pride grew especially after 1450, when Russian victory over the Tartars increased the feeling of inner superiority over the infidels by revealing the external strength of the Russian state. At the same time the Turks conquered Constantinople, and wandering Greek monks, in repayment of Moscow gold, endowed Moscow with the title of the Third Rome, with pretensions to a unique role in the Christian world. Through these circumstances our national *amour propre* received its theoretical justification.

In the period of Kiev the Greeks were independent and possessed a superior culture. Their influence on the Russians was on the whole beneficial. It imposed the discipline of history on a young people and forced the Russians to recognize the spiritual superiority of another nation. The regrettable excesses of Byzantinism did no great harm because they were balanced by opposite Western influences. In the Muscovite period this situation changed radically. The Greeks no longer represented a great Christian realm or a great civilization. They were now the slaves of the infidels, and they came to Russia as flattering supplicants. Inevitably, therefore, they strengthened the national *amour propre* of the Muscovites. At the same time, Moscow's spiritual isolation made it possible for the Byzantine ideas, in their most excessive and crude form, to penetrate the Russian mind. As the result of these historical conditions—isolation from Europe, Tartar action, one-sided Byzantine influence—the spiritual and temporal structure of the Muscovite state lost its authentically Christian character. Its basis was religious, but the religion consisted totally in an affirmation of Orthodoxy and in ritualistic piety without any moral content.

In the Muscovite state, as earlier in Constantinople, religious and moral principles were not applied to political and social relations. In these fields, instead of the universal ideal of Christianity, purely heathen concepts prevailed. The nation and state were endowed with the absolute values which Christianity had denied them. In Muscovite Russia, still ignorant and isolated from the civilized world, the reaction against Christian universalism was in full force. Our ancestors regarded themselves as the only Christian people and state and scorned all the others as "heathen dogs," thereby abandoning the true character of Christianity. The first victims of this national idolatry were to be the Byzantine Greeks who had helped to introduce that idolatry into Russia. These Greeks had so highly extolled the Muscovite state as the only defender and protector of the true faith and of the divine law that the Muscovites finally asked themselves whether the Greeks, subjected to alien rule, were still capable of preserving the purity of the true faith and the plenitude of piety. The Russians solved this problem by deciding that they were the only Christian kingdom. Thus Christianity lost its universal significance in the mind of Muscovite Russia and became the religious element of the Russian nationality. The Church ceased to be an independent social group and became merged with the state. The Church, now one with the state, made the political mission and the historical destiny of the Russian state its own. The best spiritual forces of the Russian people, represented by the Church, were devoted entirely to the historical task of building and unifying the state.

I do not exaggerate Peter's merit and value. It is personally difficult for me to call him a great man, not because he lacked external greatness but because he lacked humanity. This historical giant resembled the giants of fairy tales. Like them, he represented an elemental and prodigious force in human form, and this force was turned outward. Peter the Great did not clearly recognize the final goal of his activities or the profound destiny of a Christian state in general and Russia in particular. But he intensely felt what was needed for Russia at that moment in her history, and he directed her on the path which could bring her nearer to her final goal. This he did with all his might. What counts is the fact that Peter the Great's work was indispensable, and that he accomplished it with force and power.

The main events of the seventeenth century, particularly the religious schism, had revealed in the Russian people the existence of great and profound forces. At the same time there was manifest a complete absence of ideas. It was clear that no spiritual fruit could fully ripen in such a soil. The cause of this sterility was Russia's separation from the rest of the world and her abandonment of Christian universalism. The situation was remedied by Peter's work. For in spite of appearances, the reform of Peter the Great had a profoundly Christian character. It was based on a moral and religious act of national self-criticism. To make Russia truly fertile, this moral act had to be repeated again and again. Russia could not suddenly be reborn. Peter's reform opened for her only the possibility of a progressive movement and the opportunity to strive for perfection. If receptive to this possibility, Russian society should have perpetuated a feeling of self-awareness in order to become conscious of its vices and weaknesses. And in reality, since Peter the Great, Russia's political and cultural growth has always been connected with a series of such moments of self-recognition, which undoubtedly form the most original part of our literature. Each great period of post-Petrine history has had its own secular prophet who denounced the lies of our social life. The first half of the reign of Catherine is marked by the satirical comedies of von Wisin. The Russia of Alexander I found its accuser in Griboyedov, that of Nikolai I in Gogol, and the fertile period of Alexander II has given us the unique treasure of Saltykov's satires.

These stages of awareness corresponded to the positive accomplishments of Russia as a Christian state. The first step, most important and difficult, was to effect a change of attitude regarding other peoples, the recognition of their equal participation in mankind and their cultural superiority to us. The recognition of universal interdependence has made Russia a truly, not merely nominally, Christian nation. A series of domestic changes corresponded to this changing attitude. These domestic changes have slowly made Russia more Christian too. The "very pious Russia" of old Moscow looked upon man with heathen eyes, considering him an object which could belong wholly to someone else. The Muscovite serfdom was not essentially unlike ancient slavery. The owner who killed a serf ran no real risk and was subjected only to a formal ecclesiastical penance. Thus it became necessary to restore in the Russian conscience the elementary Christian concept of human dignity. Peter the Great accomplished this by declaring that the killing of a serf was equal to any other homicide. And in 1721 he ordered his people "to put an end to the sale of individuals, or at least not to sell them singly as cattle, which is done nowhere, but only as whole families." The horrible punishments and tortures in which Muscovite Russia excelled then began to trouble the legislator and were subjected to certain limitations. The cruel persecutions of schismatics at the end of the Moscow period were stopped by Peter, who declared that "Christ alone reigns over the human conscience."

All these indications of a Christian policy were still very weak, but they were important because they pointed out the right path to Russia. Peter's successors were to follow and broaden that path. The suppression of capital punishment under Elizabeth, the abolition of tortures under Catherine, the liberation of the serfs under Alexander II—these were the essential results of that Christian orientation which Peter the Great, whom many Russian nationalists called the anti-Christ, gave to Russian domestic policy.

It would be superfluous to prove that Russia owes all its present culture and its literary treasures to Peter's reform.

The two greatest names of Russian literature and culture in the nineteenth and eighteenth centuries, those of Pushkin and Lomonosov, which are indissolubly linked with Peter's name, should be sufficient to satisfy any doubters.

The only method which will allow Russia to develop all her positive forces is a growing adoption of the principles of Christian civilization and an ever vigilant critical attitude towards her social realities. By these means alone, Russia will be able to realize her true character and to take an active and independent part in the universal march of history. The value of this method is proved not only by its positive results—all that has been valuable among us has been built on these foundations—but also by the evident insufficiency of the Russian mind whenever it turned away from this Christian orientation and returned, under one form or another, to the heathen character of old Moscow, to the period before Peter the Great.

XII

Russia and the Revolution II
LENIN

By the start of the twentieth century, forces of economic progress were penetrating the Russian Empire. Its formerly stagnant life began to stir with new energies. The old autocratic form of government did not allow sufficient scope for the expanding activity. The middle classes and industrial labor were still numerically very weak, but discontent among them grew fast, stimulated by the closer contact with Europe. The many oppressed non-Russian nationalities of the vast empire demanded their freedom. Methodical reforms could have satisfied the various needs. The obstinate and ill-advised government refused any concessions to public opinion. It apparently believed in its own strength and the loyalty of the masses. But the administrative and economic strain caused by two and a half years of the First World War revealed the government's total incapacity and unpopularity. In March 1917 the government collapsed. The monarchy disappeared, and the new régime immediately abolished the police state and introduced full civil liberties. For the first time, the Russians and the various peoples of their empire tasted freedom. The Russian revolution had succeeded at the very time when Russia was the ally of the Western democracies. The moment of Russia's full integration with the West seemed to have arrived.

But the revolution did not pursue the road to freedom. The chaos created by defeat and economic disintegration was too great; the roots of individual liberty under law were too tenuous in the soil of Russian tradition and in the life of the Russian masses. The liberal forces had no effectual and daring leadership which would have allowed them to establish liberty among the peoples of the Russian Empire on an enduring basis. Meantime, the anti-Western forces found a leader in Nikolai Lenin, who in November 1917 succeeded in overthrowing the short-lived free régime of Russia.

Lenin's real name was Vladimir Ulyanov. Like Trotsky, Stalin, and others of his revolutionary co-workers, Lenin has entered history under his assumed revolutionary name. He came from a family of the lesser nobility. As a student he dedicated himself to the ideal of revolution, which he, like so many Russian young men of the time, conceived as a total and immediate transformation of society into a just and perfect order, barring forever exploitation and strife. For his revolutionary activities he was exiled to Siberia for five years; after this he lived abroad from 1900 to 1917. He remained there, absorbed entirely in Russian problems, and became the leader of the extremist faction of the Russian (Marxist) Social Democratic Party.

That party was founded in 1898 abroad, because at that time all political activity was banned in Russia. In 1903 Lenin split the party. The extremist faction under his leadership won a temporary majority on the party's central committee and was therefore called the majority or Bolshevik faction, as against the Menshevik or minority group. The latter wished to follow the example of the European Social Democrats and to achieve political liberties and a mass following. Lenin, on the contrary, put his trust in the resolute and ruthless action of a small minority of highly disciplined and trained professional revolutionists who would be ready in time of crisis to impose their will upon the people and lead the masses. Lenin interpreted Marxism in the light of Russian conditions and traditions, and he adhered to his brand of Marxism with fanatical devotion, claiming from the start the undisputed leadership of the party and relentlessly attacking in pamphlets and speeches all those who disagreed with him.

The "father" of Russian Marxism, George Plekhanov, opposed the Bolshevik theory and tactics as antidemocratic. In the First World War he strongly supported the democratic Allied cause. Lenin on the other hand attacked both warring camps with equal vehemence. He wished to overthrow all existing governments through an international class war. After the March 1917 revolution, the German military authorities helped Lenin, who was residing in Switzerland, to return to Russia, in the well-founded hope that he might destroy Russia's value as an ally of the democracies. Upon his return to Petrograd, as St. Petersburg was called during the First World War, Lenin immediately assumed the leadership of the extremist forces. With unusual determination, strategic skill, and ruthless realism, Lenin laid the foundations for the first Marxist state, against overwhelming odds of economic chaos and civil war. He emphasized those elements in Marxism which coincided with the Russian revolutionary tradition: the ever-repeated forecast of the doom of Western society, the faith in a utopian future, the acceptance by the masses of forceful leadership from above.

The Russian authoritarian tradition also fitted the dreams of a few Western individuals whom Kropotkin characterized aptly: "Every revolutionist dreams of a dictatorship, whether it be a dictatorship of the proletariat, i.e., of its leaders, as Marx said, or a dictatorship of the revolu-

tionary staff, as the Blanquists maintain. They all dream
about revolution as a possible means of destroying their
enemies in a legal manner, with the help of a revolutionary
tribunal. All of them dream of capturing power, of creating
a strong, all-powerful totalitarian state which treats the
people as subjects and rules them with the help of thousands
of bureaucrats. All the revolutionists dream of a Committee
of Public Safety whose aim is to eliminate everyone who
dares to think differently from those who are at the helm
of the government. Thinking, say many revolutionists, is an
art and a science which is not devised for common people."
The period of the Terror in the French Revolution lasted
a few months. It was not directed by an infallible leader or
a closely knit party. The terror in Lenin's revolution has
become a permanent institution. Lenin combined the wild
dreams of a small and ineffectual Western minority with
the traditions of the Russian masses. In that respect his relation to the West became the very opposite of Russia's encounter with the West as envisaged by Solovev.

Lenin rejected the democratic elements in Marxism
which the Western Social Democrats emphasized. "Classes
are led by parties," Lenin said in 1918, "and parties are led
by individuals who are called leaders. This is the ABC. The
will of a class is sometimes fulfilled by a dictator. What is
necessary is individual rule, the recognition of the dicta-
torial powers of one man. All phrases about equal rights are
nonsense."

In the last article that Dostoevsky wrote, he had advised
the Russians to turn to Asia. There they would find the
strength and the allies to win Russia's fated struggle against
the West. Lenin shared this conviction. He was deeply convinced that the Russian revolution of 1905, which had made
almost no impression on the workers in the West, had decisively influenced the Asian masses. In reality it was not so
much the Russian revolution as Japan's victory over Russia

in the same year which inspired the intelligentsia in Turkey and Persia, in China and India, to follow the Japanese example of modernization and reform. Yet Lenin was right in believing that conditions in Asia, both among the Westernized intelligentsia and among the agrarian masses, resembled those in Russia rather than those in the West. At the Bolshevik conference in January 1912, Lenin greeted the Chinese revolution and declared that it is "from our point of view an event of world importance towards achieving the liberation of Asia and the overthrow of European mastery."

In 1913, on the thirtieth anniversary of Marx's death, Lenin wrote an article "The Historical Fate of the Teaching of Karl Marx." In it he pointed to the fact that after the Paris Commune of 1871, European socialism entered a period of peaceful development. For this "decay" Lenin held the treacherous character of Western Socialist leadership responsible. To counter the "decay," Lenin set his hope on the Asian revolutionary movements which started in 1905 and which he vainly expected to rekindle the revolutionary fire among the Western workers. Ten years later, in one of his last utterances, Lenin lined up Russia and Asia for the impending victory over the West: "The outcome of the struggle for the control of the world depends on the fact that Russia, India, China, and so on, contain the vast majority of the world's population. This majority has progressed more rapidly every year on the road to freedom, and in this sense there can be no shadow of a doubt as to the final outcome of the world struggle."

Lenin was an internationalist, but he viewed the world with Russian eyes. He regarded the Western socialists as traitors to Marxism, and Moscow's Third International as the sole guardian of true Marxism. Similarly, Orthodox Russia regarded Western Christians as heretics, and Moscow as a Third Rome and the center of world salvation.

Lenin thought the Western proletariat incapable of real revolutionary action. The case was different in Russia. "In Russia gigantic historical events are taking place," Lenin wrote in January 1905. "The proletariat has risen against Tsarism. The proletariat of the entire world now looks with feverish expectation upon the Russian proletariat. The fall of Tsardom in Russia, heroically begun by our working class, will be a turning point in the history of all countries. The example of the proletarian heroes of Petersburg stands before all eyes."

With similar pride Lenin addressed the Third Congress of Workers' Cooperatives on October 27, 1918: "Formerly, the Western nations regarded us and our whole revolutionary movement as a curiosity. They used to say, 'Let these people amuse themselves, we shall see what will come of it. What funny people these Russians are!' Well, these funny Russians have shown the world what their amusement means. Everyone can see that this is only the beginning of a great world-wide revolution. We, the backward, funny Russian people, started this great revolution. History moves in strange ways: it has fallen to a backward country to have the honor of leading the van of a great world movement."

Lenin's expectation of the proletarian revolution in Europe and America was not realized. Western society and civilization proved stronger than Tyuchev and Lenin had foreseen. Even after the temporary sufferings brought about by great wars, the workers of the West, especially those in the most developed capitalistic countries, remained faithful to Western ideals. In Britain and the United States, social, economic, and political conditions improved rapidly and steadily. The Leninist revolution succeeded only in countries of non-Western governmental tradition and precapitalistic social conditions.

In Russia, Lenin's revolution cut off the struggle for liberty under law which had been the glory of Russia's great age from December 1825 to March 1917. The Leninist revolution immensely increased the pace of industrialization and popular education which had begun under the last tsars, but equally it intensified the efficiency and ruthlessness of the authoritarian police state as it had existed under the early tsars. Above all, Lenin's revolution separated Russia from the West, reducing her to the isolation she had known before her great age dawned, and turned her towards Asia.

ON MARXIST ORTHODOXY

[From "Our Program," 1899]

INTERNATIONAL democracy is going through a period of theoretical vacillations. Up to the present the doctrines of Marx and Engels have been regarded as a firm foundation of revolutionary theory, but nowadays voices are raised everywhere declaring these doctrines to be inadequate and antiquated. Anyone who calls himself a Social Democrat and has the intention to publish a Social Democratic organ must take up a definite attitude regarding this question, which by no means concerns German Social Democrats alone.

We base our faith entirely on Marx's theory; it was the first to transform socialism from a utopia into a science, to give this science a firm foundation, and to indicate the path which must be taken to develop this science further and to elaborate it in all its details. This theory discovered the nature of present-day capitalist economy and explained the way in which the purchase of labor power, the enslavement of the millions who possess no property, by a handful of capitalists—by the owners of the land, of the factories, of the mines—is concealed. . . . It has taught us to see through the disguise of ossified habits, political intrigues, intricate laws, and cunning theories to the class struggle—the struggle between the various species of the possessing classes and the mass without property, the proletariat, which leads all those who possess nothing. It has made clear the real task of a revolutionary socialist; and this is not to set up projects for the transformation of society, not to preach sermons to the capitalists and their admirers about improving the position of the workers, not to instigate conspiracies, but to organize the class struggle of the proletariat and to carry on this struggle, whose final aim is the seizure of political power by the proletariat and the organization of a socialist society.

We now ask: What new elements have the touting "renovators" introduced into this theory—they who have attracted so much notice in our day and have grouped themselves round the German socialist Bernstein? Nothing, nothing at all. They have not advanced by a single step the science which Marx and Engels adjured us to develop; they have not taught the proletariat any new methods of fighting. They are only marching backwards; for they adopt the fragments of antiquated theories, and they preach to the proletariat not the theory of struggle but the theory of submissiveness, submissiveness to the bitterest enemies of the proletariat, to the governments and bourgeois parties who never tire of finding new methods of persecuting socialists. . . .

We know that on account of these words we shall be drenched with a flood of accusations; it will be shouted that we want to turn the Socialist party into a holy order of the "orthodox," who persecute the "heretics" for their aberrations from the "true dogma," for any independent opinion. We know all these nonsensical phrases which have become the fashion nowadays. Yes, but there is no shadow of truth in them, not one iota of sense. There can be no strong socialist party without a revolutionary theory which unites all socialists, from which the socialists draw their whole conviction, and which they apply in their methods of fighting and working. To defend a theory of this kind, the validity of which one completely upholds, against unfounded attacks and against attempts to debase it, does not mean that one is an enemy of criticism in general. We by no means regard the theory of Marx as perfect and inviolable; on the contrary, we are convinced that this theory has only laid the foundation stone of that science on which the socialists must continue to build in every direction, unless they wish to be left behind by life. We believe that it is particularly necessary for Russian socialists to work out the Marxist theory independently, for this theory gives only general precepts, the details of which must be applied in England rather than in France, in France rather than in Germany, and in Germany rather than in Russia. For this reason we will willingly devote space in our paper to articles about theoretical questions, and we call upon all comrades openly to discuss the matters in dispute.

What are the main questions which arise in applying the common program of all Social Democrats to Russia?

We have already said that the essence of this program consists in the organization of the class struggle of the proletariat and in the conduct of this struggle, and the final aim is the seizure of political power by the proletariat and the construction of a socialist society. The class struggle of the proletariat is divided into the economic fight (the fight against individual capitalists, or against individual groups of capitalists for the improvement of the workers' position) and the political fight (the fight against the government for the extension of the rights of the people, i.e., for democracy, and for the expansion of the political power of the proletariat). Some Russian Social Democrats regard the economic fight as incomparably more important and almost go so far as to postpone the political fight to a more or less distant future. This standpoint is quite wrong. All Social Democrats are unanimous in believing that it is necessary to help the workers in their daily fight against the employers, to direct attention to all kinds and all cases of chicanery, and in this way to make clear to the workers the necessity of unity. To neglect the political for the economic fight would, however, mean a digression from the most important principle of international Social Democracy; it would mean forgetting what the whole history of the labor movement has taught us. . . .

No economic fight can give the workers a permanent improvement of their situation. It cannot, indeed, be carried out on a large scale unless the workers have the inviolable right to call meetings, to join in unions, to have their own newspapers, and to send their representatives to the National Assembly—as do the workers in Germany and all European countries (with the exception of Turkey and Russia). In order to obtain these rights, however, a political fight must be carried on. In Russia, not only the workers but all the citizens are deprived of political rights. Russia is an absolute monarchy. The Tsar alone promulgates laws, nominates officials and controls them. For this reason, it seems as though the Russian Tsar and his government were dependent on no class and cared for all equally. In reality, however, all the officials are chosen exclusively from the ruling class, and all are subject to the influence of the large capitalists who obtain whatever they want—the ministers dance to the tune the large capitalists play. The Russian worker is bowed under a double yoke. He is robbed and plundered by the capitalists and the landowners, and, lest he should fight against them, he is bound hand and foot by the police, his mouth is gagged. Any attempt to defend the rights of the people is followed by persecution. Any strike against a capitalist brings down the military and the police. Every economic fight turns of necessity into a political fight, and Social Democracy must indissolubly combine the economic with the political fight in a united class struggle of the proletariat. . . .

The Russian working class will see its way to carrying on an economic and political fight alone, even if no other class comes to its aid. The workers are not alone, however, in the political fight. The fact that the people is absolutely without rights, and under the unbridled arbitrary rule of the officials, rouses the indignation of all who have any pretensions to honesty and education, all who cannot reconcile themselves to the persecution of free speech and free thought. It rouses the indignation of the persecuted Poles, Finns, Jews, and Russian sects; it rouses the indignation of small traders, of the industrialists, of the peasants, of all who can nowhere find protection against the chicanery of the officials and the police. None of these segments of the population is capable of carrying on an adamant political fight alone. If, however, the working class raises the banner, it will be supported on all sides. Russian Social Democracy will place itself at the forefront of all battles for the rights of the people, at the head of all fights for a democracy, and then it will be invincible.

UPRISING AS AN ART

[*From* On the Eve of October, *1917*]

Among the most vicious and perhaps most widespread distortions of Marxist practices by the prevailing Socialist parties is the opportunist lie which says that preparation for an uprising and the treatment of rebellion as an art constitute Blanquism.

Bernstein, the leader of opportunism, has long since

gained sad notoriety by accusing Marxism of Blanquism, and our present opportunists, by shouting against Blanquism, do not really improve or enrich the meager ideas of Bernstein.

To accuse Marxists of Blanquism for treating uprising as an art! Can there be a more flagrant distortion of the truth, when there is not a single Marxist who denies that it was Marx who expressed himself in the most definite, precise, and categorical manner on this score; that it was Marx who called uprising an art, who said that uprising must be treated as an art, that one must gain the first success and then proceed from success to success without stopping the offensive against the enemy, making use of his confusion, etc. . . .

We have before us all the objective prerequisites for a successful uprising. We have the advantages of a situation in which only our victory in an uprising will put an end to the most painful thing on earth, the vacillations that have sickened the people; a situation in which only our victory will put an end to the game of a separate peace [with the Germans] against the revolution by openly offering a more complete, more just, more immediate peace in favor of the revolution.

Only our party, having won a victory in an uprising, can save Petrograd, for if our offer of peace is rejected, and we do not even obtain a truce, then we shall become "defensists"; we shall place ourselves at the head of the war parties, we shall be the most "warring" party, and we shall carry on a war in a truly revolutionary manner. We shall take away from the capitalists all the bread and all the shoes. We shall leave them crumbs. We shall outfit them in bast shoes. We shall send all the bread and all the shoes to the front.

And then we shall save Petrograd.

The resources, both material and spiritual, of a truly revolutionary war are still immense in Russia; there are ninety-nine chances in a hundred that the Germans will at least grant us a truce. And to secure a truce at present means to conquer the whole world.

Having recognized the absolute necessity of an uprising of the workers of Petrograd and Moscow for the sake of saving the revolution and of saving Russia from being partitioned among the imperialists of both coalitions, we must first adapt our political tactics at the conference to the conditions of the maturing uprising. Then, we must prove that we accept, and not only in words, the idea of Marx about the necessity of treating uprising as an art.

At the conference, we must immediately consolidate the Bolshevik faction without worrying about numbers, without being afraid of leaving the vacillators in the camp of the vacillating: they are more useful to the cause of the revolution there than in the stronghold of the resolute and courageous fighters.

We must compose a brief declaration in the name of the Bolsheviks in which we sharply emphasize the futility of long speeches, the irrelevance of speeches generally, the necessity of quick action to save the revolution, the absolute necessity of breaking completely with the bourgeoisie and of completely severing relations with the Anglo-French imperialists who are preparing a partition of Russia, and the urgency for the immediate passage of all power into the hands of revolutionary democracy headed by the revolutionary proletariat.

Our declaration must be the briefest and sharpest formulation of this conclusion; it must relate to the points in the program of peace for the people, land for the peasants, confiscation of scandalous profits, and a halt to the shameful damage to production done by the capitalists. . . .

Here is the other point. In offering an immediate peace without annexations, in breaking at once with the Allied imperialists and with all imperialists, either we obtain an immediate truce or the entire revolutionary proletariat will join the forces of defense, and a truly revolutionary war will then be waged by revolutionary democracy under the leadership of the proletariat.

Having made this declaration, we must appeal for decisions and not talk; we must take actions and not write resolutions; we must push all our forces into the factories and barracks. The place of the Bolsheviks is there; the pulse of life is there; the source of saving the revolution is there; the moving force of the Democratic Conference is there.

In heated, impassioned speeches we must make our program clear, and we must put the question this way: either the conference accepts it fully, or an uprising follows. There is no middle course. Delay is impossible. Otherwise the revolution will perish.

Having put the question this way, having concentrated our entire forces in the factories and barracks, we shall correctly estimate the best moment to begin the uprising.

And in order to treat uprising in a Marxist way, i.e., as an art, we must at the same time, without losing a single moment, organize the staff of the insurrectionary detachments; detail the forces; move the loyal regiments to the most important points; surround the Alexander theater; occupy the Peter and Paul Fortress; arrest the general staff and the government; move against the military cadets (such detachments will die rather than allow the enemy to move to the center of the city). We must mobilize the armed workers, call them to a last desperate battle, occupy the telegraph and telephone stations immediately, place our staff at the central telephone station, connect it by wire with all the factories, the regiments, the areas of armed fighting, etc.

Of course, all this amply illustrates the idea that at the present moment it is impossible to remain loyal to the revolution without treating uprising as an art.

RUSSIA AND ASIA

*[From "The Historical Fate of the Teaching
of Karl Marx," 1913]*

The second period in the history of socialism (1872–1904) differs from the preceding one in its "peaceful" character, in the absence of revolutions. The West has finished with bourgeois revolutions. The East has not yet grown up to them.

The West enters the field of peaceful preparation for the period of future changes. Everywhere proletarian parties, socialist in essence, are formed which learn how to use bourgeois parliamentarianism, how to create their daily press, their educational institutions, and their cooperatives. The teaching of Marx wins a complete victory and spreads. Slowly and undeviatingly the process of selection and gathering of the proletarian forces goes forward—the preparation for coming battles.

The dialectic of history is such that the theoretical victory of Marxism compels its enemies to reclothe themselves as Marxists. Internally decaying liberalism tries to revive itself in the form of socialist opportunists. The period of preparation of forces for great battles is interpreted by them as a turning away from these battles. In the struggle against wage slavery they explain improvement of conditions as a surrender by the slaves, for a penny, of their rights to freedom. In cowardly fashion they preach social peace (that is, peace with the slave owners) and renunciation of the class struggle. They have many supporters among socialist parliamentarians, various officials of the labor movement, and the "sympathetic" intelligentsia.

Hardly had the opportunists succeeded in boasting of social peace and the fact that revolutionary storms were no longer inevitable under "democracy," than a new source of great world storms was discovered in Asia. The Turkish,

Persian, and Chinese revolutions followed on the Russian revolution of 1905. We are now living right in the midst of the epoch of these storms and their reflex action on Europe. Whatever may be the fate of the great Chinese revolution, against which various civilized hyenas are now sharpening their teeth, no forces in the world will restore the old serfdom in Asia or eradicate from the earth the heroic democracy of the popular masses in the Asiatic and semi-Asiatic countries.

The long postponement of the decisive struggle against capitalism in Europe has driven a few people, who are inattentive to the conditions for preparing and developing the mass struggle, to despair and anarchy. We now see how short-sighted and poor-spirited was this anarchist despair. . . .

The Asiatic revolutions have shown us the lack of character and the cowardice of liberalism. Anyone who talks about non-class politics or non-class socialism after the experience of Europe and Asia should simply be put in a cage and exhibited along with some Australian kangaroo.

After Asia, though not in an Asiatic manner, Europe also has begun to stir. The peaceful period 1872–1904 has gone forever. The high cost of living and the yoke of the trusts are causing an unheard-of sharpening of the economic struggle—which is shaking the liberalism of even the most corrupted sections of the English workers. A political crisis is ripening before our eyes even in the most die-hard bourgeois-junker country, in Germany. Furious piling up of armaments and the policy of imperialism are creating in contemporary Europe a kind of social peace which most nearly resembles a powder barrel. Meanwhile, the decay of all the bourgeois parties and the maturing of the proletariat go unswervingly forward.

XIII

Communism and Russian History
BERDYAYEV and FEDOTOV

With Lenin's victory over the weak Russian democratic and Westernizing trends, Russian thought and creative art were forced into a strait jacket of orthodoxy to a degree unknown even in the time of Nikolai I. The lively debate which had filled Russia's great age was silenced under Communist rule. Only among the Russian scholars and thinkers in exile could the debate continue. The old problems were now viewed in the perspective of the Communist revolution. To what extent was the revolution an outcome of Russian history? How did it continue the old struggle between Westernizers and Slavophils? Among the answers given to these questions, those by Nikolai Berdyaev and Georgii Fedotov shed much light on the formation of the modern Russian mind, on Russia's past and future. Of these two men, both philosophers and theologians, Berdyaev occupied a position closer to the Slavophil tradition, whereas Fedotov was one of the most profound representatives of the Westernizing trend.

Berdyaev belonged to the brilliant young generation of Russian thinkers and poets of the beginning of the century, who, partly under the influence of Vladimir Solovev, fully participated in European intellectual and artistic life. Symbolist and "decadent" poetry pushed the utilitarian views of literature propagated by the nihilists of the sixties into the background; Sergei Diaghilev started in 1897 the famous art review *Mir Iskusstva* (*The World of Art*), one of the most beautiful in Europe, and Konstantin Stanislavsky founded the Moscow Art Theatre. Moscow merchants acquired perhaps the most outstanding pre-1914 collection of modern French painting, from the Impressionists to Picasso. Diaghilev in 1908 brought the Imperial Ballet and Russian opera to Europe and revolutionized European choreographic art and stage setting. "Never before," Vladimir Weidlé writes, "had cultured Russia such a sense of being naturally European, of being a nation with a natural place among the nations of Europe. Differences were recognized but no longer regarded as irreconcilable. The contrasts between Russia and the West were admitted, but stress was laid on natural affinities, on the features that were either harmonious or complementary." Out of a closer acquaintance with the West a new and better understanding of Russia's past was gained.

In his youth Berdyayev was influenced by Marx and by Nietzsche. The failure of the Russian revolution of 1905 caused him and some of his friends to reconsider their position. As a result of their disillusionment they published in 1909 a collection of essays under the title *Vyekhy* (*Landmarks*). In it the authors professed a religious nationalism which was akin to the Slavophil position. Yet Berdyayev always emphasized the need for spiritual freedom, and this made the simple submission to church tradition impossible. "Mankind has known Hamlet and Faust, Nietzsche and Dostoevsky, has experienced humanism, romanticism, the revolutionary spirit, and the signs of modern times, and these experiences cannot be obliterated."

In 1922, at the age of forty-eight, Berdyayev left Russia

and settled in Paris, where he published a number of important works, *Freedom and the Spirit, The Meaning of History,* and *The Russian Idea,* which developed his thoughts about Russia and the West. In 1937 he wrote a book on *The Origin of Russian Communism,* showing the roots of Lenin and Leninism in the Russian tradition.

The outlook of Fedotov was different. He too left Russia after the Communist revolution to settle in Paris, where he taught Orthodox theology. During the Second World War he came to the United States, and there he published *The Russian Religious Mind* and *A Treasury of Russian Spirituality,* two important works for a better knowledge of the religious depth of Russian Christianity. Deeply steeped in the spiritual traditions of his native land, he had at the same time the fullest understanding of the Western concept of liberty and of the need for integrating Russia into the Western world. In the time of Stalin, Fedotov asked the same fundamental question which Chaadayev has asked in the reign of Nikolai I: what was Russia's place in the history of the development of the human mind. Their answers were essentially similar, though Fedotov's came from an incomparably deeper knowledge of Russian history, which had benefited from the very great advance of Russian scholarship in the intervening one hundred and twenty years. Chaadayev and Fedotov, in spite of differences of background and period, were at one in their love for individual freedom and human dignity.

At the end of the Second World War, when under Stalin's leadership Soviet Russia turned to an extreme anti-Western Slavophilism, Fedotov wrote an article "Russia and Freedom," resuming the great struggle for full Russian participation in the intellectual life and political thought of the West. "Russia and Freedom" not only illuminates the millenary course of Russian history, it also carries forward, into the unknown future, the legacy of Russia's great age of ever richer intercourse with Europe.

THE ROOTS OF RUSSIAN COMMUNISM

[*From Berdyayev's* The Origin of Russian Communism, *1937*]

GENERALLY speaking, Russians only understood poorly the meaning of the relative, the fact that historical progress advances by stages, the differentiation of various cultural spheres. Russian extremism is due to this. The Russian spirit craves for wholeness. It yearns for the Absolute and desires to subordinate everything to the Absolute, and this is a religious trait. But it easily leads to confusion, takes the relative for the Absolute, the partial for the universal, and then it falls into idolatry. It is characteristic of the Russian mind to switch over the current of religious energy to non-religious objects, to the relative and partial sphere of science or social life. . . .

In the seventies a notable exponent of the theory of revolution was Peter Nikolaevich Tkachev. He more than anyone should be regarded as Lenin's forerunner. He edited a revolutionary paper abroad, *Nabat* (*The Tocsin*), which expressed the most extreme views. He was the first during the seventies to tell the Russians about Marx. In 1875 he wrote a letter to Engels about Russia's own particular line of development and about the special character of the coming Russian revolution. . . . He had no desire to allow Russia to be transformed into a constitutional and bourgeois state. He considered the absence of a developed bourgeoisie as Russia's greatest advantage facilitating the social revolution. The Russians were socialists by instinct. Tkachev was not a democrat; he affirmed the

authority of the minority over the majority. . . . His
fundamental idea was the seizure of power by a revolutionary minority. This required the disorganization of the
existing authority by terrorism. The masses in Tkachev's
opinion are always ready for revolution, because they are
only the material which a revolutionary minority uses. . . .
Tkachev was one of the few Russian revolutionaries of the
past, almost the only one, who thought in terms of authority, of capturing and organizing it. His desire was that
the revolutionary socialist party should become a government. And in this respect he resembles Lenin.

Georgy Valentinovich Plekhanov, the founder of Russian Marxism and Social Democracy, was already writing
decisively and sharply against Tkachev in the eighties. This
controversy is of great interest because it sounds as though
Plekhanov was arguing against Lenin and the Bolsheviks
before they even existed. Plekhanov rebelled especially
against the idea of a seizure of power by the revolutionary
socialist party. He considered such a seizure would be the
greatest misfortune and pregnant with future reaction.
. . . But Tkachev was right in his opposition to Engels,
and his rightness was the historical rightness of the Bolsheviks against the Mensheviks, of Lenin against Plekhanov.
In Russia it was not a communist revolution which turned
out to be utopian, but a liberal bourgeois revolution. . . .
The greatest paradox in Russian life and the Russian revolution lies in this, that liberal ideas, ideas of rights as well
as of social reform, appeared in Russia to be utopian.
Bolshevism showed itself to be much more faithful to certain primordial Russian traditions, to the Russian search
for universal social justice, understood in an extremist
sense, and to the Russian method of government and control by coercion. This was predetermined by the whole
course of Russian history, but also by the feebleness of
creative spiritual power among us. Communism was the

inevitable fate of Russia, the inward moment in the destiny of the Russian people.

Lenin was made of one piece; he was a monolith. In him characteristics of the Russian sectarian intelligentsia existed side by side with characteristics of the Russians who had made and shaped the Russian state. He united in himself traits of Chernyshevsky, Nechaev, Tkachev, with traits of the Grand Princes of Moscow, of Peter the Great and the Russian rulers of the despotic type. In this lies his originality. He was both an out and out revolutionary and a statesman. . . . Lenin was not a theoretician of Marxism like Plekhanov, but a theoretician of revolution; everything he wrote was but a treatment of the theory and praxis of revolution. . . . Hence his narrowness of outlook, his concentration upon one thing, the poverty and asceticism of his thought, the elementary nature of the slogans addressed to the will. Lenin's type of culture was not very high, every refinement of thought and of the life of the spirit repelled him. He read a great deal and studied much, but for a definite purpose, for conflict and action and for controversial purposes, in order to settle accounts with heresies and deviations. . . . He fought for wholeness and consistency in the conflict, which was impossible without an integrated dogmatic outlook, without a dogmatic confession of faith, without orthodoxy. He permitted any method in the fight to achieve revolution. Lenin's revolutionary principles had a moral source; he could not endure injustice, oppression and exploitation, but he became so obsessed with the maximalist revolutionary idea, that in the end he lost the immediate sense of the difference between good and evil; he lost the direct relationship to living people; he permitted fraud, deceit, violence, cruelty. He was not a vicious man, he was not even particularly ambitious or a great lover of power, but the sole obsession of a single idea led to a dreadful narrowing of thought and to a moral transformation which permitted entirely immoral methods in carrying on the conflict.

Lenin combined in himself two traditions: the tradition of the Russian revolutionary intelligentsia in its most maximalist tendency, and the tradition of the Russian government in its most despotic aspect. The Social Democrat Mensheviks and the Socialist Revolutionaries remained in the stream of the first tradition only, and that in a mitigated form. But combining in himself traditions which in the nineteenth century had been in mortal conflict, Lenin was able to fashion a scheme for the organization of a communist state and to realize it. However paradoxical it may sound, Bolshevism is the third appearance of Russian autocratic imperialism, first presented by the Muscovite Tsardom and then by the Petrine Empire. Bolshevism stands for a strong centralized state. It achieved a union of the will to social justice and the will to political power, and the second will was the stronger of the two. Bolshevism entered into Russian life as a power militarized in the highest degree, but the old Russian state also had always been militarized. . . .

Bolshevism made use of everything for its own triumph. . . . It made use of the Russian traditions of government by imposition, and instead of an unfamiliar democracy of which they had had no experience proclaimed a dictatorship which was more like the old rule of the Tsar. It made use of the characteristics of the Russian mind in all its incompatibility with the secularized bourgeois society. It made use of its religious instinct, its dogmatism and maximalism, its search after social justice and the kingdom of God upon earth, its capacity for sacrifice and the patient bearing of suffering, and also of its manifestations of coarseness and cruelty. It made use of Russian messianism and faith in Russia's own path of development. It made use of the historic cleavage between the masses and the cultured

classes, of the popular mistrust of the latter, and it easily
destroyed those of the intelligentsia who did not submit.
It absorbed also the sectarian spirit of the Russian intelligentsia. It fitted in with the absence among the Russian people of the Roman view of property and the
bourgeois virtues; it made use of the breakdown of patriarchal life among the people and the dissolution of the old
religious beliefs. It also set about spreading the new revolution by methods of violence from above, as Peter had
done in his time; it denied human freedom, which had
been unknown to the masses before, and had been the
privilege of the upper cultured classes. It proclaimed the
necessity of the integral totalitarian outlook of a dominant
creed, which corresponded with the habits of the Russian
people. The Russian mind is not prone to scepticism, and a
sceptical liberalism suits it less than anything. The mind
of the people could easily pass from one orthodoxy to another orthodoxy which embraced the whole of life. Russia
passed from the old Middle Ages to a new Middle Ages,
avoiding the ways of modern history with its seculariza-
tion, its autonomy of various cultural activities, its liberalism and individualism, its triumph of the bourgeoisie and
of capitalism.

The old consecrated Russian empire fell and a new one
was formed, also a consecrated empire, an inverted
theocracy. Marxism, itself so un-Russian in origin and
character, assumed a Russian style approaching Slavophilism. Even the old Slavophil dream of transferring the
capital from St. Petersburg to Moscow, to the Kremlin, was
realized, and Russian communism proclaimed anew the
old idea of the Slavophils and Dostoevsky—*ex Oriente
lux*. Light shines from Moscow, from the Kremlin, to
lighten the bourgeois darkness of the West. Marxism in its
Russian form proclaims the dominance of politics over
economics, the power of the government to change the life

of the country in any way it likes. In its grandiose schemes which were always on a world-wide scale, communism makes use of the Russian disposition for making plans and castle-building which had hitherto no scope for practical application. Lenin desired to overcome Russian sloth, the product of the life of the gentry and of serfdom, to conquer Oblomov and Rudin, the "superfluous people," and in this positive task it seems he was successful. . . .

The Soviet communist realm has in its spiritual structure a great likeness to the Muscovite Orthodox Tsardom. The same feeling of suffocation is in it. The nineteenth century in Russia was not an integrated whole; it showed divisions; it was the century of free enquiry and revolution. The revolution created a totalitarian realm in which the free spirit was stifled and free enquiry disappeared. In it the experiment is being made of subjecting the whole people to a political catechism. Russian *étatism* always had Russian anarchism as its obverse. The Communist revolution in its day made use of anarchist instincts, but it arrived at an extreme *étatism* which suppresses every manifestation of those instincts.

The Russian people have not realized their messianic idea of Moscow the Third Rome. The ecclesiastical schism of the seventeenth century revealed that the Muscovite Tsardom was not the Third Rome; still less, of course, was the Petersburg empire. In it a final cleavage took place. The messianic idea of the Russian people assumed either an apocalyptic form or a revolutionary; and then there occurred an amazing event in the destiny of the Russian people. Instead of the Third Rome in Russia, the Third International was achieved, and many of the features of the Third Rome were transferred to the Third International. The fact that the Third International is not international but a Russian national idea is very poorly understood in the West. Here we have the transformation of

Russian messianism. Western communists, when they join the Third International, do not understand that in joining the Third International they are joining the Russian people and help to realize its messianic vocation. . . . Something has happened which Marx and the Western Marxists could not have foreseen, and that is an identification of the two messianisms, the messianism of the Russian people and the messianism of the proletariat. The Russian working class and peasantry are a proletariat; and the proletariat of the whole world from France to China is becoming the Russian people—a unique people in the world; and the messianic consciousness of the working class and proletariat is bringing about an almost Slavophil attitude towards the West. The West is always identified with the bourgeoisie and capitalism.

RUSSIA AND FREEDOM

[From Fedotov's article, 1945]

The harassing problem of our days is that of freedom in Russia. It is not the problem of whether or not freedom exists in the USSR. No one, except ignorant tourists can entertain any doubt on this score. What preoccupies all of us is the feasibility of the resurrection of democracy in victorious Russia. Only reactionary hoodlums can feel happy in a Moscow reviving the spirit of Ivan the Terrible. Apologists for the Moscow dictatorship, yesterday's Socialists and liberals, lull their conscience by a belief in Russia's early liberation. The anticipated evolution of the Soviet regime impels them to accept light-heartedly, or even triumphantly, the enslavement by the Soviet Government of more and more European and Asiatic nations. The prospect of life in the freest and happiest community in the world of the future makes for them a few years of oppression well worth their while.

Yet Russia's past does not seem to warrant much optimism. For centuries Russia was the most despotic monarchy
in Europe. Her rather frail constitutional regime lasted
only eleven years; her democracy, which was an enuncia-
tion of principles rather than their materialization, lived
seven months. [From March to November, 1917.] Having
just rid themselves of the Tsar, the people, though against
their will and after some struggle, submitted to a new
tyranny, compared with which Tsarist Russia seems the
incarnation of liberty. This is why some . . . believe that
despotism . . . is rooted in the Russian national spirit or
geopolitical destiny, and that despotism is the best form
for the fulfillment of Russia's historic mission.

Are we to choose between the two extremes: between
the firm belief and firm disbelief in Russian liberty? This
writer belongs among those who crave for a free and peaceful completion of the Russian revolution. But bitter experience has taught him to keep desire and reality apart.
Rejecting the doctrine of historical determinism, he believes that every nation has a choice among various ways of
development. Yet this freedom of choice is limited by a
nation's past, by the painful or beneficial weight of tradition. After a revolutionary flight into the unknown, Russia
is now reverting to her historical track and her future depends on her past more than seemed likely yesterday. Without indulging in prophecy, one may attempt to discern the
hazy outlines of the future in the dim mirror of history.

There are at present few historians who believe in the
existence of general laws of the development of nations.
With the broadening of our cultural horizon, the idea of
variety of cultural types has become prevalent. Only one
of them, the Christian, Western-European type has produced liberty in the contemporary, political meaning of

the word, the kind of liberty that is not threatened with extinction. As far as Russia is concerned, the problem of her freedom coincides with the question whether she belongs to the nations of Western culture, since the notions of freedom and of Western culture are inseparable. If Russia does not belong to the West, is she an Eastern nation? Or is she a separate entity, unlike both East and West? And if she belongs to the East: what kind of East is it? Let us begin with the last question. By East, as contrasted with West, is usually meant the succession of Near-Eastern cultures which descend in an uninterrupted line from Sumero-Accadian time down to modern Islam. Ancient Greeks fought against that culture in the Persian wars: they were victorious, but retreated spiritually step by step until finally, in the Byzantine epoch, they succumbed to the East. The mediaeval West waged wars with, and learned from, that culture of the East, represented by the Arabs and Turks. Ancient Russia faced it at first in the Iranian, later in Turkish or Tartar outskirts of the East which at the same time influenced and educated her through Byzantium. Contact with this East revealed to Russia the two aspects of its culture: the pagan and the Greek Orthodox. Russia came into being on the periphery of two cultural worlds—the West and the East. Her relations with them were of an intricate nature: fighting on two fronts, against both Romanism and paganism, she was at times anxious to conclude an alliance with one against the other. In asserting her own individuality, Russia herself usually considered it as an Orthodox-Byzantine heritage, rather complex in character. Byzantine Orthodoxy was Orientalized Christianity, but it was Christianity first and foremost, and it included a great deal of Greco-Roman tradition. This religion and this tradition created a bond between Russia and the Christian West even in periods when she denied this kinship.

During the thousand-year history of Russia, her fundamental problem, that of West and East, appeared in four
different aspects. At first, in the Kievan period, Russia
freely accepted the cultural influence of Byzantinism, of
West and East. The time of the "Tartar yoke" was a period
of artificial isolation and painful choice between West
and East (Lithuania and the Tartar Horde). Muscovy represented a state and a society of an essentially Eastern
type; but as early as the seventeenth century it began to
seek contact with the West. Modern history, from Peter
the Great to Lenin, marks a triumph of Western civilization throughout the Russian Empire. This essay proposes
to study but one aspect of this West-East problem, the fate
of freedom in ancient and modern Russia and in the
USSR.

In the Kievan period all the conditions under which
freedom at that time germinated in the West, existed in
Russia, too. Her Church was independent of the state,
while the semi-feudal state, though different in type from
that in the West, was similarly decentralized and lacked
unified sovereignty. Christianity came to Russia from
Byzantium and it would seem that Byzantinism, including
its political features, provided the natural form for the
development of the young Russian nation. But Byzantinism
was a totalitarian culture with a sacred authority of the
state, which kept the Church in a firm grip. Byzantinism
makes the germination of freedom impossible.

Fortunately, Byzantinism could not take root in Kiev
where the social prerequisites for its advance were utterly
lacking. There was neither an Emperor (Tsar) nor a King
(or even Great Prince) who could have claimed power over
the Church. In [Kievan] Russia, too, the Church had her
Tsar, her Anointed one, but this Tsar lived in Constanti-

nople. To eastern Slavs his name was the ideal symbol of the unity of the Orthodox Church—but nothing more. The Metropolitans of Kiev, Greeks by origin and Byzantine subjects, were least of all willing to transfer the high dignity of the Tsars to princes of barbarian nations. There was only one Tsar-Emperor on earth. Hence the Church tenet of the divine institution of state power could not endow the state in Russia either with a sacred or an absolute character. The Church lived separately from, and high above, the state. Therefore the Church could prevail upon the princes to submit to certain ideal rules in private and political life, as for instance loyalty to treaties, the preservation of peace and justice. Saint Theodosius, in the eleventh century, denounced the usurper-prince, and Metropolitan Nicophorus, in the twelfth century, declared to the princes: "We are commissioned by God to keep you from bloodshed."

This freedom of the Russian Church was made possible by the fact that it was not yet a national Church, but considered itself part of the Greek Church. The head of the Russian Church was the Patriarch of Constantinople who was safe from any encroachment on the part of local princes. Even the proud prince Andrew of Vladimir, after his conflict with the Patriarch, had to submit.

Besides, the princes in ancient Russia were not vested with full power. They had to share it with the Boyars [aristocrats], the Drujina [retainers] and the Veche [popular assembly]. They were not masters of their principalities and often left one principality for another. It was under these conditions, that a Christian, Orthodox democracy, unique in its kind, was established in Novgorod. The supremacy of a Popular Assembly does not in itself guarantee true liberty, and under the Veche individual freedom was not safer than under the princes. At its tumultuous meetings it sometimes dealt high-handedly with the citi-

zen's life and property. Yet the division of power—which
in Novgorod went further than anywhere else—among
"lords," the Veche and the Bishop provided a considerable
guarantee for personal freedom. And thus, seen through
the haze of centuries, life in the ancient Russian democracy
seems a haven of liberty.

During those centuries, Russia lived in close contact
with the eastern border of the "Latin world." Poland, Hungary, Bohemia and Germany, though separated by religion,
were often her allies, and their rulers were kinsmen of
Russian princes. The Russians were aware of their Christian and cultural ties with Western neighbors, while the
East appeared to them as a predatory foe. Turkish nomads,
no longer the civilized Iranians, were Russia's neighbors,
and devastated her borderlands; all her political forces
had to be mobilized for defense. The Asiatic East did not
appeal to the Russians either by its culture or by its form
of government. The Church never ceased to preach the
common struggle against the pagans, and these admoni-
tions were heeded more than were warnings of the Greek
hierarchy against the Latins.

Two centuries of the Tartar yoke did not spell the end
of Russia's freedom. It perished after liberation from the
Tartars. Only the Tsar of Moscow, as heir of the (Tartar)
Khans, was able to destroy the social forces which limited
autocracy. For over two centuries northern Russia, plundered and humiliated by the Tartars, kept intact her old
ways and customs and preserved liberty on the local level,
at least in the consciousness of her people. The Novgorod
democracy extended to more than half of Russia. In feudal
principalities the Church and Boyars, if not the Veche,
shared with the Prince, the responsibility for the nation.
The Prince still had to listen to political morals preached

by bishops and saintly monks and to consider the views of his senior Boyars. Political amorality, a result of greedy foreign domination, did not corrupt the whole nation whose culture actually became conspicuous for its loftiness and spiritual freedom, unknown even in Kiev. The fifteenth century was the golden age of Russian art and Russian saints. By their spirit of moral and religious freedom, the didactic anthologies of that time, present a striking contrast to similar works in later Muscovy and Byzantium.

There was one region in mediaeval Russia where Tartar influence was stronger. At first it was a small dot on the map, but by and by it spread until, two centuries later, it covered the whole of Eastern Russia. It was Moscow, the "unifier" of Russia. Rising to supremacy through the pro-Tartar and treacherous policy of its Princes, Moscow was able to safeguard peace and security within its territory, to attract immigrant workers and to become the residence of the Metropolitan. The blessing of the Church, which was now assuming a national character, sanctified the successes of a morally dubious diplomacy. Metropolitans, now often Russians by birth and subjects of Moscow, began to identify their ministry with the interests of Moscow policy. The Church was still superior to the state, it led the state, and in the person of Metropolitan Alexis, the Russian Richelieu, ruled over it.

But national liberation was imminent. To step up its approach, people were willing to sacrifice light-heartedly elemental justice and the very principles of a Christian community inherited from olden times. Territorial seizures and perfidious arrests of competing Princes were carried out with the support of ecclesiastical threats and interdicts. In administration, court procedure and the collection of tribute, the Moscow principality followed the Tartar pattern. From within and not from without, the Tartar spirit took hold of, and shaped, the Russian soul. This spiritual

Mongol conquest ran parallel with the political decline of
the Tartar "Golden Horde." In the fifteenth century,
thousands of baptized and non-baptized Tartars were in
the service of the Moscow Princes. They joined the ranks
of government officials, the future gentry, contaminating
them with Eastern notions and customs of the steppes.

The unification of the feudal principalities was achieved
by Eastern methods, which made it quite unlike the
simultaneous process of liquidation of Western feudalism.
In Russia the upper strata of the population were carried
away to Moscow and were replaced by newcomers. Local
habits and traditions were rooted out with such thorough-
ness that even heroic legends of the past were lost in oblivion. What inhabitant of Tver, Riazan or Novgorod in
the nineteenth century remembered the names of ancient
Princes buried in local cathedrals or heard of their deeds
recorded in the epic history of Karamzin? The names of
ancient Russian countries were quite forgotten save perhaps in derisive nicknames. Little homelands lost that
historic local color which still adorns their like in France,
Germany and England. Russia grew into all-round Muscovy, a monotonous territory under a centralized government—a natural foundation for despotism.

Yet old Russia would not surrender to Muscovy without a struggle. The greater part of the sixteenth century
was filled with tumultuous quarrels and the blood of the
vanquished flowed in streams. The northern hermits and
the Boyars tried to protect spiritual and aristocratic freedom against the Orthodox Khans. . . . The victory of the
new "democratic" group of government officials over the
old nobility amounted to the barbarization of the ruling
class, to its increasing servility and also to a mounting exploitation of the laboring classes. . . .

It is permissible to halt at this turning point of Russian
history and indulge in the daydream of what would have

happened if the "Private Council" led by men like Prince Kurbsky and based upon the "National Assembly" had succeeded in inaugurating an era of constitutional regime in Russia during the rule of Ivan the Terrible. This, however, did not happen. Prince Kurbsky, who, with a handful of Russians, had escaped from Moscow tyranny, redeemed in Lithuania the honor of the Russian name. But the people were not on the side of the reformers; they gave no support to the Boyars and bestowed their affection upon Ivan the Terrible. Their motives are obvious. They are the same motives that always prevail whenever a people supports despotism against liberty—in the time of Augustus as well as in our own days. These motives are social discord and national pride. The people, of course, had plenty of reasons to resent their dependence on the old lords and never suspected that the rule of the new gentry would bring serfdom in its wake (the bulk of the peasantry was free in the Middle Ages). They were fascinated by the sight of Tartar hordes falling one after another at the feet of the Moscow Tsar. Yesterday's tributary of the Tartars, Russia was now transformed into a great Eastern power: In the words of a Russian epic song:

> Our white Tsar is the Tsar of the tsars:
> All the hordes to him are obedient.

Though the Muscovite autocracy possessed a tremendous unity of style, its origins were of a rather complex nature. As a feudal lord, the Moscow prince was "master (*khozyain*) of the Russian land" (even Nikolai II was referred to in this way). But he was also the heir of Tartar Khans and Byzantine Emperors. In Russia, they both, Khans and Emperors, were styled Tsars. This blending of various ideas and forms of government created a despotism, rare if not unique in history. The Emperor of Byzantium was in principle a magistrate voluntarily submitting to his own laws. He prided himself on appearing as ruler of free men, and took pleasure in contrasting his rule with that of a tyrant. The Moscow Tsar wanted to reign over slaves and did not feel himself bound by laws. "I am free to bestow grace on my subjects and I am free to send them to the scaffold," Ivan the Terrible used to say. On the other hand, a true Eastern despot, not bound by the law, was bound by tradition, particularly by religious tradition. Ivan the Terrible and especially Peter the Great showed that their autocracy was little limited by tradition. The Church, which contributed most to the success and rise of Tsardom, was the first to suffer. Metropolitans were actually appointed by the Tsars, who also deposed them without much ado. One of them, perhaps two, were murdered by order of Ivan the Terrible. Even in purely religious matters the will of the Tsar was supreme. When Peter the Great decided to abolish the Patriarchate and to introduce in the Russian Church a Synod of a Protestant type, he could do even this with impunity.

All the classes were tied to the state by personal service or work. Free professions, save brigandry, were unthinkable. In mediaeval Russia there were free merchants and artisans. Now all townsmen were obliged to pay taxes in kind, and, pressed into compulsory organizations, were shifted from one place to another according to state needs. Serfdom spread throughout Russia at the time when it was on the decline in the West; it became ever more oppressive until, at the end of the eighteenth century, it was downright slavery. The historic trend in Russia was the reverse of that in western Europe: it was a development from freedom to servitude. This servitude was the outcome not of the rulers' whim but of a new national objective: the creation of an empire upon a very meagre economic basis. Only through tremendous general strain, iron discipline and gruesome sacrifices, could this beggarly, barbaric, endlessly expanding Empire exist. There is every reason to believe that in the sixteenth and seventeenth centuries the people realized better the needs and the situation of the state than they did in the nineteenth century. Wittingly or unwittingly they made their choice between a mighty state and liberty. Therefore they themselves bear the responsibility for their fate.

In the Tartar school and in the Moscow service a new Russian type was forged, the Muscovite type, the most sturdy and stable among the manifold variety of Russian characters. The striking features of this type, particularly as compared with the Russian of the nineteenth century, are his sturdiness, endurance and resistance power. The Muscovite created his tremendous empire without resounding military feats, even without military élan—the Kievan admiration of warlike prowess became extinct in Moscow—merely by superhuman endurance and discipline, by sweat rather than by blood. This passive heroism and inexhaustible readiness to sacrifice have always been the forte of the Russian soldier—until the last days of the Empire. The world-outlook of the Russian reached a very low level of simplification; the Muscovite was a primitive man even if judged by mediaeval standards. He did not indulge in abstract thinking, and took on trust a few tenets on which was based his moral and social life. But his religion contained something that was more important to him than tenets. The rites, the periodical repetition of prescribed gestures, obeisances, customs, and verbal formulas shaped his life, prevented it from degrading into chaos and even adorned it with the beauty of a formal frame. With the extermination of the mystic tendency, Christianity grew steadily into a religion of holy matter: of ikons, relics, holy water, incense, liturgic bread and Easter cakes. Food regulations became the focal point of religious life. It was ritualism, but a tremendously exacting and morally effective ritualism. As the Jew in the law, so the Muscovite in the rite found support for the sacrifice of his life. . . .

It is obvious that in a world of such a mould, there was no room for liberty. Blind obedience was the highest virtue of a monk in the school of Joseph. From monasteries it spread through the "Domostroy" ("The Book of Husbandry") into the life of lay society. To the Muscovite, liberty was a negative idea, a synonym of license, of wanton and shameful behaviour.

But what about the special magic of the "volya" (liberty), dreamed of and sung about by the people, to which every Russian heart responds? In Russian as in English there are two words for the designation of liberty or freedom. But the difference between the two Russian words "volya" and "svoboda" does not correspond to, and is more substantial, than in the two English synonyms. The word "svoboda" sounds in Russian like the translation of the French *liberté*. But the specific Russian meaning of "volya" cannot be denied. It is therefore important to realize the full meaning of "volya" as it sounds to the Russian ear.

"Volya" first of all means the possibility of living as one desires, disregarding social limitations. "Volya" is hampered by equals and by the community. Its triumph is attained by escape from society, in the immensity of the steppes, or by the domination of society and by violation of men. "Svoboda" is unthinkable without respect for the liberty of the other men, but "volya" disregards the others. It stands in no contrast to tyranny, for the tyrant possesses the "volya" in the highest degree. The brigand is the ideal of Muscovite "volya," as Ivan the Terrible is the ideal of a Tsar. Since "volya," like anarchy, is impossible in a civilized community, the Russian ideal of "volya" finds its expression in the worship of the desert, of wild nature, of nomadic life, of gypsy songs, wine, revelry, passionate self-oblivion, brigandry, tyranny and revolt.

There was something striking in the Muscovy of the seventeenth century. The people adored the Tsar. There was not a shred of political opposition, of desire to take part in the government or to get rid of the Tsar. Yet the century that passed between the "Time of Troubles" [1604–13] and Peter's reign was filled with popular and military riots. Razin's rebellion shook the state to its very foundations. These facts prove that the state burden incumbent on the people, was beyond their strength, and in particular that the peasants did not resign themselves—as they never did—to serfdom. When suffering became intolerable and "the cup of woe was filled to the brim" the people straightened up: they hit, plundered, took revenge on their oppressors until they regained composure. Then the rebels themselves would stretch out their hands to be manacled by the Tsar's police. . . .

It is easy to imagine what could have happened if Razin or Pugachov, the rebel against Catherine II, had been successful. The old Boyars or the gentry would have been exterminated, and replaced by a new Cossack officialdom. . . . There would have been no change either in the situation of the serfs or in the power of the Tsars under the new dynasty. . . . Serfdom was the product of state needs, and state instinct was vaguely alive even among the Cossacks. The people could depose the Tsar but not limit his power. What is more, they were unwilling to accept the Tsar's offer of self-government, and regarded participation in the national assemblies as a burden. Had their attitude toward state affairs been different, the Assemblies might have become the germ of Russian parliamentarism. But the state was the Tsar's and not the people's worry. His was to be the unrestricted power, and the Boyars one day would pay hundredfold for the wrongs they had committed.

If a longing for freedom glimmered at all in Muscovy, it was only among those hated Boyars. Despite Ivan the Terrible's persecutions, the aspiration to freedom found its expression in the attempts to establish constitutional restrictions of the power of the Tsars Vassily, Vladislav and Michael. The Boyars were anxious to safeguard themselves against being disgraced by the Tsar and being executed without guilt—to get a habeas corpus. And the Tsars took the oath, kissing the cross. But the people did not uphold them, because the Tsar's wrath was their only means of defense—or revenge. Thus the first Russian constitution became a "lost charter."

Muscovy meant more than just a two century period of Russian history ending with Peter. For the masses of the people, untouched by European culture, the Muscovite way of life continued until the abolition of serfdom in 1861. During the nineteenth century the merchant class and the clergy, too, preserved the old customs. On the other hand, in the course of its tempestuous existence, Muscovite Russia created a far reaching unity of culture that could not be found either in Kiev or in St. Petersburg. From the Tsar's palace to the last peasant's shack, Russia of this period was imbued with the same culture and the same ideals. There were everywhere the same superstitions, the same "Domostroy," the same ways, customs, manners of speech and gestures. There was no demarcation line between Christianity and paganism (as in Kiev) or between Western and Byzantine traditions as in Petersburg, or even between enlightened and crude types of Orthodoxy. To this unity of culture was due the tremendous stability of the Muscovite type, which many regard as synonymous with everything Russian. Be this as it may, this type outlived not only Peter, but also the golden age of Russian Europeanism; in the depths of the nation it lived until the Revolution.

It has long since become hackneyed truth that after Peter Russia lived on two cultural levels. A sharp line divided the thin upper layer that had adopted Western culture from the masses of the people who mentally and socially still lived in old Muscovy. To these masses belonged not only the serfs, but also the bourgeoisie of trade and industry and, with certain reservations, the clergy. In contrast to the unavoidable difference between classes, which existed in the West, as in every differentiated society, with regard to their cultural standard the difference in Russia was qualitative rather than quantitative. Two cultures lived side by side in Russia in the eighteenth century. One was a survival of Byzantinism, the other a primitive adoption of Europeanism. Bigger than the class dissension between the gentry and peasantry, was the wall of incomprehension between the intelligentsia and the people. Yet granting this, one has to realize the astonishing ease with which the Russian Scythians adopted alien education. They adopted it not only passively, but also in an active, creative way. A century and a half after Peter's overturn of Muscovy —a comparatively short spell—there began a period of brilliant development for Russian science. It is worthy of note that in the literary art, as well as in music, the deepest and most intimate creations of the national genius, Russia gave her best in the nineteenth century. Had Russia perished as a nation during the Napoleonic wars, the world would never have realized what it had lost.

This astounding blossoming of Russian culture in modern times was made possible by the grafting of Western culture upon the Russian wild growth. This proves that between Russia and the West there was a certain kinship, otherwise the foreign element would have crippled and ruined Russian national life. Ugliness and deformity were, of course, plentiful. But . . . the nineteenth century produced Pushkin, and . . . Tolstoy, Mussorgsky and the

historian Klyuchevsky. This shows that beneath the orien-
talism of the Muscovite type, ancient layers of the Kiev-
Novgorod Russia were still intact, and that in these layers
spiritual interchange with the Christian West proceeded
easily and freely. . . .

With Western culture, science and new customs came
also freedom. It made its appearance in two forms: the
unfettering of traditional ways of life and the promoting
of a movement for political liberation. We usually under-
estimate the freedom in everyday life which Russian society enjoyed from the time after Peter and which for a
long period obscured the lack of political freedom. The
Petersburg court tried to align itself with the courts of
Potsdam and Versailles, and the former Tsar of Moscow,
heir of the Khans and Basileuses, felt himself a European
monarch—autocratic as were most Western monarchs, but
bound by a new code of morals and decency. Somehow
we did not realize that the Russian Emperor who was
vested with the unlimited right to execute his subjects
without trial or guilt, to torture or flog them, to take away
their property and their wives, never did so. Moreover, it
is not possible to imagine that even the most despotic of
the Romanovs, Paul or Nikolai I, should ever avail himself of such rights. The Russian people would probably
have resigned themselves as they were resigned to Ivan
the Terrible or Peter the Great and would perhaps relish
the execution of the hated lords; as a matter of fact, attempts were made by the people to canonize Paul. But
the Petersburg Emperor always took his cue from his German cousins; he was brought up in their ideas and traditions. When his subjects bowed to his feet or prostrated
themselves to kiss his boots, he hardly felt gratified. When
he forgot himself and was led astray by his absolute power,
the nobility reminded him of his duty to behave decently.
The role of the nobility which sometimes raised Tsars to

the throne and sometimes murdered them, became so enhanced that the Tsar called himself the first nobleman.

Government agents belonging to the same circle followed the example of those above. The nobleman was
exempt by law from corporal punishment; by custom he
was exempt from personal outrage. He could be deported
to Siberia, but could not be struck or abused. The nobleman developed a feeling of personal honor, quite different
from the Muscovite family honor, a feeling derived from
mediaeval knighthood. The ukase about "Freedom of the
Nobility" freed the nobleman from the obligation to do
personal service to the state. Henceforth he could devote
his leisure to literature, art, and science. By the nobleman's
participation in these professions, the professions themselves became free, even when exercised by plebeians, descendants of commoners, chiefly of clergymen. Nobility
was the kernel out of which grew the Russian intelligentsia;
it imprinted upon the intelligentsia its virtues and its
vices. Apart from China, Russia was the only country where
nobility could be attained by college education. Gradua-
tion from high school, even from grammar school turned a
muzhik into a gentleman, that is, into a free man, and protected him in some measure from the administration's arbitrariness. Policemen saluted university students whom
they beat black and blue only during riots. This actual
freedom in Russia was of course a privilege, as it always is
in the initial period of freedom. This freedom was the island of Petersburg-Russia amidst the Moscow sea. Yet the
island extended continuously, particularly after the abolition of serfdom. This freedom, the most substantial and
significant cultural achievement of the Empire, was obviously a fruit of Europeanization. It was brought about in
the face of constant and stubborn resistance of the "dark
realm," that is, of old Russia.

More gloomy was the fate of political freedom. It seemed

near at hand in the eighteenth century, and still more so in the opening years of the nineteenth century. Later it receded and in the time of Alexander III seemed a fantastic dream. It came too late, when in all classes the authority of the monarchy had been sapped and the wide open gulf between the classes made a democratic transformation of the regime extremely difficult.

For a long time, perhaps up to 1905, Russian liberalism was represented by the gentry. Contrary to the Marxian scheme, the bourgeois was not the zealot of liberation. His cultural standard remained that of the pre-Petrine period, and it was the main support of reaction until the end of the nineteenth century, when a new type of industrialists and bankers appeared who had received a thorough European education. Aspiration to freedom had lived in the gentry alone, and in its highly educated upper stratum, not in its stagnant and ignorant rank and file.

It is quite possible that if in the eighteenth century constitutional monarchy had been introduced throughout Europe, it would have been adopted by Russia, too, along with the rest of European culture. The French revolution hampered this development. The wind of reaction blew over Europe, and the Russian Emperor had no desire to mount the scaffold and repeat the gestures of the King of France. Yet transplanting political institutions, though possible as the example of Turkey and Japan shows, is much more difficult and dangerous than adopting science and art.

The sixties of the last century, while contributing a great deal toward the social emancipation of Russia, dealt a heavy blow to the cause of political liberation. At that time a considerable and most active part of its partisans—the revolutionary movement—was directed into anti-liberal

channels. To the men of the lower classes, who soon
formed the majority of the intelligentsia, political freedom
did not seem a very attractive ideal. They wished a revolution that would achieve equality for all without further
delay, even at the price of the extermination of the privileged classes (the famous three million heads). They
unleashed a fierce campaign against the gentry's liberalism,
even against Herzen's liberal Socialism. At its inception in
the sixties and seventies, the populist movement opposed
the idea of introducing a constitutional regime in Russia
since it would have strengthened the bourgeois classes.
There are many explanations of this astounding blindness:
the desire to keep up with the latest political fashions in the
West, the primitive type of Russian thinking, the maximalism peculiar to the Russian intelligentsia. In addition to
this, there was a much more serious and fatal motive, one
already mentioned. The intelligentsia that did not belong
to the privileged classes stood in closer contact with the
people than did the liberals. They knew that, to the people,
freedom was an empty sound and that it was easier to arouse
them against squires than against the Tsar. But their own
hearts were with the people: equality meant more to them
than liberty. This was another by-product of the Moscow
heritage.

With time they grew wiser. Already the "Narodovoltsy"
[a revolutionary party active in the seventies and eighties]
acknowledged the importance of political liberation. In the
closing years of the century, both the Social-Democratic and
the Socialist-Revolutionary parties waged a persistent
struggle for democracy. To be sure, in the Marxist conception, freedom still remained instrumental, a mere device
in the fight for dictatorship of the proletariat. Exposing the
"bourgeois background" of the liberal movement, they
abased and depreciated freedom in the eyes of the unso-
phisticated masses. But this was no longer the old "Russian

spirit," it was a new Western air, or rather draft, that blew from the Utopian Communism of 1848 into the yet unknown and indiscernible age of Fascism.

And yet during the half century following the abolition of serfdom, the face of Russia underwent a thorough change. The intelligentsia grew a hundredfold. A new workers-and-peasants intelligentsia was on the ascent and now and then carried to the crest of the wave brilliant representatives of Russian culture, like Gorky and Shaliapin. In 1905 the age-old gulf between the people and the intelligentsia seemed to have been bridged. Having lost their faith in the Tsar, the people entrusted the intelligentsia with leadership in the struggle for "freedom and land." The gentry's swerving to the track of reaction was abundantly compensated by the development of a new liberal bourgeoisie. The old "Zemstvo" [rural self-government] was an excellent school for free public activity, and in anticipation of its democratization did very good work. Trade union and cooperative movements provided social education for the laboring classes. The elementary schools which had a ready plan for general education, rapidly disintegrated the Muscovite heritage. . . . Fifty more years and the Europeanization of Russia, down to her lowest layers, would be accomplished. How could it be otherwise? The Russian people were made from the same ethnographic and cultural dough as the gentry which successfully went through the same school in the eighteenth century. Yet these fifty years were not given to Russia.

The first contact of the Russian soul with Western civilization was in most cases frustrated by nihilism: the destruction of the old morals usually outstripped the fruits of the new education. He who had lost faith in God and the Tsar, forfeited also the principles of personal and social ethics. At the beginning of the century rowdyism in the villages became conspicuous. Upon the collapse of the revolution of 1905, and after the hasty alienation from the people of the educated upper classes, a new cleavage came into being. In his almost prophetic essays, the poet Alexander Blok tried to discern the mounting roar of the people's hate which threatened to drown the brilliant but frail Russian culture. . . . In this aspect, the modern development of Russia appears as a perilous race between the liberating Europeanization and the Muscovite revolt that would drown the young freedom in the tidal wave of the people's wrath.

Reading Blok one senses that Russia was menaced not just by a revolution, but by a reactionary one. Here, on the threshold of the disaster, it is pertinent to peer into this last reaction of Muscovy, which called itself, in Moscow style, the "Black Hundreds." At the time this political formation was underestimated because of the barbaric nature of its ideology and political methods. The "Black Hundreds" gathered the wildest and the least cultivated dregs of old Russia, but kept contact with the majority of the Orthodox episcopate. The priest John of Kronstadt, renowned for his saintliness, blessed them, and Tsar Nikolai II trusted them more than his ministers. There is reason to believe that their ideas have won in the course of the Russian revolution, and that they will outlive all of us.

Two basic tendencies can easily be discerned behind Orthodoxy and Autocracy, i.e., the Muscovite Creed: harsh nationalism befogging people with hatred toward all aliens —Jews, Poles, Germans, etc., and just as harsh a hatred toward the intelligentsia in the widest meaning of the word, including all the upper classes of Russia. Hatred toward Western life blended with class hatred toward the gentleman, nobleman, capitalist, government official— toward the whole "partition wall" between the Tsar and the people. The very term "Black Hundreds" was borrowed from the Muscovite dictionary, where it was applied to the guild of the lowest, poorest class of tradesmen. To the Muscovite ear it must have sounded as "democracy" did at the time of Tocqueville. In short, the Black Hundreds was the first Russian version of National-Socialism. With its fanatical hatred and violent methods often resulting in pogroms and riots, the movement bore in itself the potentialities of the Razin rebellion. The government and the nobility reared it—to their own destruction. Governors of the provinces were not always able to cope with it, and the example of the monk Iliodor in Tsaritsyn shows how easily a Black Hundreds demagogue turned into a revolutionary one. It is useful to call to mind this last reaction of Muscovy in those fateful years when—not in vain—Merezhkovsky recalled the old prophecy: Petersburg will be a desert.

In the twenty-eight years of its victorious, though hard, existence, the Russian revolution went through a tremendous evolution, performed a good many zig-zags and changed many a leader. But one thing has remained unaltered: the incessant, year in and year out, strangling of freedom. It seemed that Lenin's totalitarian dictatorship could not be outdone. But under Lenin the Mensheviks could carry on an open struggle within the Soviets, limited freedom of discussion within the Communist party was recognized, and literature and art were little affected. This sounds queer now. Of course, Lenin was no friend of liberty. But for a man who had breathed the air of the nineteenth century, though in a lesser degree than for a Russian Tsar, there existed certain unwritten limits of despotism, at least in the form of habits and inhibition. They had to be overcome, step by step. Even now, though the totalitarian regimes have reintroduced tortures, they refrain from resorting to quartering or public burning. Foreigners who visited Soviet Russia after a lapse of several years noted the increased oppression even in the last refuge of free activity, in the theater, music and the movies. While Russian émigrés exulted in the nationalist transformation of Bolshevism, Russia lived through one of the most gruesome stages of her Golgotha. Millions of corpses mark every turn of the dictator's steering wheel. On this last "nationalist" stage, which could be expected to inspire artists, Russian literature sank to the bottom of naive helplessness and didacticism, as a result of the disappearance of the last vestige of freedom.

There is another still more ominous phenomenon. As freedom subsides, so does the struggle for it. After the last echo of the Civil War of 1918–1920 had died away, freedom disappeared from opposition programs, even when opposition still existed. We have seen a good many Soviet citizens abroad—students, soldiers, émigrés of the new brand. Hardly any one of them shows longing for freedom, joy of having attained it. Upon the majority of them Western freedom made a painful impression of disorder, chaos and anarchy. They are disturbed by the clash of opinions in the press: is there more than one truth? They are shocked by the freedom of the worker, by strikes and by the easy tempo of work. "We have driven millions through concentration camps to teach them how to work," remarked a Soviet engineer who studied the conditions of work in American plants. And this engineer is himself a former worker, a son of a worker or a peasant. What is valued in Russia is discipline and compulsion, while personal initiative is little appreciated not only by the Party, but also by the vast mass of the new intelligentsia brought into being by the Party.

Responsible for the rise of this antiliberal man is not the system of totalitarian education alone, even though the modern technical apparatus for social "reforging" is of tremendous power. Another, demographic factor worked in the same direction. The Russian revolution was a gigantic meat-grinder into which were thrown millions of men. The entire intelligentsia was not subjected to extermination; technically needed personnel was partly preserved. Yet, however blindly the machine of terrorism turned, it hit first of all, the elements which resisted, if only morally, the totalitarian regime: monarchists, liberals, socialists, men with strong convictions or critical thought, or just independent men. There perished not only the old intelligentsia, the "Order of Chivalry" devoted to freedom and the people, but also its product: the vast near-intelligentsia of popular descent.

To be more precise, a selection took place. This popular intelligentsia split in two: one part joined the Communist ranks, the other (Socialist-Revolutionaries and Mensheviks) was destroyed. Mere Bolshevism would not tempt the intelligentsia. Those among them who did not wish to perish or flee the country, had to extinguish—during years of dire humiliations—their will to freedom, even the longing for it, otherwise their life would have become unbearable. It would not be an exaggeration to say that the whole freedom-loving Russian intelligentsia raised in the two centuries of the Empire has disappeared altogether. And then the old Muscovite totalitarian rock reappeared on the surface. The new Soviet man was not so much modelled in the Marxian school, as he crept into the light out of the Muscovite Tsardom, slightly glossed over with Marxism. The grandfathers of the generation who made the revolution lived in serfdom, their fathers were flogged in rural courts. They themselves on January 9, 1905, marched to the Winter Palace to implore the Tsar and later transferred their whole complex of inborn monarchial feelings to the new red leaders.

Behold the typical Soviet citizen—the one who shapes life, not the one trodden underfoot, harnessed in a Kolkhoz or a factory, or held behind the barbed wire of a concentration camp. He is robust, physically and mentally; he lives according to orders, dislikes thought and doubt and appreciates practical knowledge and experience. He is very ambitious and rather hard-hearted toward other peoples' suffering, a prerequisite of a Soviet career. He is willing to work himself to exhaustion, and his highest ambition is to give his life for the community—for the party or homeland as the case may be. All these features are reminiscent of the ruling class of Muscovy in the sixteenth century. More analogies suggest themselves: with the officials of the time of Nikolai I, but without the humanism imbued by Christian education, or with the entourage of Peter I, but without the fanatic attachment to the West and without national self-denial. The Soviet man is more akin to the Muscovite through his proud national consciousness: his country is the only Orthodox, the only Socialist, the first country in the world—the "Third Rome." He is disdainful toward the rest of the world, that is to say toward the West. He does not know the West, dislikes it and fears it. And as of old his soul is open to the East. Numerous "hordes" make their first contact with civilization and joining the ranks of Russian educated circles orientalize them for the second time.

Referring to the Muscovite type in connection with the dynamism of present day Russia may seem inappropriate. It is Moscow that has been set in motion with its heaviness, but without its stagnation. Yet this motion proceeds along the line of outward, mainly technical, achievements. It does not stir either heart or thought, and there is not a trace of what the Russians call spiritual pilgrimage and the French, *inquiétude*. Behind the tempestuous, even warlike outward movement, reigns undisturbed inner calm. . . .

Sources

Chapter II

RUSSIA AND THE WORLD, from "Letters on the Philosophy of History" (1829-1831), Letter I in *Sochinenia i pisma P. Ya. Chaadaeva*, ed. by M. Gershenzon (2 vols., Moscow, 1913-14), vol. I, pp. 74-93; and Letter III, *ibid.*, pp. 119-137.

RUSSIA'S INTERCOURSE WITH EUROPE, from letters to A. I. Turgenev of April 20, 1833, and May 1, 1835. *Ibid.*, pp. 165, 185. In his letter to Turgenev on May 25, 1836, Chaadayev wrote: "A profound idea of M. de Tocqueville, and which he has stolen from me, is the theory that the point of departure of nations determines their destinies." *Ibid.*, vol. I, p. 191.

THE LEGACY OF PETER THE GREAT, from "Apology of a Madman" (1837), *ibid.*, pp. 219-234.

Chapter III

THE WEALTH AND STRENGTH OF RUSSIA, from "Letter on Russian History" (1837), in Nikolai Platonovich Barsukov, *Zhizn i trudy M. P. Pogodina* (22 vols., St. Petersburg, 1888-1910), vol. V, pp. 165-175.

Chapter IV

THE BOOKS OF THE POLISH NATION, in Adam Mickiewicz, *Poems*, ed. by George Rapall Noyes (New York, Polish Institute of Arts and Sciences in America, 1944), pp. 371-380. Reprinted by permission of the Polish Institute.

CZECH and SLAV, in Karla Havlíčka Borovského *Politické spisy*, ed. by Zdeněk V. Tobolka (3 vols., Prague, 1900-1903), vol. I, pp. 32-70. The article appeared in *Pražské Noviny* in February and March 1846. It was violently attacked from the Pan-Slav point of view by Jakub Josef Dominik Malý (1811-1885) in his magazine *Květy* in April 1846. Havlíček answered in *Pražské Noviny* in May.

Chapter V

RUSSIA THE ROCK OF REFUGE, in F. I. Tyuchev, *Polnoe sobranie sochinenii*, ed. by P. V. Bykov (St. Petersburg, 1913), pp. 295-307, 344-351. The article appeared first under the title "La Russie et la Révolution" in the *Revue des Deux Mondes* in 1849.

Chapter VI

RUSSIA AND WAR, "Letter to a Foreign Friend on the eve of the Crimean War," in *Russia and the English Church during the last Fifty Years*, ed. by W. J. Birkbeck (London, 1895), vol. I, containing a correspondence between Mr. William Palmer and M. Khomyakov in the years 1844–1854, pp. 166–176. Khomyakov's letter is published there in the original French. It is here translated into English.

RUSSIA AND AUTOCRACY, "Address to the St. Petersburg Benevolent Slav Society after the Assassination of Alexander II," in Olga Novikov, *Skobeleff and the Slavonic Cause* (London, Longmans, Green, 1883), pp. 354–362.

Chapter VII

RUSSIA AND THE WEST, from "Literary Reveries" (1834), in V. G. Belinsky, *Selected Philosophical Works*, ed. by M. Yorchuch (Moscow, Foreign Languages Publication House, 1948), pp. 22–96.

THE MIRACLE OF PETER THE GREAT, from a review of *The Acts of Peter the Great, the Wise Regenerator of Russia* (author unknown) (1841), *ibid.*, pp. 120–138.

THE REFORM OF SOCIETY THROUGH WESTERNIZATION, from a letter to V. P. Botkin of September 8, 1841; from a review of *The History of Little Russia* by Nikolai Markevich (Moscow, 1842); and from a letter to Botkin, December 1847. *Ibid.*, pp. 163–165, 282–283, 502.

RUSSIA AND THE SLAVOPHILS, from "A View on Russian Literature in 1846," *ibid.*, pp. 358–363.

AGAINST GOGOL'S ORTHODOXY, from a letter to N. V. Gogol of July 3, 1847, *ibid.*, pp. 504–508.

Chapter VIII

The five readings from Chernyshevsky are from his novel *Chto delat? Iz razskazov o novykh lyudakh*, in N. G. Chernyshevsky, *Polnoe sobranie sochinenii* (Moscow 1939–1951), vol. XI. The novel was translated twice into English in America in the 1880's. The translation by Benjamin R. Tucker which appeared in Boston in 1886 was compared and partly used.

Chapter IX

THE DEVELOPMENT OF REVOLUTIONARY IDEAS IN RUSSIA, from A. I. Herzen, *Du développement des idées révolutionnaires en Russie* (Paris, 1851), passim.

APPEAL TO THE RUSSIAN SOLDIERS IN POLAND AT THE START OF THE CRIMEAN WAR, in A. I. Herzen, *Polnoe sobranie sochinenii i pisem*, ed. by M. K. Lemke (21 vols., Petrograd and Moscow, 1919–1923), vol. VIII, pp. 67 ff.

EVOLUTION AGAINST REVOLUTION and FOR A FREE FEDERAL UNION, from *The Bell*, March 1, 1859, in reply to an inquiry by Polish revolutionaries about Herzen's attitude to Alexander II and to Polish independence, *ibid.*, vol. IX, pp. 453–469.

ON RUSSIAN FREEDOM and ON RUSSIA'S FUTURE, written in March 1860 in reply to a Polish émigré publication, *ibid.*, vol. X, pp. 237–258.

FOR SOBRIETY IN POLITICS, *ibid.*, vol. XX, pp. 131–135 (written November 29, 1867); and vol. X, pp. 218–224 (written February 25, 1860).

Chapter X

THE SLAV ROLE IN WORLD CIVILIZATION is a shortened version of Danilevsky's seventeenth and last chapter in *Rossiya i Evropa. Vzglyad na kulturniya i politıcheskiya otnosheniya Slavyanskago mira k Germano-Romanskomu*, ed. by N. Strakhov with notes by K. N. Bestuzhev-Ryumin (5th ed., St. Petersburg, 1895).

Chapter XI

AGAINST THE SLAVOPHILS, in V. S. Solovev, *Sobranie sochinenii*, ed. by Sergei M. Solovev and E. L. Radlov (2nd ed., 10 vols., St. Petersburg, 1911–1914), vol. V, pp. 82–147. Written in 1888. This is a criticism of Danilevsky's *Russia and Europe* and his *Darwinism* and of N. N. Strakhov's *Borba s zapadom v russkoi literature* (*The Struggle with the West in Russian Literature*).

ON DOSTOEVSKY, in V. S. Solovev, *Sobranie sochinenii* (9 vols., St. Petersburg, 1902–1907), vol. V, p. 381. Written in 1891. See also Solovev's preceding three lectures on Dostoevsky, *ibid.*, vol. III, pp. 169, 172, 183.

AGAINST EXTREME NATIONALISM, *ibid.*, vol. V, pp. 206 ff. Written in 1889.

PETER'S REFORMS, *ibid.*, pp. 144–160. Written in 1888. English translations of other works by Solovev are available in *War, Progress, and the End of History* (London, 1915), including "A Short Story of the Anti-Christ," tr. by Alexander Bakshy; *A Solovyov Anthology*, arranged by S. C. Frank, tr. by Natalie Waddington (London, 1950); and *Russia and the Universal Church*, tr. by Herbert Rees (London, 1948).

Chapter XII

ON MARXIST ORTHODOXY, from an article "Our Program," written in 1899, though not published until 1925. It preceded by three years the writing of Lenin's pamphlet "What is to be Done?" which repeated Chernyshevsky's famous title. It is reprinted here from *Handbook of Marxism* (New York, International Publishers, 1935), pp. 571–575, by permission of the publishers.

UPRISING AS AN ART, reprinted from V. I. Lenin, *On the Eve of October* (Little Lenin Library edition, New York, International Publishers), pp. 5–10, by permission of the publishers. Written at the end of September 1917.

RUSSIA AND ASIA, from an article "The Historical Fate of the Teaching of Karl Marx," written in 1913. It is reprinted here from *On the Theory of Marxism* by Marx, Engels, Lenin, and Stalin (Little Lenin Library edition, New York, International Publishers), pp. 22–24, by permission of the publishers.

Chapter XIII

THE ROOTS OF RUSSIAN COMMUNISM, reprinted from Nicholas Berdyayev, *The Origin of Russian Communism*, tr. by R. M. French (London, Geoffrey Bles, 1937), by permission of the publishers.

RUSSIA AND FREEDOM, reprinted from *The Review of Politics*, Notre Dame University Press (January, 1946), pp. 12–36, by permission of the editor. See also Fedotov's collected essays *Novyi Grad*, ed. by George P. Ivask (New York, Chekhov Publishing House, 1952).

Selective Bibliography

General Histories of Russia

Michael T. Florinsky, *Russia: A History and Interpretation* (2 vols., New York, 1953). The best general history of Russia available in English.

Valentin Gitermann, *Geschichte Russlands* (3 vols., Hamburg, 1949).

Alexander Kornilov, *Modern Russian History* (New York, 1943).

Paul Milioukov, Ch. Seignobos, and L. Eisenmann, *Histoire de la Russie* (3 vols., Paris, 1932–33).

Sir Bernard Pares, *A History of Russia* (6th ed., New York, 1953).

S. F. Platonov, *History of Russia* (New York, 1925).

Warren B. Walsh, *Readings in Russian History* (Syracuse, N.Y., 1948).

Warren B. Walsh, *Russia and the Soviet Union* (Ann Arbor, Michigan, 1958).

Studies of Special Periods and Problems

K. E. Breshko-Breshkovskaya, *Hidden Springs of the Russian Revolution* (Stanford, Calif., 1931).

Sergius Bulgakov, *The Orthodox Church* (London, 1935).

J. S. Curtiss, *Church and State in Russia. The Last Years of the Empire, 1900–1917* (New York, 1940).

Rostislav Fadeyev, *Opinion on the Eastern Question* (London, 1871).

Readings in Russian Foreign Policy, ed. by Robert A. Goldwin and Marvin Zetterbaum (3 vols., Chicago, 1953).

Oscar Halecki, *The Limits and Divisions of European History* (New York, 1950).

Michael Hrushevsky, *History of Ukraine*, ed. by O. J. Frederiksen (New Haven, 1941).

Hans Kohn, *Basic History of Modern Russia* (Princeton, N. J., Anvil Books, 1957).

Hans Kohn, *Pan-Slavism, Its History and Ideology* (Notre Dame, Ind., 1953); revised edition, New York, Vintage Books, 1960).

Prince P. A. Kropotkin, *Memoirs of a Revolutionist* (Boston, 1899).

Ludwik Kulczycki, *Geschichte der Russischen Revolution* (3 vols., Gotha, 1910–14).

Andrei A. Lobanov-Rostovsky, *Russia and Europe 1789–1825* (Durham, N.C., 1947).

Karl Marx, *Secret Diplomatic History of the 18th Century* (London, 1889).

Karl Marx, *The Eastern Question,* ed. by Eleanor Marx Eveling and Edward Eveling (London, 1897).

Karl Marx and Friedrich Engels, *The Russian Menace to Europe* (Glencoe, Ill., 1952).

A. G. Mazour, *The First Russian Revolution, 1825. The Decembrist Movement, Its Origins, Development and Significance* (Berkeley, Calif., 1937).

D. Merejkowsky, *Le Tsar et la Révolution* (Paris, 1907).

P. N. Milyukov, *Russia and Its Crisis* (Chicago, 1906).

Boris J. Nikolaevsky, *Aseff, The Spy, Russian Terrorist and Police Stool* (New York, 1934).

Olga Novikova, *Skobeleff and the Slavonic Cause* (London, 1883).

G. V. Plekhanov, *History of Russian Social Thought* (New York, 1938).

Hugh Seton-Watson, *The Decline of Imperial Russia, 1855–1914* (New York, 1952).

Stepniak [S. M. Kravchinsky], *Underground Russia: Revolutionary Profiles and Sketches from Life* (New York, 1883).

Ludowit Stur, *Das Slawentum und die Welt der Zukunft,* ed. by Josef Jirásek (Bratislava, 1931).

A. Thun, *Geschichte der Revolutionären Bewegungen in Russland* (Leipzig, 1883).

George Vernadsky, *The Mongols and Russia* (New Haven, Conn., 1953).

Georg von Rauch, *Russland: Staatliche Einheit und Nationale Vielfalt* (Munich, 1953).

Vladimir Weidlé, *Russia Absent and Present* (New York, 1952).

Descriptions of Russian Society and Life

Alexander Brückner, *Die Europäisierung Russlands, Land und Volk* (Gotha, 1888).

Astolphe Louis Leonard, Comte de Custine, *La Russie en 1839* (4 vols., Paris, 1843). New shortened editions, *Lettres de Russie* (Paris, 1946) and *Journey for Our Time,* ed. by Phyllis Penn Kohler (New York, 1951).

J. Eckardt, *Modern Russia: Russia under Alexander II* (London, 1870).

Adam Gurowski, *Russia As It Is* (New York, 1854).

August Baron von Haxthausen-Abbenburg, *The Russian Empire, Its People, Institutions and Resources* (2 vols., London, 1856).

Anatole Leroy-Beaulieu, *L'Empire des Tsars et les Russes* (3 vols., 4th ed., Paris, 1897–98).

G. K. Loukomski, *La Vie et les Moeurs en Russie de Pierre le Grand à Lenine* (Paris, 1928).

Sir John Maynard, *Russia in Flux before October* (London, 1941).

Nikolai Turgueneff, *La Russie et les Russes* (3 vols., Brussels, 1847).

Sir Donald Mackenzie Wallace, *Russia* (rev. ed., London, 1912).

H. W. Williams, *Russia of the Russians* (2nd ed., New York, 1915).

Histories of Thought and Literature

Maurice Baring, *An Outline of Russian Literature* (New York, 1914).

N. Berdiaev, *The Russian Idea* (London, 1947).

Alexander Brueckner, *A Literary History of Russia* (London, 1908).

Nadejda Gorodetzky, *The Humiliated Christ in Modern Russian Thought* (London, 1938).

Richard Hare, *Pioneers of Russian Social Thought* (London, 1951).

David Hecht, *Russian Radicals Look to America 1825–1894* (Cambridge, Mass., 1947).

Alexander Koyré, *La Philosophie et le Problème National en Russie au Début du XIXe Siècle* (Paris, 1929).

Jan Kucharzewski, *The Origins of Modern Russia* (New York, 1948).

Waclaw Lednicki, *Russia, Poland and the West* (New York, 1954).

Fritz Lieb, *Das westeuropäische Geistesleben im Urteile russischer Religionsphilosophie* (Tübingen, 1929).

Fritz Lieb, *Russland unterwegs, der russische Mensch zwischen Christentum und Kommunismus* (Bern, 1945).

N. O. Lossky, *History of Russian Philosophy* (New York, 1951).

Arthur Luther, *Geschichte der russischen Literatur* (Leipzig, 1924).

T. G. Masaryk, *The Spirit of Russia, Studies in History, Literature and Philosophy* (2 vols., New York, 1954).

A. G. Mazour, *An Outline of Modern Russian Historiography* (Berkeley, 1939).

Paul N. Miliukov, *Outlines of Russian Culture,* ed. by Michael Karpovich (3 vols., Philadelphia, 1942).

D. S. Mirsky, *Contemporary Russian Literature 1881–1925* (New York, 1926).

D. S. Mirsky, *A History of Russian Literature,* ed. by Francis J. Whitfield (New York, 1949).

D. S. Mirsky, *A History of Russian Literature from the Earliest Time to the Death of Dostoyevsky* (New York, 1927).

Karl Nötzel, *Die Grundlagen des geistigen Russlands* (Jena, 1917).

Michael Boro Petrovich, *The Emergence of Russian Panslavism 1856–1870* (New York, 1956).

Renato Poggioli, *The Poets of Russia 1890–1930* (Cambridge, Mass., 1960).

A. N. Pypin, *Die geistige Bewegung in Russland in der ersten Hälfte des 19. Jahrhunderts,* tr. by Boris Minzes (Berlin, 1894).

Nicholas V. Riasanovsky, *Russia and the West in the Teaching of the Slavophiles* (Cambridge, Mass., 1952).

Hans Rogger, *National Consciousness in Eighteenth-Century Russia* (Cambridge, Mass., 1960).

Emanuel Sarkisyanz, *Russland und der Messianismus des Orients* (Tübingen, 1955).

Peter Scheibert, *Von Bakunin zu Lenin* (Leiden, Netherlands, 1956).

Alexander von Schelting, *Russland und Europa im russischen Geschichtsdenken* (Bern, 1948).

Bernhard Schultze, *Russische Denker, ihre Stellung zu Christus, Kirche und Papsttum* (Vienna, 1950).

Stuart Ramsay Tompkins, *The Russian Mind from Peter the Great through the Enlightenment* (Norman, Okla., 1953).

Franco Venturi, *Roots of Revolution* (New York, 1960).

V. V. Zenkovsky, *A History of Russian Philosophy,* tr. by George L. Kline (2 vols., New York, 1953).

V. V. Zenkovsky, *Russian Thinkers and Europe* (Ann Arbor, Mich., 1953).

Studies of Personalities and Their Works

Two important source works are Alexander Herzen, *My Past and Thoughts,* tr. by Constance Garnett (6 vols., London, 1924) and F. M. Dostoievsky, *The Diary of a Writer,* tr. by Boris Brasol (2 vols., New York, 1949).

Bakunins *Social-politischer Briefwechsel mit Alexander Iw. Herzen und Ogarjow,* ed. by Mikhail Dragomanov (Stuttgart, 1895).

V. G. Belinsky, *Selected Philosophical Works,* ed. by M. Yorchuch (Moscow, 1948).

Nicolas Berdiaeff, *Constantin Leontieff,* tr. by Helene Iswolsky (Paris, 1937).

Herbert E. Bowman, *Vissarion Belinski, a Study in the Origins of Social Criticism in Russia* (Cambridge, Mass., 1954).

E. H. Carr, *Michael Bakunin* (London, 1937).

E. H. Carr, *The Romantic Exiles* (London, 1933).

N. A. Dobrolyubov, *Selected Philosophical Essays*, ed. by M. Yorchuch (Moscow, 1948).

A. Gratieux, *A. S. Khomiakov et le Mouvement Slavophile* (2 vols., Paris, 1939).

Benoit-P. Hepner, *Bakounine et le Panslavisme Révolutionnaire* (Paris, 1950).

N. M. Karamzin, *A Memoir on Ancient and Modern Russia*, tr. by Richard Pipes (Cambridge, Mass., 1959).

Konstantin Kawelins and Iwan Turgenjews *Social-politischer Briefwechsel mit Alexander Iw. Herzen*, ed. by Mikhail Dragomanov (Stuttgart, 1894).

Iwan Kirejewski, *Russlands Kritik an Europa* (Stuttgart, 1923).

Hans Kohn, *Prophets and Peoples* (New York, 1946), Chapter V on Dostoevsky.

Raoul Labry, *Alexander Ivanovič Herzen, Essai sur la Formation et le Développement de ses Idées* (Paris, 1928).

Raoul Labry, *Herzen et Proudhon* (Paris, 1928).

Boris N. Menshutkin, *Russia's Lomonosov* (Princeton, N. J., 1952).

Adam Mickiewicz, Poet of Poland, ed. by M. Kridl (New York, 1951).

K. P. Pobyedonostseff, *Reflections of a Russian Statesman*, preface by Olga Novikoff, London, 1898.

Alexander Radishchev, *Journey from St. Petersburg to Moscow*, ed. by R. P. Thaler (Cambridge, Mass., 1959).

Charles Quénet, *Tchaadaev et les Lettres Philosophiques* (Paris, 1931).

David Shub, *Lenin* (New York, 1948).

Ernest J. Simmons, *Dostoevsky, the Making of a Novelist* (New York, 1949).

Vladimir Soloviev, *Conscience de la Russie*, ed. by Jean Gauvain (Paris, 1950).

D. Stremooukhoff, *La Poésie et l'Idéologie de Tiouttchev* (Paris, 1937).

D. Stremooukhoff, *Vladimir Soloviev et son Oeuvre Messianique* (Paris, 1935).

Bertram D. Wolfe, *Three Who Made a Revolution* (New York, 1948).

Avraham Yarmolinsky, *Turgenev, the Man, his Art and his Age* (New York, 1926).

Nicholas Zernov, *Three Russian Prophets, Khomiakov, Dostoevsky, Soloviev* (London, 1944).

Index

Revised Nov., 1963

hARpER ⚜ ToRchbooks

HUMANITIES AND SOCIAL SCIENCES

American Studies

Anthropology & Sociology

*The New American Nation Series, edited by Henry Steele Commager and Richard B. Morris.

†*The Rise of Modern Europe Series*, edited by William L. Langer.

RELIGION

Mathematics

H. DAVENPORT: The Higher Arithmetic: *An Intro-*
duction to the Theory of Numbers   TB/526

H. G. FORDER: Geometry: *An Introduction*   TB/548

GOTTLOB FREGE: The Foundations of Arithmetic: *A*
Logico-Mathematical Enquiry into the Concept of
Number   TB/534

S. KÖRNER: The Philosophy of Mathematics: *An Intro-*
duction   TB/547

D. E. LITTLEWOOD: Skeleton Key of Mathematics: *A*
Simple Account of Complex Algebraic Problems
TB/525

GEORGE E. OWEN: Fundamentals of Scientific Mathematics   TB/569

WILLARD VAN ORMAN QUINE: Mathematical Logic
TB/558

O. G. SUTTON: Mathematics in Action. *Foreword by*
James R. Newman. Illus.   TB/518

FREDERICK WAISMANN: Introduction to Mathematical Thinking. *Foreword by Karl Menger*   TB/511

Philosophy of Science

R. B. BRAITHWAITE: Scientific Explanation   TB/515

J. BRONOWSKI: Science and Human Values. *Illus.*
TB/505

ALBERT EINSTEIN: Philosopher-Scientist. *Edited by*
Paul A. Schilpp   Volume I   TB/502
Volume II   TB/503

WERNER HEISENBERG: Physics and Philosophy: *The*
Revolution in Modern Science. Introduction by F. S.
C. Northrop   TB/549

JOHN MAYNARD KEYNES: A Treatise on Probability.
Introduction by N. R. Hanson   TB/557

STEPHEN TOULMIN: Foresight and Understanding:
An Enquiry into the Aims of Science. Foreword by
Jacques Barzun   TB/564

STEPHEN TOULMIN: The Philosophy of Science: *An*
Introduction   TB/513

W. H. WATSON: On Understanding Physics. *Intro-*
duction by Ernest Nagel   TB/507

G. J. WHITROW: The Natural Philosophy of Time
TB/563

Physics and Cosmology

DAVID BOHM: Causality and Chance in Modern
Physics. *Foreword by Louis de Broglie*   TB/536

P. W. BRIDGMAN: The Nature of Thermodynamics
TB/537

LOUIS DE BROGLIE: Physics and Microphysics. *Fore-*
word by Albert Einstein   TB/514

T. G. COWLING: Molecules in Motion: *An Introduc-*
tion to the Kinetic Theory of Gases. Illus.   TB/516

A. C. CROMBIE, Ed.: Turning Point in Physics   TB/535

C. V. DURELL: Readable Relativity. *Foreword by Free-*
man J. Dyson   TB/530

ARTHUR EDDINGTON: Space, Time and Gravitation:
An outline of the General Relativity Theory   TB/510

GEORGE GAMOW: Biography of Physics   TB/567

MAX JAMMER: Concepts of Force: *A Study in the*
Foundation of Dynamics   TB/550

MAX JAMMER: Concepts of Space: *The History of*
Theories of Space in Physics. Foreword by Albert
Einstein   TB/533

EDMUND WHITTAKER: History of the Theories of
Aether and Electricity
Volume I: *The Classical Theories*   TB/531
Volume II: *The Modern Theories*   TB/532

G. J. WHITROW: The Structure and Evolution of the
Universe: *An Introduction to Cosmology. Illus.*
TB/504

A LETTER TO THE READER

Overseas, there is considerable belief
that we are a country of extreme conservatism and
that we cannot accommodate to social change.

Books about America in the hands of
readers abroad can help change those ideas.

The U. S. Information Agency cannot,
by itself, meet the vast need for books about
the United States.

You can help.

Harper Torchbooks provides three packets
of books on American history, economics,
sociology, literature and politics to
help meet the need.

To send a packet of Torchbooks [*] overseas,
all you need do is send your check for $7 (which
includes cost of shipping) to Harper & Row.
The U. S. Information Agency will distrib-
ute the books to libraries, schools, and other
centers all over the world.

I ask every American to support this
program, part of a worldwide BOOKS USA campaign.

I ask you to share in the opportunity to
help tell others about America.

EDWARD R. MURROW
Director,
U. S. Information Agency

[*retailing at $10.85 to $12.00]

PACKET I: Twentieth Century America

   Dulles/America's Rise to World Power, 1898-1954
   Cochran/The American Business System, 1900-1955
   Zabel, Editor/Literary Opinion in America (two volumes)
   Drucker/The New Society: *The Anatomy of Industrial Order*
   Fortune Editors/America in the Sixties: *The Economy and the Society*

PACKET II: American History

   Billington/The Far Western Frontier, 1830-1860
   Mowry/The Era of Theodore Roosevelt and the
     Birth of Modern America, 1900-1912
   Faulkner/Politics, Reform, and Expansion, 1890-1900
   Cochran & Miller/The Age of Enterprise: *A Social History of
     Industrial America*
   Tyler/Freedom's Ferment: *American Social History from the
     Revolution to the Civil War*

PACKET III: American History

   Hansen/The Atlantic Migration, 1607-1860
   Degler/Out of Our Past: *The Forces that Shaped Modern America*
   Probst, Editor/The Happy Republic: *A Reader in Tocqueville's America*
   Alden/The American Revolution, 1775-1783
   Wright/The Cultural Life of the American Colonies, 1607-1763

*Your gift will be acknowledged directly to you by the overseas recipient.
Simply fill out the coupon, detach and mail with your check or money order.*

HARPER & ROW, PUBLISHERS · BOOKS USA DEPT.
49 East 33rd Street, New York 16, N. Y.

Packet I ☐   Packet II ☐   Packet III ☐

Please send the BOOKS USA library packet(s) indicated above, in my
name, to the area checked below. Enclosed is my remittance in the
amount of _____ for _____ packet(s) at $7.00 each.

_____ Africa   _____ Latin America

_____ Far East   _____ Near East

Name_____

Address_____

_____

NOTE: This offer expires December 31, 1966.